Run School Run

Run School Run

Roland S. Barth

HARVARD UNIVERSITY PRESS
Cambridge, Massachusetts
and
London, England
1980

Library of Congress Cataloging in Publication Data

Barth, Roland S
  Run school run.

  Bibliography: p.
  Includes index.
  1. Angier School. 2. Educational innovations—
Massachusetts—Newton. I. Title.
LD7501.N743B37   372.9′744′4   79-25686
ISBN 0-674-78036-1

To Carolyn

Contents

Foreword

A S A WRITER on educational topics, Roland Barth is a rare bird. Indeed, he and a handful of others—Sylvia Ashton-Warner, Herbert Kohl, and Vivian Paley are three whose names jump to mind at once—come close to qualifying for the status of an endangered species. For they all are, or have recently been, practitioners. When they write on the inner workings of schools, they know whereof they speak.

To readers unfamiliar with textbooks in education and with the bulk of the writing that fills educational journals, the length and recency of Barth's immersion in the daily life of a school—eight years as an elementary-school principal—may not seem like unusual qualifications. The truth is that much of what passes for educational wisdom these days flows from the pens of people whose practical experience, if they ever had any at all, is both brief and remote. Barth suffers neither handicap: his tenure as a school administrator is sufficiently long and his knowledge up-to-date.

But practical experience is by no means the only qualification Barth brings to his work as an author. Though he is too modest to say so, it is evident from the contents of his book that he was an unusually able principal. Thus what he has to tell us about schools commands our attention, not simply because it is being said by someone who has been there for a time, and recently so, but also because that someone was obviously good at his job.

In seeking to summarize these observations about the use Barth makes of his first-hand knowledge of schools, I thought initially of the old admonition to practice what we preach. It seemed, in a nutshell, to epitomize one of the book's major strengths. However, that idea was followed in short order by the realization that *Run School Run* was actually an instance of the ancient advice being played backward. In this book, my second thought informed me, Barth was in fact preaching what he practiced! A rather nice way of putting it, I said to myself; but a compulsion for accuracy quickly destroyed my self-congratulatory mood.

For there is nothing at all preachy about *Run School Run*, at least not in the usual holier-than-thou sense. As a matter of fact, Barth goes out of his way to make it clear that he is not trying to tell other principals and teachers how to run their schools. He confesses early on to being unsure about whether the ideas and practices he describes "can or should be applied to other schools, even very similar ones."

But if Barth is not out to sermonize, what is he trying to do? The answer to that question is crucial to a proper understanding of the book. "Rather than offering solutions for others to replicate," Barth explains in his preface, "my purpose in writing is to attempt to identify issues central to elementary education, to enlarge the universe of alternative solutions to problems, and to provoke others to think about their schools and ask themselves if their institutions are as they want them to be."

With these as criteria, how well might we say Barth succeeds in accomplishing what he sets out to do? Each reader is free to answer that question on his own, of course, but I for one would give him high marks in all three categories of his avowed purpose.

To begin with, he certainly seems to have put his finger on many if not all of the key issues that keep cropping up in elementary schools. In what classrooms should students be placed as they move from grade to grade? How, if at all, can parents have a say in the classroom placement of their children, without at the same time encroaching on the legitimate authority of teachers and administrators? How can teachers with diverse and often conflicting views of education, and with quite disparate teaching styles, work together harmoniously in the same school? How can teachers arrive at a way of evaluating their students in a manner that is at once thorough, honest, and constructive? How can a principal exercise authority without threatening the autonomy of the staff, yet also without abdicating responsibility for the overall functioning of the school? These are some of the perennial questions that confront practicing educators, as anyone who has been around schools for any length of time knows full well. As an identifier of the common woes that beset those who work in elementary schools, Barth is right on target.

There is more to this list of conundrums than its accuracy, however. One of the points Barth keeps repeating, and one that serves to explain his disavowal of the preacher's role, has to do with the generalizability of educational problems and the uniqueness of their solutions. In essence he asserts that what is common among schools is the set of problems they face; what is unique to each institution is the set of solutions it devises. That assertion is not new, but in these days of magic formulas for the supposed cure of our educational ailments and in a time when the admirable goal of social equality finds its clearest expression in the demand for uniformity, an insistence on the uniqueness of each student, each teacher, each classroom, and each school deserves the emphasis Barth gives it.

This set of considerations stands behind Barth's warning that the particular arrangements he and his teachers have worked out are not to be looked upon as "solutions for others to replicate." Indeed, he remarks upon the impermanence of these homemade remedies even within his own school. Institutional repair work, whether or not undertaken by people who know what they are doing, has a way of becoming unglued when administrators' backs are turned. And Barth is well aware of this fact.

It certainly does not follow that practitioners should hesitate to try variations of Barth's modus operandi in their own schools. Where it seems appropriate, they may even wish to adopt in their entirety the procedures he describes. This experimentation is what Barth hopes for, I'm sure, when he tells us that he is out "to enlarge the universe of alternative solutions to problems." If we understand alternative solutions to mean alternative ways of responding to recurring problems, some of which may turn out to be solutions (even though temporary) in some school settings, then I think we have to acknowledge that *Run School Run* does quite well in this second category of its author's striving.

How close Barth comes to his third goal, "to provoke others to think about their schools and ask themselves if their institutions are as they want them to be," is difficult for me to say. Like Barth himself I no longer am a practicing school administrator. I no longer have a particular school to think about and question whether it is as I want it to be. I do remember vividly that when I did have a real school to worry about, I certainly did not need a book to provoke me into thinking about it—nor did I need anyone prodding me into asking myself whether I was doing all I could to make the school in which I worked a better place to learn.

Quite the opposite, in fact. Whenever possible, which as I recall wasn't too often, I turned to books to escape from such worries! So with due respect for Barth's candor about his reasons for writing *Run School Run*, I suspect his talk about encouraging practicing educators to think about their work may describe a superfluous task. Indeed, I would hope that his book might give such readers the opportunity to forget the nitty-gritty of their own school situations for a few restful hours.

Although I do not buy the "provoking them to think" goal in the general way Barth states it, I think I do understand what he was driving at in more specific terms and, measured by these more refined standards, I suspect his book stands an excellent chance of achieving this goal as well. As I would phrase it, the third purpose served by *Run School Run* is that of showing its readers how far it is possible to go in the direction of liberalizing and democratizing the inner workings of a school without having the institution come apart at the seams. This demonstration is of great importance and is particularly timely given today's rising spirit of neoconservatism. The oldest excuse of all for hanging onto outmoded and authoritarian practices on the part of administrators and teachers alike is the fear that any move to relinquish authority or to increase the sharing of responsibility is to place the school on a slippery slope whose downward path ends in chaos and anarchy. The experiences related in this volume show convincingly that such an outcome is by no means inevitable and may thereby encourage those among its readers who have been holding the reins a bit too tightly to loosen up.

So I wind up giving the book you are about to read straight A's on the checklist of its author's avowed intentions. But these three high marks do not complete my evaluation. I would append a fourth category of purpose to those the author mentions, though I acknowledge that he comes close to adding it on his own at several points. This unstated function of *Run School Run*—its hidden message, so to speak—has to do with strengthening our faith in schools as institutions.

Many readers, I predict, will feel better about our nation's schools and what can be accomplished in them when they finish this book than they did when they began it. For practitioners, this alteration should translate into a deepened sense of pride in their profession and a renewed vigor in carrying out their work. For readers who are not themselves educational practitioners, it should nurture the conviction that well-run and educationally sound schools, like the one Barth describes, are neither as rare nor as difficult to create as many recent critics of our educational system would have it seem.

What it takes, as Barth demonstrates, is a reasonably well-trained and dedicated staff, willing to work together, to try out new ideas, and to learn from mistakes. That may sound like a tall order, but I suspect that many schools in our nation are already blessed with these essentials. All they need to launch out in the direction of an improved educational program is the kind of encouragement waiting for them in the pages of this book.

Philip W. Jackson
Department of Education
University of Chicago

Preface

I AM A COLLECTOR. In my barn in Maine I hoard, revel in, and trip over an assortment of stuff that in most households would long ago have found its way to the dump. From rain, sun, and snow I protect abandoned trucks, mowing machines, wheels, boards, and baling wire. I even have a rusty old hog scalder rescued from a neighbor's field. And a moth-eaten bearskin robe. Like the New England dowager who carefully maintains a shoe box labeled "string too short to use for anything," my dump is empty, my cupboard full. When asked why I so painstakingly and unselectively retain what appear to be pieces of junk, I can only respond, "You never know when you might need them."

So it has been with my experience as an educator. For twenty years, first as a teacher of third, fourth, fifth, and sixth grades in New Jersey, Massachusetts, and California, then as a principal in urban Connecticut and suburban Massachusetts, I have collected. Whenever something especially noteworthy or satisfying or problematic occurred in the class-room or the school—a particularly successful meeting, a remarkable change in a child, a heated letter from a parent, a sudden insight from a teacher—I jotted it down and added it to the sedimentary deposit form-ing in the bottom drawer of a desk. I never knew when I might need it.

In the winter of 1978 I set out for the Maine farm with a leave of ab-sence, my family, and an auto trunk filled with three bushel baskets of those recorded anecdotes and incidents. For two months I played card-sorting games: I placed each item in a variety of shifting categories until some piles persisted and each piece of paper came to rest in an accommo-dating category—or in the wastebasket. (I had to rationalize throwing away by using the discards to kindle the fire on chilly mornings.) Each of the enduring piles became the basis for a chapter in this book.

Within each pile I shuffled, arranged, and rearranged until I was able to find, or impose, some meaning and organization. I have a dreadful memory, which seldom allows me to recall names and events, let alone details. But I found each item I had squirreled away gave rise to a train of associations and rich reminiscences with which I was able to recall the details of long-forgotten incidents. Without the frayed, dusty notes scribbled on the backs of envelopes and interoffice memos, even noteworthy occurrences would have vanished. "You never know when you might need them."

Effective writing is usually reflective, clear, rational, well-organized, and linear. I hope that this account of a school will be so. But the reader should not be deluded. Schools and the lives of schoolpeople, despite our best efforts, can seldom be characterized by these adjectives. Existence in even the best of schools is by nature unpredictable, hurried, agitated, disjointed, occasionally even chaotic. The medium of the written word here, no matter how carefully groomed, should not be allowed to distort the frequently untidy message.

Whereas my previous book, *Open Education and the American School*, was the product of a doctoral student making use of the resources of a great library, what follows here is the product of a school practitioner and makes full use of the resources of another great institution—American public schools. This is a work that, quite literally, has emerged from my experience as teacher and principal.

No matter how many years one spends in how many schools collecting how much information, one can experience, observe, and convey only a mere slice of public elementary education. I find the contexts of the individual school, particular teacher, and specific principal probably the largest units I can fully examine, comprehend, and compare. Generalizing from these particulars to other settings is often unwarranted and dangerous, leading only to the discovery of an extraordinary variability among classrooms, schools, and school districts. Indeed, as I look back I find that much of what I have written here, based largely upon one suburban school, is not applicable to other settings in which I have worked. Some of what follows is no longer applicable even to the school about which it is written.

It is important, at the same time, not to be too parsimonious about generalizing. We educators seem to have the remarkable characteristic of being fascinated with what others are doing in other schools—and at the same time the capacity to generate inventive reasons why many of the innovations of others are impossible in our particular setting. The informal classrooms in many British primary schools are all well and good—but the British are another culture, with much greater self-control and respect for authority; the exciting program in an inner-city school is commendable—but they have all that Title I money and a teacher aide in every classroom; the careful, individualized instruction students receive in an independent school is noteworthy—but they have classes of fifteen pupils and selective admission; the methods of an innovative suburban school are impressive—but inappropriate for us because, well, we all know what suburban kids are like; and the dynamic program in a consolidated rural school system is great, but it wouldn't work for us because they have that fancy new open-space building. In short, promising educational practices elsewhere provide an occasion to dismiss the practice of others and perhaps to excuse our own. Often with good reason. Often not. There is a reluctance among educators to generalize from anything about anything, adding to the extraordinary momentum to preserve the status quo in our schools. I find this unfortunate.

As different as schools and their settings are, it seems to me that many of the issues and *problems* of education—pupil evaluation, discipline, staff development, principal effectiveness—are indeed endemic and generalizable from one setting to another, whether it be Massachusetts or California; public or private; urban, suburban, or the rural elementary school my daughters attended for a year. It is the *solutions*, if there are solutions, that tend to be idiosyncratic and particularistic, and much less generalizable from context to context.

This book, then, is an account by one principal about one school at one time in one district in one part of the country. It offers neither an idealized prescription for a principal nor a model for school reform. I am not sure whether the developmental stages I observe are universal. I am even less sure if the ideas and practices I describe here can or should be applied to other schools, even very similar ones. Rather than offering solutions for others to replicate, my purpose in writing is to attempt to identify issues central to elementary education, to enlarge the universe of alternative solutions to problems, and to provoke others to think about their schools and ask themselves if their institutions are as they want them to be. Ultimately, it remains for the readers to make their own generalizations and draw their own conclusions on the basis of their own experiences.

Schools are among the most studied, least understood, most critical, and most criticized institutions in American society. Three out of ten citizens are engaged in education. Yet surveys show dissatisfaction with discipline, curriculum, teachers, administrators, and integration, and less than a third of the public reporting confidence in American education. We have passed through a decade or two of policy debates conducted at the macro level about schools. We have learned a great deal about the effects of race, social class, poverty, and inequality upon children's lives. There is much about American education that is debilitating and deplorable. Macro analysis tells us a lot about *what* to change, but precious little about *how* to change or where to begin. The crucial micro realm of individual practitioners in individual schools has been sorely neglected.

Only recently have educational policy makers come to realize, for instance, that the school principal has an extraordinary influence over the quality of education and the quality of life under the roof of the schoolhouse. The principal stands at the intersection, mediating between the resources of the school system and the needs of children and their parents; between the school board and superintendent on the one side and teachers on the other; between theory and practice. The principal influences and is influenced by all the participants of the educational enterprise. The school principal has the opportunity to make it all work—or not.

Although principals are directly responsible for running schools, their voice is largely unheard in debates about education. This is not because principals have nothing to say, but because they have neither time nor opportunity to say it. I have found that my lenses as a school principal provide a remarkable window through which to view the world of education, and I have spent the past decade as participant-observer in that complex social institution called a public school. Unlike most principals I have also had the chance to step out of the consuming hustle and bustle for two years, to reflect and recollect. In a sense, then, this is a book written from the point of view of a practicing school principal about the principalship, an attempt to take a principal's look at schools and share what I see.

I argue that principals matter a great deal more to the health of schools than people outside the schools realize. At the same time, I don't believe principals can or should go it alone. To change schools we need to build grass-roots coalitions among the three key groups of adults concerned with schools: teachers, parents, and principals. So although this is a principal's view of things, I am eager for teachers and parents as well to read what I have to say. The interests of the three groups may not always overlap, especially in embattled schools and school systems where conflict is endemic, but all of us have an equal stake in developing good schools.

This is also a book about the relation of schools to society. Schools may be the last place in our society where people of different values, philosophies, backgrounds, races, and income levels are expected (and compelled by law) to work closely together for long periods of time. We can choose when and with whom to worship, travel, drink beer, or go to the movies. By and large, we cannot choose where and with whom our children will receive their schooling. Heterogeneity and compulsory attendance laws taken together frequently transform schools into battle-fields over race (With children of what color will my child attend school?), resources (Which school in the district will close?), philosophy (Which style of teaching will prevail in the school?), or politics (Who decides and controls major decisions?). These ingredients produce good schools and bad ones. Any attempt to sort it all out must come to grips with the question of uniformity and diversity. What follows is an account of one attempt to make the most of what we have: limited resources and unlimited diversity.

This book addresses a major problem in American education: how to create cooperative institutions, characterized by mutual respect and learning, in a pluralistic society where growing parent militancy, teacher power, student activism, and federal, state, and local regulation all threaten simultaneously to paralyze and inflame schools. There has been much talk about alternative schools within a district and alternative programs within a school. Personally, I am committed to an institution characterized by "alternative people"—where it is both possible and safe for teachers and students to be themselves, not actors in some elaborately constructed, monolithic program directed by others. I have explored the possibilities and drawbacks of a school where classrooms differ significantly in appearance, instructional style, and teaching philosophy. I have often found it possible to transform differences among children, teachers, parents, and administrators into powerful educational assets.

It is my firm belief that life within a public elementary school can reflect and celebrate the pluralism of our society and that schools can be productive, viable, and valuable. This is an account of what happens when a school community resists many of the institutional pressures toward uniformity and moves instead toward diversity. It is a description of one attempt by teachers, parents, and principal to achieve an acceptable diversity of program, personnel, and style on the one hand, and comply with important expectations for uniformity on the other. How this balance is determined and by whom is as complex and important a process as public education itself.

Acknowledgments

A book, like a school, is the product of many efforts and minds. Because in one sense this is the autobiography of a school, first and foremost I must thank the members of the Angier Elementary School in Newton, Massachusetts—faculty, parents, and students—for the unending insights, opportunities, and problems they provided me. I want to bless Ann Finnelli, who like all good school secretaries, was "out front" doing her work so the principal could be somewhere else doing his. I gratefully acknowledge the assistance of the other twenty-one Newton elementary-school principals, who shared freely with me their ideas and practices and supported me in mine. And I thank Aaron Fink, superintendent of the Newton public schools, who had the perspicacity to appoint me and then the personal confidence and professional courage to entrust me with a school.

I am indebted also to Mary Winslow, former partner in the Leadership and Learning Cooperative, for helping me become more conscious of my leadership style and philosophy. Paul Houts, director of publications of the National Elementary School Principals Association, kindly gave me permission to use materials I wrote earlier for the *National Elementary Principal;* portions of Chapters 1, 3, 4, 5, and 8 appeared in various issues of that publication between 1974 and 1980, and part of Chapter 2 appeared in *Saturday Review/World* in 1973. I acknowledge with gratitude the confidence and assistance of the John Simon Guggenheim Memorial Foundation, which has enabled me to write rather than administer.

My thanks go to the many readers who scrutinized and commented on early drafts of the manuscript: Norman Colb, Thomas Edwards, Aaron Fink, Helen Herzog, Deborah Horwitz, Barry Jentz, Jerry Katz, Sarah Levine, Sara Lawrence Lightfoot, Peggy Newman, Arthur Powell, Lillian Radlo, Vincent Rogers, Ann Sawyer, Israel Scheffler, Vincent Silluzio, Judy Smith, Sheldon White, Joan Wofford, and particularly Joseph Featherstone. I am grateful to Captain Snydah for the use of his text-processing equipment.

Finally, I acknowledge the efforts of Faith Weinstein Dunne, Joseph Barth, and Vivian Wheeler, in helping edit a ponderous manuscript, transforming it from something approaching a sow's ear to something approaching a silk purse. And of Vanessa Barth who typed it. Last of all, my thanks—and love—to Beth, for holding it all together during my years as principal and author.

R. S. B.

Run School Run

CHAPTER ONE

Uniformity and Diversity

The search for diversity is never free from an element of risk.

— Amiya Chakravarty

A S I LOOK back over eight years as an elementary-school administrator in three different systems, it seems my greatest difficulties and most abiding satisfactions have been concerned with uniformity and diversity. Underlying most of the day-to-day problems, decisions, and conflicts I recall so vividly lies a fundamental question: on what occasions must all teachers and all children in a school behave in the same way, and when is it acceptable — even desirable — for them to differ? Of course, this dilemma is not unique to principals or to schools. It is a question posed, for instance, by state legislatures to their municipalities, by the federal government to the states, and by the United Nations to member countries. In short, the problem of maintaining both personal autonomy and collective membership is one that vexes our society.

Schools are especially vulnerable to this dilemma. They are expected to respect individual differences on the one hand and maintain standards and develop specified skills and competencies on the other. They are criticized for bland, even blind, uniformity — for their tendency to sacrifice individual expression to institutional norms — yet at the same time are attacked for their permissiveness and failure to teach the basics and respect for adult authority.

Many school leaders have responded by opting for homogeneity, seeking to minimize differences among classroom teachers, instructional styles, and programs. I have found many reasons for this. First, uniformity tends to reduce friction and competition among staff members. If everyone is doing the same thing in the same way, teachers get along. But if Miss Jones has three reading groups and Miss Brown across the hall has

1

an individualized program, tension is more likely to grow and, ultimately, to erupt into conflict. Faculty warfare is seldom good for teachers, students, or administrators.

Second, uniformity of teachers, classrooms, and programs conveys the reassuring appearance that the school has found the one best way to teach everything and everybody. "We use the Ginn reading series," a principal can say to a parent with the authority of a person who has found The Answer. Such assurance is not likely to come from the school leader committed to diversity. Uniformity makes school boards, superintendents, curriculum coordinators, parents, and even children feel secure that we educators know what we are doing, and that we know how to do it well.

Third, uniformity of teaching style and practice is the cornerstone of what we all refer to as "scope and sequence." We assume that children's cognitive development is predictable and sequential as they pass through school. The instruction each child receives, therefore, should also be predictable and sequential. If a child is taught subtraction by a third-grade teacher using Houghton Mifflin materials, it follows logically that the same child, as a fourth grader, should be taught multiplication using the same publisher's methods.

There is a powerful logic to this formulation, one that withstands parental scrutiny. I recall the questions our Parent-Teacher Association asked me to address one evening at a meeting on the English curriculum:

(1) Are there language-arts guidelines for the system?

(2) Are teachers required to comply with these guidelines?

(3) Do we at Angier follow these guidelines?

(4) Can you guarantee that my child will know all of the things included in the guidelines for his grade?

(5) How do you (the principal) do this?

Many messages are implicit in these questions. One is that parents desire uniform, consistent curriculum guidelines. Another suggests that all children must achieve minimum competence levels at each grade. A third message is that the instructional program of each teacher must be part of a larger curriculum if children are to learn properly. Furthermore, in order to evaluate how much and how well teachers are teaching and children are learning, we must have uniform expectations. If teachers act autonomously, children may fall between the cracks in the floor; it becomes difficult to hold either child or teacher accountable for a year's work. Finally, whatever the minimum competencies may be, they must be uniform.

It is seldom clear just where desirable teacher variability stops and responsibility to continuity and consistency in curriculum begins. But it is clear that diversity suggests whimsy and capriciousness, while uniformity of curriculum, teaching style, and methodology is defensible in PTA meetings. This in itself is a powerful pressure toward uniformity in the schools.

A fourth press toward uniformity comes from standardized tests. To the extent that parents and school people are concerned about pupils' scores, the curriculum is subtly, and sometimes blatantly, shaped to anticipate and prepare for these tests. Because the tests are "standardized" (that is, the same instruments are administered throughout the nation), the instructional programs of classes within schools, schools within districts, and districts within states become remarkably similar — and uniform.

Any principal who has to place children in classrooms each spring is familiar with a fifth impetus. Uniformity of teachers and classrooms makes the annual assignment of students to teachers a relatively easy administrative task. The principal can go home one evening and randomly put children's names into three equal piles, with balanced numbers of boys and girls, leaders and followers, bright and slow. The next day children, parents, and teachers are notified of the decisions and no one can complain (or I should say no one has any justification for a complaint) because, as they are told, "every child will have exactly the same program, the same kind of teacher, the same learning environment." Accordingly, the class into which a child is placed "does not matter."

A rapidly growing array of collective-bargaining agreements, while protecting the interests of teachers, also constitutes a strong force toward uniformity in schools: "All teachers shall leave the building at 3:30"; "No class shall exceed twenty-five pupils"; "No teacher may be asked to assume noninstructional responsibilities without compensation"; "Each teacher shall have thirty minutes for lunch each day."

Economies of scale create a final pressure toward uniformity. When a school or a school system buys in quantity, the unit cost is considerably smaller than when individual schools, or individual teachers, buy different things. Uniform "stuff" — instructional supplies, materials, books, equipment — is cheaper than differentiated "stuff." Given our present (and probably permanent) period of severe budgetary constraint, concern to save dollars and cents becomes another powerful push to uniformity.

Thus uniformity has interpersonal, pedagogical, political, administrative, legal, and economic survival value in schools — and survival is not to be taken lightly in these especially troubled times. Yet at the same time that schools and principals are dealing with strong pressures toward uniformity, equally strong forces are pushing them toward *diversity*. These pressures come from four sources: faculty, parents, children, and principals. Pressures toward multiformity, always in the background, are becoming ever more pronounced and more difficult to handle.

The last decade has seen a marked change in the teacher market. School systems today can hire almost anyone they want — from an old electronics engineer to a new Phi Beta Kappa. Most schools are seeking out and finding the best people available. These teachers are, as we say, "highly qualified," much more so than they used to be. This is a blessing to public education, as anyone can attest who compares the teachers who left school last June with those who came in to replace them. However, with their high qualifications new teachers are bringing into schools different attitudes toward their role. A few years ago they said, "Here I am; tell me what you expect of me and I'll do it," and they adapted to whatever local uniformity prevailed. Today the message is apt to be, "Here I am, Highly Qualified. Here's what I intend to do; here's how I intend to do it. What I need from you, Principal, is support while I do it." This is an orientation closely akin to what universities call academic freedom. Academic freedom works pretty well in colleges and graduate schools because the burden rests upon students to integrate their disparate courses, teachers, and classes. As I have suggested, however, elementary-school teachers under the direction of the principal must assume the burden of supplying sequence and continuity for their young students. In this setting academic freedom often runs counter to the system's function. Public schools do not enjoy what Justice Felix Frankfurter once termed "the four essential freedoms of the university — to determine for itself — who may teach, what may be taught, how it shall be taught, and who may be admitted to study." To some extent we are faced with a choice: hire pedestrian, mediocre teachers who comply willingly with imposed uniformities, or hire highly qualified, imaginative teachers who demand a great deal of instructional autonomy. I'm not sure we can have it both ways: there just aren't many highly qualified sheep to teach in our schools.

To the school with strong-willed and increasingly well-qualified staff, add a few other pressures: growing teacher militancy (which has instructional as well as economic consequences); low faculty turnover; a large proportion of tenured staff (this year nearly 85 percent of Newton's teachers are tenured, as opposed to 50 percent five years ago). The result is a school staff that is mature, secure, assertive, able — but also increasingly diverse.

Pressure toward diversity also comes from parents who are becoming active and powerful forces in the education of their children. Earlier parents simply demanded quality education and let professional educators determine what was meant by "quality" and, for that matter, what was meant by "education." Now, stimulated by the consumer movement, provoked by rising taxes, and encouraged by the new pluralism legitimized by ethnicity and by the "alternatives movement," many parents feel a right and a responsibility to intervene in the educational decision-making process. It has been said of Newton parents that "they know what they want and in order to get it they will start at the top and work up." This is increasingly true of parents across the country.

It might be possible for a school principal to contend with these demands if all parents wanted the same thing. But, in spite of the PTA's yearning for a uniform curriculum, the principal finds among that parent body some who want a military-academy education with corporal punishment, others who want a traditional education complete with phonics drills and teachers in skirts, others who insist on a totally child-centered environment. Some want individualized reading instruction, or a programmed approach; others want to go back to the Cardinals, the Bluejays, and the Crows. Parents are ready to go to the wall for what they know to be "right." And most of them send their children to a common neighborhood school. How is the principal to respond to these conflicting and strong demands? In the past, a uniform, middle-road approach sufficed. Teachers followed a single methodology, not far enough to the right or left to offend anyone, with elements designed to satisfy most. Today such compromise rarely works. Schools instead must somehow provide a variety of teachers, programs, instructional styles, and philosophies under one roof. In short, diversify.

A third pressure generating diversity within the schools comes from children. Schools formerly offered a uniform curriculum taught in uniform ways. We assumed this was appropriate for all but a few children. Those days are over, replaced by an era of individual differences in which almost nothing is considered good for everyone. Schools are faced with the message in neon lights (and frequently backed by law) that children are different and must be treated differently. Diverse practices emerge, partly from a need to have our actions agree with our rhetoric and partly from a realization that most schools are, in fact, becoming more and more heterogeneous. Compulsory busing has caused student populations to more closely reflect society as a whole. While this is a commendable change, it is one with tremendous instructional, as well as social, implications. Many school systems are instituting open-enrollment policies. And more and more parents are voluntarily transferring their children from the neighborhood school to a magnet school across town because of educational preferences. While this practice may promote uniformity of educational philosophy within each school, it also has the intended effect of promoting a racial, economic, and occupational diversity. Furthermore, mainstreaming has expanded the range of children in schools and classrooms. If children with pronounced social, emotional, physical, and academic needs are placed in regular classrooms for at least part of every day, those classrooms must be differentiated enough to accommodate their needs.

In short, a powerful force for diversity comes into school each morning with the students.

Finally, schools and classrooms differ because principals differ. Observers find in each school a unique "climate," which appears to be closely related to the personal and professional characteristics of its chief administrator. The phrase "my building" or "my school" is commonly heard. School principals, like others, pride themselves on their individuality and attempt to place a unique stamp on the learning environment in accordance with their particular — and idiosyncratic — values and needs.

Strong pressures for educational diversity in public schools come, then, from teachers, parents, children, and principals — the major parties to the educational enterprise. Schools and principals face a disturbing, discouraging, often destructive dilemma: on the one hand, they are expected to provide a standardized instructional style, method, and appearance — common educational means and ends. The consequences for those who do not read these signals are severe. On the other hand, teachers, parents, and children are demanding diverse instructional styles, methods, and appearances — diverse educational means and ends. These demands for pluralism cannot be violated with impunity either. Schools have always been buffeted by conflicts between uniformity and diversity, but now these conflicts seem to be intensifying. Public schools are one of the few remaining institutions in our society where diverse backgrounds, values, ideas, and behaviors must coexist over long periods. And the school principal must somehow manage the inevitable conflicts and transform them into stability and learning. It is against this general backdrop that we shall now consider a particular school.

Yellow Walls and Orange Pipes

I had been principal only a few days when I was confronted with an apparently trivial decision. Several heroic parents had undertaken the job of painting my office. The question: What would be the latest in the long succession of colors to cover the peeling, sedimentary deposits of institutional greens and dirty browns on the walls? I chose a cheerful yellow. The next question: What about the pipes? Two corners of the room were dominated by an assortment of hot water, cold water, heating, and sewage-discharge pipes, that for reasons known only to a 1920s school architect passed through my office on their way to service the floors above and below. The alternatives were two: paint the pipes yellow to blend into the woodwork, so to speak, or paint them a contrasting color to highlight their existence. I chose bright orange.

That choice of yellow walls and orange pipes turned out to be more revealing than I knew. It became emblematic of an attitude toward differences that shaped the six years I spent at the school. My educational decisions, like my choice of paint for the walls and pipes, deliberately tilted toward diversity. Why?

A School in Trouble

Angier is a K-6 public elementary school. The sixty-year-old, three-story brick building is located in a middle- to upper-middle-class neighborhood of the suburban city of Newton. Its four hundred fifty pupils are predominantly white. Of the perhaps 10 percent black students, most are voluntarily bused each day from adjoining Boston. While the Angier community is fairly uniform in race, class, income level, and professional occupations, it includes large proportions of Catholics, Protestants, and Jews. More importantly, while most parents buy homes in Newton because they expect excellent education, few agree on what that implies.

When I first came to Angier in the early '70s I found a bitterly polarized school. Several teachers had resigned or transferred. Large numbers of parents had withdrawn children from the school. Many of the students were abusing school rules, the school building, schoolteachers, and one another. The principal had been removed as a result of teacher and parental unrest. Those who would rather "fight than switch" remained. It was during this period that I received letters appropriately misaddressed to the "Anger School" and the "Angrier School."

Many of the school's problems clustered around the classic battle of liberal versus conservative — or, in this context, open versus traditional. Would desks be arranged in rows, clusters, interest areas, or would there be no desks at all? On one side were parents and teachers who believed that children learn best and most when adults control learning and behavior, thereby assuring coverage and competence in many subject areas; on the other were those who believed children learn through their own direct, and often untidy, experiences with a wide range of objects, people, and ideas of the real world. Tensions and conflicts battered at the institutional requisites of trust, respect, stability, and productivity.

Diversity of thought was accompanied by militant action. Teachers told the principal they didn't believe in three reading groups and were setting up individualized programs; parents refused to have their children placed in open classrooms; a group of students wouldn't come to school if required to write reports on the explorers (and those who came might not write the reports anyway).

Contributing to the animosity and desperate infighting was the powerful assumption, based upon generations of precedent, that uniformity must prevail, that every classroom in the school would be similar in curriculum, appearance, and in children's and teachers' behavior. Given this assumption, teachers and parents *had* to be intensely involved in the struggle. If you get your way and have gerbils, I will have to have gerbils; if I get my workbooks, you will be required to have them too. So ingrained in our educational system is the presumption of uniformity that differences within schools frequently become the basis for winner-take-all competitions.

Although many were uncomfortable with both sides, all felt pressured to align themselves. In that first year, every move I made was carefully scrutinized to determine whose side I was on. To me it seemed a classic case: if you move to the left you get shot, if you move to the right you get shot, if you don't move at all you get shot tomorrow rather than today.

Why Uniformity?

School principals try to respond to conflicts by using a rule of thumb: minimize dissonance and maximize productivity. Usually we are able to find a formula, a line to walk neither too far to the left nor to the right, a line that represents a sometimes happy medium among a variety of competing possibilities. But in the fragile, volatile context I had inherited what response could minimize dissonance and maximize learning? David B. Tyack describes the history of American education as a quest for "the one best system."[1] I too recall a tremendous urge to create, maintain, and enforce similar expectations and practices for all teachers and students — if only I could figure out *which* uniform expectations and practices to choose and how to enforce them. What compelled me at that time to respond to militant diversity with even more militant uniformity?

Perhaps the strongest and yet most subtle force toward educational homogeneity emanates from the culture of education itself. I have visited many schools in parts of this country where food, architecture, climate, topography, and dialect are noticeably different. But the differences remain outside school walls. Like other observers, I've seen remarkable similarity inside schools, for no apparent reason. Why do all twelfth graders study American history? Why do children enter school at age five? Why do students fill out workbook pages? Why do teachers pass out assignments, correct papers, grade them, hand them back, and go over them with their students? Why do principals hold faculty and parent-teacher meetings? Sometimes it seems as though an invisible national ministry of education were determining philosophy, curriculum, appearance, and procedure for all. But there is no such ministry, no mandated uniformity.

There doesn't need to be. The lives of teachers and students in this country are closely wedded to an implicit, persistent "transmission-of-knowledge" model of learning. This model assumes the existence of an accumulated body of knowledge, from Plato to nuclear physics. The proper business of teachers is to transmit this knowledge to students as efficiently as possible. And the student is expected to assimilate this knowledge quickly and to display it upon demand. Students are evaluated according to how much knowledge they have acquired and how fast and ably they can demonstrate it.

Certain deep-seated assumptions seem to underlie the transmission-of-knowledge model:

(1) The ultimate purpose of education is the acquisition of knowledge.

(2) Knowledge is what has been learned and recorded over the ages. It is categorized into the disciplines of mathematics, chemistry, history, and so on, each of which has a content and a structure that can be taught and learned.

(3) There is a minimum body of knowledge in each subject (the curriculum) that everyone must know before leaving school.

(4) Adults are best suited to make important choices about what children should learn.

(5) If children are given much choice about how and what they learn, they will wander from the best path to knowledge.

(6) Children are not naturally drawn to academic work and must therefore be externally motivated.

(7) Children play on their own time, out of school. During school time they work.

(8) The student who is having a lot of fun probably isn't learning very much. If learning involves some pain, it's likely to be good for a child.

(9) Children learn most in settings where there are few distractions.

(10) When children work together, cheating is more likely.

(11) Some children are bright, some average, some slow.

(12) There are individual differences among children, but if we group them by ability and vary the rate at which we present material to them, they will all have an equal opportunity to learn.

(13) The student who knows something is able to display that knowledge publicly, at the request of the teacher. The student who can't display knowledge doesn't have it.

(14) Errors are mistakes. Mistakes are undesirable and must be eliminated.

(15) Acquisition of knowledge can be accurately measured.

(16) The best way of evaluating the effect of the school experience on a child is through a battery of standardized tests.[2]

Most so-called innovations in American education accept and only tinker with the transmission-of-knowledge model. The "new curriculum" selects new details from the accumulated wisdom; team teaching changes the transmission agents, as do instructional TV, computers, programmed instruction. Nongrading, like ability grouping, rearranges students so they can become better knowledge receivers.

While the transmission-of-knowledge model seems to provide a crude learning theory by which schools are organized and operated, it is the classroom teachers who create homogenized (sometimes pasteurized) classrooms. Asked why they do what they do, teachers' frequent response is "Because of pressures from above." Colleges determine the curriculum for high schools, high schools for junior highs, and so on down to kindergarten and nursery school. Each dog is wagged by the tail above. Teachers and schools are measured by the yardstick of standardized tests: Scholastic Aptitude Tests, Preliminary Scholastic Aptitude Tests, the Stanford Achievement Test, and various reading readiness tests.

The pressure for a standardized "preparation" curriculum seems but to intensify as students go through the grades, as one superintendent observed in his annual report to the school board:

> By far the greatest flexibility and greatest differences in individualization are in the elementary schools. We tend to think that as children become older and better able to assume responsibility for their own education and their own behavior, that we provide greater opportunities for them to work on their own. There is actually almost an inverse relationship within the school system between the child's age and the degree of flexibility and openness. In the elementary schools teachers do not seem disturbed about children working in small clusters or doing things on their own . . .

> It is clear that as kids go through the school system the program becomes much more formal and much more rigid. We talk a great deal about the independence of high school students, but in fact find many more opportunities for independent activity for children at the elementary school level.[3]

When teachers talk about "pressures from above," they also mean superiors within the system — the school board, members of the central administration, and principals. "I'm doing what 'they' tell me to do," a teacher will say when questioned about the classroom. "They," in turn, formulate their policy in response to national waves — "humanize the schools" or "back to basics" — that frequently affect the outcome of school board elections. New boards, representing a new mandate of the people, replace the superintendent or prevail upon the existing administration to carry out more fashionable policies.

One public school board distributed a document that illustrates both the extent to which those above perpetuate the transmission-of-knowledge model and how the model promotes uniformity among principals, teachers, and students:

In assuming responsibility for the school system in these challenging times the Board adopts the following principles and policies as guide posts for the professional conduct of our schools:

(1) The principal aim of the schools shall be the development of the minds and the acquisition of knowledge by all children. All other aims, however important and desirable they may appear in themselves, shall be subordinated to this primary aim.

(2) The curriculum will be strengthened by designing a specific program which all students can follow. Such programs, supported by appropriate credits and minimum requirements for promotion and graduation, shall be designed to insure a true basic education for every child. Recognizing as a matter of course the difference between individual children with respect to intellectual capacity, maturity, emotional pattern and background, we hold that these differences must not be allowed to interfere with the fundamental education each child receives. Consideration for the individuality of the child cannot obscure the real purpose of the schools, which is to provide a measurable standard of education for all children . . .

(3) Children, being by definition immature, are not generally equipped to choose subjects, topics, methods or rates of learning or teaching. The teacher shall assume responsibility for planning and teaching the subject matter to be covered in a given period in accordance with an approved outline of study at each grade level.

(4) It is the intent of the Board to have comparable standards of performance and coverage of subjects, grading and promotion throughout the School District. Within limits, autonomy of the individual schools and teachers is desirable so as to encourage the development of distinctive institutions with close ties to the parents and children in the various areas. However, the desire for autonomy cannot be permitted to extend to the curriculum prescribed by the Board nor to the basic materials and methods employed in teaching. The Board is charged with the responsibility for maintaining standards of education in the School District. It cannot effectively do so unless it is assured that a uniform policy will be followed and comparable standards will be observed throughout.[4]

This is "they." This kind of formal statement may be unusual in American school systems, but centralized, hierarchical thinking is not. Board or administration dicta are frequently benevolent and well intentioned, but they reduce diversity and promote conformity within schools far more than they improve the state of teaching and learning.

The "from-the-top-down" model of school district organization appears to be based upon certain assumptions about schoolpeople: they have a limited capacity; they will behave responsibly and productively only when objectives are specified for them and when they are held accountable by others for achieving these objectives.

Granted, there are teachers in every system for whom these assumptions are warranted. But I find there are many more for whom the assumptions are not only unwarranted, but debilitating, seriously inhibiting their best efforts. Incompetent or lazy principals and teachers must be reckoned with directly and firmly — and individually — without poisoning the lives of others. To organize an entire enterprise on the basis of the characteristics of a few of its members is a dubious practice. And the results are predictable: expecting the worst from everyone elicits the worst from everyone.

Why Diversity?

Recently, I was reading an article in a farm journal about asparagus culture in central Maine. It soon became evident that the author, an asparagus grower, was a public-school teacher as well. Although her article was written for farmers, not educators, it is instructive for both:

> The year I discovered the asparagus, a new language program was started in the school where I teach. Each of my seventy students was expected to complete a nice, fat workbook before the end of May. Like many educational programs that are cheerfully promoted by those who do not have to be shut up in a classroom with dozens of resistant students, this one generated animated animosity. By the time we had suffered through to the final pages, the workbooks — inside and out — contained a fine collection of graffiti expressing the students' feelings. Some celebration seemed necessary.
>
> So we marched the bedraggled, never-to-be-used-again books out to my car and I promised to bury them near the manure pile. Slave labor was promptly volunteered. The students who came out to the farm enthusiastically labored at lugging the workbooks down the hill, laying them out along the sides of my new asparagus bed and over the area where I planned to extend the bed. Then we covered the workbooks liberally with hay. During the summer months when students stopped by to swim, they always made a pilgrimage to the asparagus bed to lift the hay and gloat over the decay of the detested pages.
>
> By the next spring the earthworms had industriously demolished most of the heavy sod and reduced the language workbooks to compost. I was able to dig a trench and set out my new asparagus roots.[5]

No wonder authenticity is not always characteristic of those who inhabit schools. Too often what goes on in classrooms and schools reflects not the judgments of schoolpeople, but uniform expectations from above. Sad to say, I know of no teacher (or principal) who does not have a substantial accumulation of "asparagus mulch."

In education, it seems, everyone wants control. The ultimate prize is influence over what teachers do with children in classrooms. The federal Office of Education, state departments of education, local school committees, superintendents, curriculum coordinators, principals, educational critics, parents — and even teachers — want to determine the nature of the interaction between teacher, child, and subject matter. The Statement of Principles represents one attempt to control. The asparagus mulch is one response. The issue is not whether workbooks are valuable educational materials; they often are. The issue is who determines which educational materials children use, how they are used, and on what basis.

Unfortunately, most attempts to control by regulation fall into the category "if you call a moose a duck, it can fly." To be sure, rhetoric is frequently effective in promoting the *appearance* of equal and quality education. All classrooms look similar, as if they contain the same opportunities. All teachers behave in similar ways, as if they share the same educational philosophy and desire to follow the system's guidelines with uniform diligence. All children sit in similar seats doing similar work, as if they are complying with uniform, minimum expectations of performance. Despite the rhetoric of equality and the stalwart attempts of schoolpeople to comply with that rhetoric, the myth of uniform, quality education that so preoccupies America is laid bare whenever the veneer is scratched. Because, of course, all teachers aren't the same, nor are all children. Teachers and children are not marionettes whose strings can be pulled at will by those who would control what happens in classrooms.

Anyone observing schools in a given district will see that some have better morale or worse science programs than others. Even in a single school, one third-grade teacher will use a different reading method from another, and children will learn to read in different ways. A cup-of-coffee-length visit in any faculty room reveals an enormous diversity of philosophy, personality, and ways of thinking about children. Schools, classrooms, teachers, and children differ in marked ways; despite attempts to paint them out, these differences stubbornly reveal themselves.

Schoolpeople are aware of the pronounced discrepancy between rhetoric and practice. Their awareness breeds apprehension lest someone discover that they are not doing what they are supposed to be doing, that fearful consequences may follow. Repeatedly calling a moose a duck and expecting it to fly promotes defensiveness and self-protection. Schoolpeople expend extraordinary amounts of time and energy going through unchosen motions to which they have no commitment, and for which they feel little sense of responsibility. Externally imposed decisions and statements of principle undoubtedly supply a surface coating of coherence, but they also have a chilling effect upon the quality of education in the schools. As Vivian Paley has observed, "Homogeneity is fine in a bottle of milk, but in the classroom it diminishes the curiosity that ignites discovery."[6]

Fear is not conducive to anyone's best performance. In an important study Gerald Becker and his associates [7] found pervasive fear a recurring characteristic of bad schools. I have found this true in my experience as well. Fear leads to enmity among those within the building. And fear leads to an embattled coalition of those inside the building against those outside — and to asparagus mulch.

I remember a teacher who visited Angier in a state of panic to observe open classrooms. It had been announced, she said, that over the summer walls in her school were to be torn out, basal texts removed, and children grouped across many ages, all because the school board wanted some "open classrooms." She was thoroughly confused, frightened, and, needless to say, unenthusiastic about what was expected of her. I doubt that the quality of education in that teacher's classroom was enhanced by this innovation.

The primary problem with public education is not that teachers and principals aren't doing their jobs. The problem is that they are frequently under pressure to behave in ways dictated by others — school committees, superintendents, curriculum directors, John Holts, or Hyman Rickovers — whether or not these ways violate or coincide with what their own experience suggests is best for children. When a teacher is preoccupied with dictates from above, there is little chance to respond to different children differently, to make flexible use of the widest possible repertoire of instructional materials and practices. When a principal sees his job as complying with the policies of the Board of Education, the school becomes more an institution than a place of learning. Indeed, an administrator or teacher worried about complying with mandates from without has little time to know or care what is best for children.

Much of the push and pull toward school uniformity I felt at Angier was coming, then, from the transmission-of-knowledge model and expectations from above. In the school culture homogeneity — almost any homogeneity — is expected and rewarded. Pluralism — almost any pluralism — is usually neither welcomed nor condoned. Yet I was unable to resolve Angier's difficulties by determining uniform goals and methods, because promulgating a uniform position and making certain everyone abided by it offered little hope of a solution. Attempts to determine and enforce educational uniformity — whether uniform workbooks, uniform gerbils, or uniform hair lengths — seem to create rather than minimize dissonance and impede rather than enhance learning.

It is lunacy to try to function this way in today's schools. Daily we school administrators face important decisions — to ability-group or not, to administer standardized tests or not, to require homework or not — and we usually find about 55 percent of our constituents on one side and 45 percent on the other. On issue after issue, we're damned if we do and damned if we don't. It is important to know where everyone stands and why, before we make decisions. Still, no good solution can be found by counting up the largest number of votes. If we are going to be damned anyway, it might as well be for doing what we think is right. That way we avoid the thankless trap of trying to justify a judgment that violates personal or professional integrity. Although some administrators may try to enforce uniformity with the hope of avoiding damnation, they find no cool place there either. In schools there is no uniform course that will be accepted, let alone respected, by all teachers, parents, or children. We can no more paint out differences of values, styles, and methods than we can cause the pipes to disappear by making them the same color as the wall. Differences in our schools will always exist because teachers and students are people, and a fundamental characteristic of people is diversity. It's time we realized that to acknowledge variability of people and programs in our schools is not to create it; to respect diversity and make use of it need not promote inequity. It is possible to nurture substantial differences, all of high quality.

As a principal, I have found myself sorting educational decisions into two baskets. Basket one contains areas in which I feel teachers and children must behave in similar ways. Basket two contains situations in which it is acceptable, often desirable, for teachers and children to differ. I suspect that many principals engage in this kind of exercise. But my objective over the years has been to minimize the items in the first basket while maximizing the items in the second. Rather than viewing differences among children and teachers as problems to be solved, I have explored the flip side of the coin. I have tried to find ways in which differences can be turned to educational advantage and enlisted in the service of personal and intellectual growth for those within the school. By abandoning the fruitless, frustrating search for "the one best system" and insisting on similarity only where it is crucial to institutional survival, I have come to find fewer and fewer entries for the "all-the-same" basket and more and more for the "it's-okay-to-differ" hopper. And, as we shall see, I have found that when teachers are teaching in ways consonant with their own personal style and professional philosophy, both they and their students appear to benefit.

School administrators over the last twenty years have been accustomed to solving problems by plugging in new resources from the central office. But times have changed. Resources have diminished — often vanished — leaving the solution of a problem to the imagination and resourcefulness of schoolpeople. Today many of us find that the best we can do is identify a problem (or, more frequently, acknowledge a problem that is identifying itself), and then *rearrange* the problem or exchange it for another. I often attempt to trade what I call an "unproductive problem" for a more productive one. And, equally often, I find that unproductive problems are related to uniformity — how do I find a math series that will satisfy all teachers from kindergarten to sixth grade? — while the productive problems are related to diversity — how shall we place seventy-five very different children in three very different classes next fall? In short, I am finding the problems of determining and enforcing uniformity to be less satisfying, interesting, and productive than the problems associated with diversity. When I can choose, I pick the productive problems of diversity every time.

The givens today seem to be a growing diversity and increased voice among teachers, children, and parents and the diminishing success of any uniform approach to education. A principal can deal with these realities either by denying or attempting to suppress diversity, often watching authority erode, or by acknowledging and trying to make constructive use of diversity, and thereby, I believe, gaining a more creative kind of authority.

Pluralism rather than uniformity, eclecticism rather than orthodoxy, offer our greatest hope for minimizing dissonance and maximizing learning. The discussion of the Angier experience in the following pages suggests that acknowledging and taking advantage of the diversity that invariably emerges in schools can solve many problems in ways that make both political and educational sense. Diversity is abundant and free. Used wisely, deliberately, and constructively, it offers an untapped, renewable resource available to the public schools. We should learn to use it well.

CHAPTER TWO

Alternatives to Uniformity

Sameness depresses; differences stimulate.

— Ancient Chinese proverb

W E LIVE IN A SOCIETY that sees education as the major avenue to personal, professional, and economic success. Yet we provide families with little choice about going to school, about which school a child will attend, who the teacher will be, and what the child will do within the classroom. In fact, schools have displayed little capacity to provide choices for anyone — administrators, teachers, parents, or children. Recently I received this letter from a troubled parent in the Midwest, which conveys the intensity of confusion, helplessness, and hopefulness that characterizes the current relationship between parents and the public schools:

Dear Mr. Barth:

. . . Gordon is an elementary school serving approximately 300 children under a five-year approach called Continuous Progress; however, because of administrative changes from Superintendent to Principal the original proposal has been all but scuttled. The entire city school system appears to be experiencing confusion as to expectations, goals, policy, etc. The greatest hope for many of us is the opening of the Roswell School — an open education concept in plans and facility. We are all presently stunned by recent test scores done by an outside firm at the request of the school committee. These results appear to show significantly below national norms and in many areas far below scores here in past years. Another element of hope and yet some healthy trepidation is our position of needing a new Superintendent by June.

Generally, the parent community is uninvolved but those who want to be or in fact are very involved lack the necessary information. Programs are discussed and often implemented with little administrative in-

17

formation to parents and thus when problems arise, the parental response is to discredit the entire program concept. At this time, because of the opening of the Roswell School and the influence of the media, discussions about open/self-contained education, structured/unstructured classrooms, discipline/lack of discipline, pervade school committee meetings, PTA events, and coffee klatches.

In summation, parents are generally unhappy about their children's school experiences without knowing exactly why, and yet any discussion of change brings the fear of the unknown out front — both from parents, staff, and administration. The highlights are those committed principals and teachers sprinkled throughout the system who go forward on their own to create exciting, beautiful experiences with their individual classes. Perhaps there's a message in the fact that these teachers are requested by parents for their children overwhelmingly.

As long as it could be assumed that somewhere, somehow, we could find a single, coherent, acceptable educational system, lack of choice was tolerable. The distress so apparent in this letter suggests that concerned parents, like David Tyack, have come to realize that the search for a single pedagogical model to provide a panacea for the education of all children is fruitless. As a result, schools, although locked into compulsory attendance laws and a tradition of uniformity, are being forced to accommodate differences in philosophy and method. Educational alternatives have proliferated, and public schools are being moved, kicking and screaming, toward diversity.

Alternative Schools

Some systems are providing alternative schools within a district. One school might offer a back-to-basics curriculum, complete with hair codes and demerit systems; another might provide all informal classes, with no walls and a ten-year supply of gerbils; a third school might be organized around behavior modification techniques. There are now thousands of these alternative public schools in the United States; Berkeley and Milwaukee are examples of cities offering an extraordinary array. The existence of alternative schools reduces faculty and parental dissonance, since only those who share a school's prevailing philosophy and methodology need associate with it. Gerbil lovers have no gerbil haters to contend with; instead, at least in theory, they have a school filled with teachers who like gerbils, principals who like gerbils, children who like gerbils, parents who like gerbils, and even custodians who like gerbils (or at least know a lost cause when they see one).

Alternative schools within a district have made diversity legitimate in public education. And by carefully controlling the admission of students, many have contributed to peaceful racial integration, an extraordinary accomplishment. Alternative schools have serious limitations, however: people are drawn to alternative schools because they share an educational philosophy. But as soon as a decision has to be made — about a chewing-gum policy or a reporting system — the assumed compatibility vanishes, and the conflicts so typical of most schools reappear, to the astonishment and dismay of the participants. It's a bit like ability grouping: we put together people similar in one characteristic, only to find a wide variation along most other dimensions. Differences within groups are as dramatic as differences between groups. Failure to recognize this fact has been the shoal on which many alternative schools have foundered.

Alternative schools within a district also make difficult the flexible placement of children. If a parent chooses to send a child to a school that offers only highly teacher-directed instruction and it turns out that the youngster clearly needs another kind of learning environment, there are two equally unfortunate possibilities: the child must either stay and be miserable or must leave the school. Furthermore, homogeneous schools attract a homogeneous group of people who reinforce one another rather than examining and challenging what goes on in the school. In such an environment teachers and parents are often lulled into unquestioning acceptance of whatever is going on, and the school stops changing and growing.

Homogeneous schools also have a disturbing tendency to further segregate our already segregated society. In some instances where parents and teachers are given a choice of schools without admission quotas, the student body becomes skewed toward one racial or ethnic group. Schools become all black, all white, all Jewish, all Catholic, all rich, all poor. This self-selection process diminishes the cultural diversity that many alternative schools value and espouse.

Finally, alternative schools within a district, the magnet schools, tend to siphon off the questioning, active parents; this leaves the "regular" schools even more homogeneous and uniform, bereft of possible agents for change. In short, developing a school system with different kinds of schools, each of which is internally homogeneous, solves some problems but perpetuates — and often increases — uniformity within each school.

Alternatives within a School

A second response to pressures for diversity has been the creation of alternatives within a school. This approach also offers the possibility of allowing parents to choose an educational system compatible with their values. Faculty can be selected to reflect a range of deliberately cultivated pedagogical positions. With luck and careful planning, different philosophies can be represented at grade levels and parents can request a teacher each spring for the following year. Ideally, there is no question of a child having a "good" or a "bad" teacher; all children will have good teachers with different teaching styles. The objective is to achieve an optimal match between teacher and parent. This arrangement has clear advantages. Teachers can teach in a manner closely approximating their personal values; parents can place children in a learning environment approximating theirs. Under these circumstances the teacher can devote time to instructional questions rather than political ones, while children, no longer in the middle between dissenting adults, can enjoy their school, teacher, and enhanced learning.

A typical school might offer as alternatives an open or a traditional program. One school I visited had open classrooms on one side of a long corridor and regular classrooms on the other.[1] Another school divided its teachers and children into three categories:

I. Structured Learning Mode:
   The child learns best with a high degree of teacher direction and supervision. While there is some opportunity for independent work, most classroom activities are primarily teacher directed.

II. Semistructured Mode:
   The child learns best in a classroom situation that offers equal amounts of teacher-directed learning and independent work. The child can work independently for periods of time after teacher assistance. Classroom activities are designed for initial teacher instruction and direction and with opportunities for self-directing and independent work.

III. Independent Learning Mode:
   The child learns best in a classroom where activities are designed by the teacher to capitalize on the student's ability and competency to work independently. The child spends much of the class time working independently on learning activities.[2]

I find juxtaposing different methods, materials, and philosophies under one roof works better than creating alternative schools within a district. Parents remain within the school even though they disagree among themselves. And children can be placed each year in whatever classroom closely corresponds to their learning style, without leaving the school. Because they are exposed to a variety of instructional practices each day, teachers are more likely to examine and question and, frequently, to change what they are doing. Finally, it is possible for children to spend some of each day with other children who represent a range of ability, race, background, and social class.[3]

Still, there are disadvantages to having alternative classrooms within a building. Often the alternatives are initiated by outsiders: school committees, superintendents, or parents. Teachers are asked (or told) to affiliate with one of the two or three prevailing methodologies. What is usually achieved is a "closest approximation." The fit between teacher and label is only partial, raising several disturbing questions for teachers to answer as best they can: "Which am I?" "What do they want me to do?" "Will I be able to assume a mode that is in part incompatible with my own beliefs and practices?" "Do I have to?"

These uncertainties can have grim effects. Some teachers try to assume new characteristics, generally with considerable resentment, resistance, undermining . . . and asparagus mulch. Others assume only some of the more visible elements of the advertised philosophies. They move the desks into rows or out of rows while continuing to teach in their own styles. Others accept any label assigned but do what they have always done, the new sign on the door notwithstanding. It is not surprising that most schools that try alternatives within the school soon begin to offer some octane blendings. Frequently, successive deviations from the original learning modes lead to classrooms the way they used to be. Labels, if they have any meaning at all, serve only as code words for "Whose class is my child in?"

Alternative classrooms within a school attempt to offer a selection of ideologies and thereby reduce political problems and increase educational advantages. These attempts replace a single uniformity with two or three uniformities. Unfortunately, the results are often little different from living within a single uniformity. The principal must comply with the superintendent's mandates, the teachers must comply with the principal's mandates, and children must comply with what everyone mandates. The language changes, but subordinate, compliant behavior does not.

In America we tend to exchange new educational orthodoxies for old the way we trade in our automobiles. We seem pathologically susceptible to new ideas and remedies that offer immediate salvation. We seize upon a "free school" or an "open school" or a "traditional" classroom or "open space" or "back to basics" as the answer with the same eagerness we show for front-wheel drive or diesel engines. The alternatives movement has been a welcome antidote to the pallid uniformity that preceded it. But it has a central flaw. Proponents of each alternative have seen it as a "new car" and have tried to replace the prevailing district orthodoxy and uniformity with their own orthodoxy and uniformity. We should realize by now that neither teachers nor students are likely to do their best in situations where a formula — any formula — has been supplied or imposed from without. Innovations from outside the classroom usually bring with them more rigid practice and less effective learning than whatever they replaced.

Alternative People

I should like to suggest a third way of responding to diversity: developing schools characterized not by alternative ideologies, not by *any* ideologies, but by alternative people. That is, attempting to provide conditions under which each teacher can discover, develop, refine, and implement a distinctive, authentic, idiosyncratic form of instruction. As succeeding chapters will reveal, this alternative was my response to a troubled Angier School.

There is considerable documentation to suggest that no particular methodology can be associated with successful learning for all children. Indeed, there is surprisingly little evidence that *any* instructional style, method, or philosophy works consistently better than any other. Educators and parents are beginning to realize that there are many diverse conditions under which children learn well. We need to stop the search for that Holy Grail, the ultimate way, and instead learn to listen to the initiatives emanating from people in the school. If pluralism is to become an educational asset as well as a political one, schools must provide a forum where different educational ideas and methods can be developed, examined, and challenged.

Different methods work better in concert than in isolation. Good education is neither gerbils nor workbooks; it is not externally prescribed behavior for teacher or student. Rather, good education is rooted in a teacher's personal belief about how children learn best. Good education grows in a situation where the teacher's behavior is a response to first-hand observations of children's behavior. Thus good education necessarily varies from classroom to classroom, teacher to teacher, year to year.

Alternative schools within a district are preferable to no alternatives at all; alternative classrooms within a school are preferable to alternative schools within a district; and best of all I believe are schools where classrooms reflect the rich diversity of those who inhabit them.

Alternative-People Schools — Can they Work?

There is precious little precedent for organizing schools around alternative people. The very idea has a dangerous sound, contrary to the American creed of equality and equal educational opportunity, remote from bureaucratic, centralized, chains of command, difficult to rationalize and justify in terms of familiar educational rhetoric currently so full of "accountability" and "measurability." Thus, we have little idea of how such a nonideology might work in practice.

The British have perhaps come closest to providing examples of primary schools with alternative people. Britain has a long tradition of respecting diversity. Schools there offer about as much uniformity among classrooms as among teachers — very little. Indeed, the excitement of British schools is not in uniform open classrooms, but in diverse thinking and behavior from person to person, classroom to classroom, and school to school. British superintendents usually accord school headmasters (their term for principals) great responsibility. Most heads tend to do likewise with teachers, who, in turn, do likewise with children. In this atmosphere teachers and children tend to involve themselves productively — and to learn.

Not surprisingly, classrooms differ considerably, each reflecting the teacher's special interests and areas of competence. One may be stocked with a huge range and number of exciting books; another may be dominated by objects related to nature study, plants, and animals; a third may be full of mathematical materials. Similarly, teaching practice may be different in each room. Some teachers, for instance, never address the total class; others do so occasionally; for still others this is the common means of instruction. Some teachers work alone, some in pairs, some in larger teams. By continually observing and responding to children, teachers develop their own beliefs about learning. These beliefs become the basis of classroom practice.

The major contribution of the British schools is not the stuffed reading chairs or the litany of "interest areas" and "facilitated learning." British primary schools have dramatically expanded and enriched the range of useful instructional methods and materials available to teachers and children. Thoughtful, timely selection from this extended repertoire makes learning for all children a more attainable goal. British classrooms have provided important precedents that can help us move with security from mechanical, homogenized classrooms toward more humane, diverse, and academically respectable learning environments.

Unfortunately, the real significance of the British experience has not been appreciated in this country. Numbers of us, fed up with obvious inadequacies in our own schools, saw in the British informal classrooms a new way to deal with children — a way that allowed the youngsters freedom, dignity, and close individual attention. We wanted similar things to happen in American schools. For a decade many of us tried to re-create those schools in a variety of contexts — with mixed success. We worked hard. We identified the basic beliefs about children, learning, and knowledge that seemed to underlie British practice: children are innately curious; play and work are indistinguishable in early learning; much learning takes place independent of teacher direction. We described, in great detail, what an open classroom should look like — the interest areas, the carpeting, the cubbies, the ubiquitous gerbils. We also delineated a distinctive function for the classroom teacher: provide materials; observe and record each child's progress; move from child to child giving help when needed; facilitate learning as each child goes about his work independently. We believed the task was clear. Find teachers who would accept these assumptions about children's learning, train them, and equip their classrooms correctly. Then we knew we would have the right learning environment at last — the open classroom. All the benefits for children and adults so visible in England would be ours.

What we did, of course, was create a new orthodoxy, one more rigid formula to be imposed on the schools from the outside. This is educational reform, American style: academic analysis, prescribed (and proscribed) materials and equipment, codified and circumscribed teaching behavior, and, presumably, uniform display of desirable behavior by adults and children.

In America we have packaged informal British classrooms for wholesale distribution — we have produced attractive vocabulary, materials, and classroom arrangements and sold them to the schools. But we have failed to adopt the process that led to the product, a process that precludes packaging. Consequently, resemblance between what happens in Britain's informal schools and in most American open classrooms is often coincidental.

We must remember that the distinguishing characteristic of British primary schools is that each classroom teacher has primary responsibility for what happens in the classroom. Alice Yardley, principal lecturer in education at the Nottingham College of Education, has noted:

> I think never in our country have educationists or theorists told teachers what to do. It is necessary for teachers to think out for themselves what their view of children is and what they believe about the education of children.

It is not surprising that in turn

> teachers see children not as fodder for the state, not as malleable material out of which they make good citizens. They see children as people — little people — who have the right to be individualists, to become themselves and nobody else. They see children as people who have the right to formulate their own beliefs and attitudes toward society and then to live by those beliefs. The challenge for educators is to provide the opportunity for the child's personality to unfold. We see education as a means for providing the opportunity for a child to become the architect of his own personality. This is what we mean by freedom.[4]

If we learn nothing else from British primary schools, I hope we can see that good things happen to children in classrooms where teachers have considerable responsibility for instructional decisions. The only teacher-proof curriculum is the one the teacher designs and manages.

I see signs that American school systems may be moving in the direction of according principals and teachers more responsibility (and more accountability). Sadly, this is not being done so much through the thoughtful choice the British employ, but by default. In the current "crisis in the classroom," pragmatism is winning over ideology. Principals, superintendents, and school committees less often tell teachers what to do because in the face of a plethora of different methods and problems they are no longer sure they know. Administrators do know that if they direct teachers to use certain materials in certain ways and it doesn't work, the finger of accountability will point at them. Consequently, the unwritten policy in many public schools is becoming, "Teachers, do what you want and we won't stop you, as long as parents don't make angry midnight phone calls to the school board members; as long as the children don't destroy the building, the teachers or one another; and as long as standardized measures of achievement show growth." While the basis for such practices may not be commendable, some of the results are promising.

The plain truth is that we who work in schools — teachers, principals, psychologists, children — cannot deliver on promises of uniform achievement made by others. To dictate that "by June, all fourth graders will have mastered . . .", whatever the blank, makes no sense. If we want good things to happen in our schools we must start with people — children and teachers — not ideology or minimum competencies. Ultimately, effective education will not come from alternative schools within a system, alternative classrooms within a school, or even alternative people within a school. The essence of effective education lies in teachers who can find alternative ways of responding creatively to each of twenty-eight children. Alternatives within a classroom are the critical instructional alternatives. Classrooms, too, need orange pipes and yellow walls.

CHAPTER THREE

Organization

No man does well against his will, even though that which he does be good.

—Saint Augustine

EVERY SPRING, with the predictability and hopefulness of new-flowing sap and swelling buds, the question of staff organization comes to a school. One year the givens might be: four hundred children, sixteen teachers, eighteen classrooms. The challenge: to arrange personnel to offer the best instruction to children and at the same time meet the needs of teachers, parents, and central office. The *Rules and Regulations of the Newton School Committee*, under "Principals and Their Duties," devotes just two words to this responsibility: principals shall "assign teachers."[1] It is not that simple; nor is it that limited.

I have suggested that it is important for adults to be authentic when working with children. The institutional consequence of this conviction is a school of openly, honestly different and authentic people, offering children a multitude of "selves." Stefan Vogel, an elementary-school principal in Hanover, New Hampshire, put it this way in a memo to his staff:

> Children should be exposed to the individualities of teachers as human beings, so they can learn the give and take of personal relationships, and ways of coping with these relationships. Schools should be committed to providing children with the very best examples of the adult world they can hire. And the best doesn't mean "same." Children need many models of the adult world; diversity in experience, in talent, in temperament, in intellect, and in attitude should be a prime goal of staffing a school.[2]

We educators reel off, sometimes ad nauseum, the phrase, "Respect the individual differences of children," but I have seldom heard the cry, "Respect the individual differences of teachers" — although teacher differences have as much impact on students as any other factor. When

26

teachers behave in accord with their own personal styles and professional philosophies, both the teachers and their students benefit. Accordingly, in organizing the faculty each year we at Angier have evolved a process that tries to acknowledge, accept, and encourage differences in teacher style, method, and philosophy; that finds general acceptance from parents; and that capitalizes on the variety of teacher strengths and characteristics to the children's advantage.

Many experienced teachers feel trapped. They feel they have few significant options; there is little they can do next year other than repeat what they did this year. They have little sense of choice or commitment. Such captive teaching takes its toll on teachers and their students, leading to the sad, familiar portrait of the older teacher counting the days to retirement. An able senior staff must pursue new ideas and practices if it is not to become drowsy and mean-spirited. If schools can give teachers room to grow, such a picture is unnecessary. If teachers have choices — including the choice to take time off for personal renewal — and if teachers can be encouraged to develop new and important elements in their professional lives within·the school, their entire personal and professional being will be enhanced.

About mid-March at our school, after teachers have committed themselves to employment for the following year, I meet individually with each staff member and ask, "If you could decide under ideal conditions what you would like to do next year, and with whom, what would it be?" I provide one boundary condition: "You must work in the school in some way with children." In short, I invite teachers to disregard all practical constraints for a few moments to reflect upon their jobs as educators, to consider current interests, ideas, skills, and relationships, and to engage in some "if only . . . " brainstorming. These conferences explore and make explicit not what I would like teachers to do, not what they have been doing, but what they themselves would like to do. My assumption is that teachers are always changing, always developing, and would if they could always be growing. This assumption legitimizes change and often stimulates real growth.

My objective is for all of us to come to school each September with at least one significant new element in our professional (and therefore personal) lives — something to dream about, think about, worry about, get excited about, be afraid about, lose sleep about, become and remain *alive* about. Each fall children return to a new grade with a different teacher and a fresh combination of friends. Teachers too often return to the same school with the same colleagues teaching the same grade in the same room using the same books in the same way. This is a formula for personal and professional atrophy. Teachers find renewed vitality only from a new class of students. But the burden of staff renewal should not rest upon the children. Teachers should keep themselves alive and thereby enrich the lives and education of their students. Exploring how this may be done is a central issue of this book.

Teachers respond to the annual organization conferences as one might expect — differently. Many express the wish to do "the same thing" next year. Of these, a few may be too settled in or too worn down to change; others may recently have become involved in something so important and exciting that they are not ready for another change. For instance, two teachers may have worked out a teaming arrangement that allows one of them to teach math and science to both classes while the other teaches language and social studies. This kind of endeavor cannot be exhausted in a year. The teachers need time to master its complexities and savor the satisfactions.

Most teachers anticipate the conference, and give a great deal of thought to "if only . . . " Many share dreams they may not yet be ready to carry out. For instance, a teacher aide wants to become a librarian, a teacher wants to become a principal, a physical education teacher wants to become a director of physical education, or a teacher who runs a very teacher-directed class wants to develop a more child-centered classroom. We talk about these dreams, trying to break them down into smaller, more attainable stages, each less dramatic and threatening than the totality.

Many of the fantasies, and most of the changes in organization, are related to what the teacher would like to do next year, with which children, and in partnership with which other teacher. These are the sorts of dreams ready to be realized:

> I've been teaching half-time while my own children were in school. Now I'd like a full-time position.

> I've worked alone all these years. I'd like to try teaming with another teacher.

> I've taught fourth, fifth, and sixth grades. Now I'd like to try first grade.

> Linda and I would like to share responsibility for a single class of children, each of us working half time.

> We'd like to add a third member to our team.

> I'd like to concentrate on developing strengths in math next year.

The danger in asking the honest question, "Ideally, what would you like to do?" is that you generally get honest answers. These answers create expectations. The lively problem then is what to do with them. While I encourage teacher fantasies, value them, and take them seriously, I make it clear that these dreams are *starting* points. I will do the best I can to make them work if it is administratively possible to do so — and in the best interests of the children and the school. Often, unrealized fantasies cause disappointment and hard feelings. More frequently than one might suppose, though, we have been able to make a teacher's "if only . . . " come true. Our results suggest that following the best interests of teachers is often in the best interests of children and the school.

All year we make use of the information generated in the fantasy conferences. A teacher who wants to become a principal may assume many administrative responsibilities in the school. The teacher interested in making a classroom more materials-centered can visit model rooms in other schools. If we begin with the assumption that there always is a fantasy — a growing edge for teachers — then there always is a basis for growth and change. If we express the hope that everyone will do the same thing in the same way as last year, professional stagnation is likely to follow.

Obviously, working from individual fantasy conferences leads to diversity in classroom organization. While this diversity enriches professional development and enhances children's learning, it also poses a variety of intriguing, knotty problems. Among these are three issues of classroom organization: team teaching, cross-age grouping, and classrooms labeled according to some prevailing educational ideology.

The Issues

TEAM TEACHING: WHY TWO IS COMPANY

When I came to Angier, most teachers from kindergarten to fourth grade worked in self-contained classrooms, and the fifth- and sixth-grade staff worked as a large team. But it was a team in name only. The teachers involved demonstrated an extremely primitive level of cooperation, respect, and communication. As a consequence, everyone was doing something and no one was doing everything. The children lost out. After the first year I set a limit: no more than two teachers might team together.

The Koran tells us that a man should have four wives: one is not enough; two pits one against the other and fosters intense competition; three, like three siblings in a family, lends itself to "two against one." Thus, four is the smallest stable number. By similar reasoning, I have concluded that in most cases *two* is the optimal number of teachers to work with a group of children. A teacher working alone can lead a lonely, isolated existence. Outnumbered twenty-five to one, the teacher often becomes more and more childlike; the children may not become more and more adult. The absence of professional interaction leaves the teacher with little support when the going gets rough. The solitary teacher must face without backup the angry parent in confrontations of "your word against mine"; the single teacher must face without relief the usual two or three very disturbed or disturbing children. The teacher must cover assorted daily responsibilities like recess and lunch duty without benefit of cooperative arrangements to reduce the hours of duty. If by some lucky chance the school favors and fosters adult communication, cooperation, and interdependence, the self-contained teacher may draw upon the resources of colleagues. Unfortunately, this is seldom the case.

If the teacher in a self-contained classroom must cope with traditional professional problems, the multiteacher team faces other difficulties. Typically, each member of a large team is responsible for a different sub-ject area, the common organization of junior and senior high schools. Even in high school this model has limitations; at the elementary level, the drawbacks are severe. Organizing the child's day by subject matter — math, science, language, social studies — disintegrates learning ex-periences. Children's experiences do not sort themselves into tidy categories corresponding to the various disciplines. A field trip in the autumn woods has elements of science ("Why do the leaves fall?"), art ("What colors of leaves can we see?"), social studies ("Why are there trees around some schools and not others?"), math ("Can we estimate the number of leaves on a full-grown maple tree?"), and so on. If we divide the curriculum, we must then reintegrate subjects through artificial devices like cross-disciplinary courses in the "humanities." The larger the number of adults working together, the greater the tendency to fragment knowledge, and the more contrived and limited children's learning ex-periences become.

Scheduling problems also beset departmentalized programs. Each child and each teacher must have a schedule and must stick to it. English begins at 10:00 A.M. and ends at 10:55. Math begins at 11:00 and ends at 11:55. But during English the class becomes excited about making its own thesaurus. Everyone has an idea at once. A moment of great learn-ing is at hand. Sorry, "It's time for math." The self-contained classroom teacher can, of course, extend the language period all day. In a team of two teachers one can pop into the other's classroom and ask, "Can I keep the kids another half-hour?" In a larger team, however, few teachers would violate a schedule by trying to secure a consensus that would disrupt the schedules of perhaps a hundred students. In large team efforts the clock is the independent variable governing what, when, and with whom a child will be learning. The larger the team, the more inexorable the clock.

Communication is another major problem in large teams. If five adults divide Andrea's time into subjects, who will worry about her problems that do not deal specifically with math, science, language, or social studies? Who cares about her learning disability, the divorce at home, her short attention span? If these kinds of non-subject-matter problems are to be addressed by a team organized around disciplines, there must be meetings. Compound Andrea's needs by those of one or two hundred other children and there must be *many* meetings. In large teams meetings among teachers, with administrators, and with parents consume large amounts of time, leaving less for children.

When the meetings are satisfying and substantive, this use of time is justified. All too frequently, however, they are fruitless efforts to reach agreement on some minor issue. Can our children go to the library without a teacher escort? Shall we permit gum chewing in the classrooms? Shall we hold parent night next week or the week after? Members of a team of five people rarely hold the same views about anything. Teachers are people of extraordinary conviction and variability. Agreement between two teachers usually represents a considerable accomplishment; members of a five-person team are likely to spend much of their time speaking or working at odds.

The difficulties of team meetings are eclipsed only by the difficulties of *not* meeting. Without frequent, direct communication, a team may soon become a collection of isolated prima donnas, each of whom touches a piece of each child each day, but none of whom can assume responsibility for all of the child or all of the children.

And "communal marriages" have interpersonal difficulties. These problems become especially visible in open-space schools. A prerequisite to the successful sharing of living space is some measure of mutual respect, cooperation, and consensus among those who occupy it. I remember visiting the faculty room of one open-space school and talking with a teacher who was considering playing soft music in order to keep the noise level down. Then she added, "But they'd never let me." When I asked who "they" were, she replied, "Why, the other teachers in the room, of course." The tyranny of the majority exacts a particular toll upon teachers who share membership on a formal team or who share classroom space. I have never seen a team of four or five where each member had a satisfactory relationship with every other member. Generally, each member of a large team has a strong relationship with one or two colleagues, and an awkward relationship — or none — with the others.

Two members make the best team. Two form a support system as accessible as the door across the hall; two allow ready alteration of schedules; two provide mutual visibility, which fosters questioning, healthy competition, personal insight, and a context for growth; two can specialize some of the time, but range across disciplines as opportunities arise. And with a team of two, responsibility and accountability for children's progress is focused on a manageable number of pupils.

Finally, a two-person team has an interpersonal advantage. Like marriage, a team relationship between two teachers is apt to have much personal intensity, meaning, frustration, and satisfaction. I have seen many examples of two teachers forming successful teaching marriages. I have also seen some divorces. Like marriage, each teacher must decide whether to make (and maintain) the commitment and to whom. Neither the "arranged" marriage nor the "arranged" teaching team has much of a record of weathering the inevitable strains. For that reason I encourage teachers to work together, but I stay away from matchmaking.

When two teachers decide to team, the three of us sit down and talk. It may be a simple exchange: "You take my kids for math, and I'll take yours for language." It may be a more elaborate arrangement in which teachers share responsibility for teaching all subjects or treat their classrooms as one big instructional setting. There are many variations; the constant is the relationship with another adult who is always involved, listening, caring, and available.

Our final organization each year finds about half the staff teaching in self-contained classrooms (by their choice), about half in some form of two-person team (by their choice), and none working in teams larger than two (by my choice). Teams, properly formed and encouraged, are a valid form of classroom variability. Badly managed by teachers or administrators, they are disasters.

Cross-Age Grouping: Who Benefits?

ANGIER GREENSHEET

[the school's weekly newsletter, so named because it is printed on green mimeograph paper]

November 3

WE HOPE YOU WILL

join us on Wednesday evening, November 12, at eight o'clock for a discussion of cross-age grouping in the elementary school. The discussion will be both more lively and more profitable if you are willing to do some homework. The PTA Program Committee, members of the Angier faculty, and I have prepared the following list of questions in the hope that between us we can find some answers and stimulate further questions.

(1) How is continuity of curriculum retained within cross-age classes?

(2) In what ways are older children treated the same/differently as younger children within a multiage classroom?

(3) How do we decide which children to place in cross-age classes?

(4) Why are many parents disturbed about having their child placed in the older end of a cross-age group, but comfortable about having their child placed in the younger end?

(5) What is the relationship between multiage classes and more informal classrooms?

(6) What is the effect on the variability in a class (in terms of ability, behavior, interests) of doubling the age range?

(7) Who benefits, in what ways, when older children help teach younger children?

(8) Why mixed-age classes? What are some advantages and disadvantages for children who are in a classroom with other students representing a two- or three-year age range?

We hope you will join us Wednesday evening for a discussion of these and other questions.

Roland

"Cross-age grouping," "family grouping," "mixed groups"; "nongraded" or "continuous-progress" classes — whatever you call them, these classrooms have a common characteristic: children of different ages are placed together for instruction. And, whatever you call it, this practice generates questions, anxiety, and misunderstanding among teachers and parents.

Cross-age grouping is one of those educational practices that trades old problems and solutions for new problems and solutions. At Angier, on balance, cross-age groups have been productive for teachers, children, and the school. Other schools have had different experiences.

Each year at organization time many teachers ask to teach a mixed-age class — a K-1, a K-1-2, a 3-4, or a 5-6. We have even considered K-6 fantasies. As many flatly refuse to consider a mixed-age class — with equal strength of conviction. Few have no strong feelings. When the dust settles, we find about half the faculty, half the students, and half the parents involved in cross-age groups; about half are committed to straight-age classes.

A mix of cross-age and single-age groups within the school promotes unending discussions among staff, parents, and administration, as the PTA meeting announcement suggests — a good example of the productive problems that accompany diversity. It is a rich, recurring, and sometimes heated dialogue. Typically, it goes like this:

QUESTION: Why do we have multiage classes?

ANSWER: Because we begin the organizational process with teacher preferences and many teachers prefer a mixture of age levels in their classes. When teachers are teaching under conditions they feel best, they put more of themselves into teaching and their students get more out of it.

QUESTION: Why do some teachers prefer mixed-age classes?

ANSWER: Many believe a child benefits from being with others who differ along important dimensions — including age. These teachers make deliberate, constructive use of differences to foster learning, a practice that is less possible in a more homogeneous class. I have found that teachers who prefer mixed-age groups are especially sensitive to sex differences in children as well. And teachers who prefer mixed-age groups often prefer individualized programs. They are accustomed to an ability range of two, three, or four years and have little difficulty in preparing for a class of different ages. Many use children as peer tutors, which is clearly easier in a class where many older children "have it" and many younger children do not.

QUESTION: Why do many teachers *refuse* to teach a cross-age class?

ANSWER: Teachers with strong objections to teaching a cross-age class value large-group projects. They also tend to group children by ability. In a mixed-age class these teachers would have to work with many small groups, which means more lessons to plan, more materials to procure, more work to do, and perhaps fewer large-group activities. Mixed ages have the effect of increasing variability among children; teachers feel they can be more effective by decreasing student variability.

Some of the variability in the cross-age groups is illusory. The evening of the PTA meeting, we discovered that in each multiage class the fastest and the slowest children were the same age. Doubling the age range does not double the range of ability. Ever-widening variation in ability is inevitable as children go up through the grades. Most second grades show about a two-year ability span; sixth grades have perhaps a six-year range. The cross-age group may *appear* more heterogeneous — some children will be much larger and more mature than others — but the ability span will not differ as radically from the straight-age class as some might suppose. Teachers who individualize instruction, whether in straight or cross-age classes, swim with the inevitable current; those who group children by ability swim against it. Teachers who expect children to differ will have their expectations fulfilled; those who expect children to be similar will be disappointed.

Cross-age groups generate many problems outside the classroom. Parents are particularly sensitive to experiments starring their children. After one debate on cross-age grouping, a mother wrote:

Many parents last visited a classroom when they themselves were in school — and they only recall a bit of that. It is difficult for them to comprehend a classroom of several age levels. It must be seen to be believed. Parents who don't know anything about cross-age grouping encounter problems new to *them* but probably not new to all of you. Problems like a child moving from a mixed-age class to a straight one — or vice versa. Problems like what happens when kindergarten children leave a K-1 class at noon. What's it like for the K's and for the 1's? Problems of concentration, competition, and differences in skill level. And lots of other problems you will hear about but can't predict!

By allowing parents to participate in these decisions and discussions, you are inviting attack by those whose position you do not honor, but I hope the heat will not dampen the school's spirit of openness and flexibility. Good going!

This letter is from a friendly parent; many are not nearly so positive. The teacher who asks for a cross-age class also asks for a year-long selling job, as suggested by another parent's confusion of the words *multiaging* and *mutilating*. The teacher must show, to the satisfaction of the parents, that a mixed-age class is just as good as a "regular" class. This job is made still more difficult by the routine association of mixed-age classes with the now tainted concept of open classrooms. The following letter suggests both the confounding of the two concepts and some of the problems that arise:

Dear Mr. Barth,

Can you stand another comment from another parent? I have missed all the meetings about cross-aged classes because I didn't know they were happening. It sounds as if Angier is in some sort of mental crisis which directly affects my daughter Sally, who is entering second grade.

As you can guess, I am pulled by what I have learned in graduate school but also by ten years of having children at Angier. I know that teaching facts is out of style and that the goal of making children self-directed is a worthy one, but most parents in this community are worried about any more loss of structure. I really think that this is because there is so little structure left in the lives of these kids. I suspect that we can't transpose open classrooms, English style, to this environment because the English upbringing is different. Perhaps somehow those children have some built-in restrictions which Americans don't have. I resist quoting Bronfenbrenner! My own experience as a parent, for what it's worth, is that it is almost impossible for a teacher to keep tabs on each child in an interest-centered classroom. For one reason or another, my children have been able to avoid the basic hard work of learning certain skills unless they are lucky enough to be forced by a concerned teacher. Sally has been "saved" by Mr. Roberts, and John, now in seventh, has slid through without ever being made to write and is in serious difficulty.

My point, I guess, is that I am afraid of a 2-3 or a K-1-2 setup because most of the time children will be working in their interest areas. I don't believe children choose what they need. In fact, they avoid what they need. The activity-oriented trend in education seems to me to be for children who don't have our rich background. Newton children don't need entertainment; they don't need "interests"; they don't need trips to the zoo. They need study habits, ability to produce, meet a challenge, and maybe even a little criticism. They can bake all the cupcakes they need at home. What they can't seem to do is tackle and finish something that is hard work. I *do* lay this directly at the feet of the school system. I'm afraid if you disperse the attention of one teacher over too many levels of learning, he/she will not be able to demand enough from each child. I'm not saying that something has to be painful to be good for you, but that often we get turned on only after a good deal of nose-to-the-grindstone. I have been most grateful for conscientious, demanding teachers.

I think parents need more than reassurance that school is not becoming an entertainment center. They need to be shown that something is expected of their children. The word "open" certainly sets up all kinds of alarms.

I apologize for taking your time, but as you know by now, Angier parents are notorious for "helping" in school affairs.

Sincerely,

In some ways this parent is right. Teachers who favor individualized instruction and diversity of sex, race, and age are often the same teachers disposed toward more student-centered, informal, and material-centered classrooms. And teachers committed to both cross-age groups and more informal classrooms tend to cluster in the primary grades, where parents and children often experience a particularly high level of school anxiety.

The teacher of a cross-age group, in addition to making it work for twenty-five children — a burden for any teacher in any kind of classroom — must assume the 180-day burden of making it work for an even larger number of skeptical, often hostile, parents. Saddled with overtones of "tentative," "experimental," and "open," and foreign to parents' own school experiences, the mixed-age class flies red flags. Only teachers deeply committed to cross-age grouping are prepared to take on the political battle of creating legitimacy in addition to the educational battle of making it work. Since teachers, like other people, have a finite supply of time and energy, it is not hard to see why some regard cross-age grouping with all the enthusiasm with which they might confront an irritated cobra.

The double burden of running and selling a cross-age class makes it perilous to impose such an organization on a teacher uncommitted to it. On one or two occasions over the years I have asked (or "told," depending on who was telling the tale) a teacher to take on a mixed-age class. At best, the experience was unsuccessful; at worst, it was a lot worse. The reluctant teacher treats the mixed class as two separate groups — a fourth and a fifth grade, for instance. This works badly, augmenting the teacher's fears, doubts, and resistance. Teacher anxieties corroborate, substantiate, and compound parents' fears, doubts, and resistance. When both teacher and parents lack confidence in a class, children have a rough year. So does the teacher. So do the parents. So, let me assure you, does the principal. After a few of these experiences, I learned to assign like-age groups to teachers who want them and mixed-age groups only to teachers who prefer them, avoiding conditions likely to produce failure.

Principals can — and often do — avoid the entire situation by vetoing mixed-age classes and organizing school, teachers, and children into straight grades. Why not do this all the time? There are both pedagogical and administrative reasons. I value diversity within a classroom just as I value diversity within a school, and for many of the same reasons. Diversity in race, sex, ability, maturity, social background, and age exists in the real world; representing those differences in the classroom can have great instructional potency, particularly if orchestrated by a teacher who values and can make instructional use of human variability.

There are good reasons, however, for maintaining both like-age and cross-age classes in a school. Certain children appear to learn better in groups of like-age peers, some as members of the younger part of a mixed-age class, and others as members of the older part of the class. Having both like and mixed-age classes enables us to match individual learning styles with appropriate classrooms.

The presence of mixed-age groups also contributes to the professional development of the staff. When significantly different forms of classroom organization coexist within a school, questions like those on the agenda of the PTA meeting are asked — questions that promote constant examination of what all of us are doing, and how, and why. Uniformity inside schools discourages and stifles such questions.

The pedagogical reasons for including cross-age grouping in an elementary school organization are reinforced by administrative considerations such as class size. Most school systems determine the size of a school's teaching staff by dividing the total number of students by the system-wide average class size. Recently Angier had 400 pupils and the average class size in the system was 24. Thus, we were given 16.5 teaching positions that year. However, the number of pupils at any grade level could not be neatly divided by 24:

Grade	Number of pupils
K	49
1	52
2	50
3	68
4	47
5	76
6	58
	400

If there were *no* mixed-age classes in the school, the organization and distribution of 400 children over 16.5 teachers might look like this:

(half time)	K	17	1	26
(half time)	K	16	1	26
(half time)	K	16	2	25

2	25		5	25
3	22		5	26
3	23		6	19
3	23		6	20
4	24		6	19
4	23			400
5	25			

This (or any other plan we might devise) sets up inequities in class size. One kindergarten teacher would have only 16 children; in the room next door, a first-grade teacher would have 26. Despite research that questions the importance of class size to children's learning, my experience suggests that it does make a difference — to the child, the parent, and the teacher — whether a youngster is a member of a class of 16 or a class of 26. Cross-age grouping can very nearly equalize class sizes throughout the school. Unexpected influxes of students at particular grade levels can be absorbed among five or six teachers rather than three or four. With cross-age grouping, the same 400 children with the same 16.5 teachers might be distributed this way:

K	22		3-4	25
K-1	22		4	24
K-1-2	49 (two teachers)		4-5	24
1	22		5	24
2	24		5	24
2-3	22		5-6	24
3	23		6	24
3	23		6	24

School boards inevitably are reluctant to add teaching positions (about 75 percent of the typical school budget is already expended on personnel). They voraciously cut every position made vulnerable by dwindling enrollments. Thus if class sizes are to be kept at equitable levels, the burden will fall on the organizational pattern within each school.

This is not to deny the problems facing an administrator whose school has cross-age classes. The principal must be prepared to join teachers in a perpetual effort to describe, explain, defend, and legitimize cross-age groups and at the same time not discriminate against single-age classes. The effort is likely to be unsuccessful if the administrator has serious doubts about mixed-age grouping.

Furthermore, cross-age grouping runs counter to many conventional school practices that conveniently categorize children by age. For instance, all third graders in the Newton system learn to play the recorder. Second and fourth graders do not. The system sends all sixth graders (but only sixth graders) on a week-long camping experience. Cross-age groups constantly run counter to such conventions. If half the members of a cross-age class have an experience that for some reason is not available to their classmates, *two* classes emerge within the class, and the possibilities for integration and cooperation across age groups dissipate. But if the entire cross-age class is to have an experience, additional funds, materials, and personnel are needed. Even if the necessary resources can be found, two new problems arise: curriculum continuity and equity. If the second graders in a 2-3 combination learn to play the recorder this year, what do they do next year while their peers learn beginning recorder? And if *they* receive recorder lessons, what about the other second graders in straight second grades? Shouldn't they have the recorder option too? Is the principal trying to deprive the children in "normal" classes?

I have resolved (if not solved) the equity question by establishing a rule of thumb: all children in a mixed-age group may participate in all activities offered to children within that class. My answer to teachers and parents whose children (say, second graders) are excluded from an activity (say, recorder) that is available to children in a mixed class (say, a 2-3) is "That's one of the benefits of being in a cross-age class." This always generates interesting conversation.

I leave this discussion of cross-age grouping as I have left most discussions of this issue — with several unanswered questions:

What is the effect upon children of being in a cross-age group rather than in a straight-age class?

How is the experience of the younger children in the class different from that of the older?

What problems of program discontinuity are associated with cross-age groups?

Are cross-age groups more suitable for primary children than for intermediate?

Are there certain age groups that should not be placed together (for instance, mature sixth graders [who are preadolescents] with immature fifth graders)?

Until I see evidence to the contrary, I shall continue to support cross-age classes because I find this organization desired by some teachers and because, as we shall see when we discuss placement, cross-age classes appear to be especially beneficial for some children. It is hard to ask more of a staff organization.

Avoiding Labels: Each Classroom Its Own Place

Classroom labeling is a third complex problem besetting the organization of a pluralistic school. I have discouraged class labeling as vigorously as I have encouraged personal authenticity. Whatever may be their good uses, labels create inevitable and useless conflicts. No matter how carefully constructed, no matter how thoroughly explained, any educational label carries a burden of associations and prejudices that make the task of teacher and principal more difficult. I have found few compensating benefits.

Take, for example, a current educational hot potato — open classrooms. The presence of an educational label like "open" demands a definition and description to convey what the teachers who wear that label mean by it. After interminable meetings teachers in one school succeeded in hammering out a description to which they reluctantly agreed to subscribe:

AN OPEN CLASSROOM

An open classroom has tables and chairs, not desks in rows. Pupils work in small groups or individually but seldom in large groups. They are free to move about the room or go outside to get materials or assistance. Walls and corridors offer lovely displays of children's work. Often there are rugs on the floor and the room is arranged into cozy interest areas in language, art, math, science, and social studies. Teachers attempt to provide individualized instruction suitable for each child's special needs and skills. The room offers many activities: books, paints, sand, batteries, and bulbs, math balancers, animals, and plants to observe and care for. Pupils learn to take responsibility for their own time. They decide when to move from one activity to the next as they are finished.

Open-classroom teachers look for assets children bring to school. This requires keen observational skills and close cooperation between child and teacher. Stress is placed on what children can do, not on what they cannot do; on success and not failure. Teachers teach children but children also learn from each other. Peer learning is aided by the practice of placing children of different ages in the same class — such as groups of K-1-2's.

A good open classroom helps children become resourceful and independent in using their time. Another objective is to teach the basic literacy skills of reading, writing, and arithmetic. These skills, while not taught and learned in conventional ways, are taught and learned.

A thoughtful, innocuous statement. It sounds like a good place, a classroom in which we might all like to have our children placed. But the effect of broadcasting such a description can be deadly. What about the classrooms that do *not* operate under the "open classroom" label? Are they inflexible? uncomfortable? boring? unresponsive? characterized by failure? Teachers not included in the description take exception to these implications and hard feelings arise — "I do that, too!" "Who do they think they are, anyway?" It is hardly surprising that this leads to faculty dissension and the undermining wish for colleagues to fail.

Teachers unanimously take exception to a description of an educational practice that does not include them — and only a few do not take exception to a description of a practice that *does* include them. A labeled program usually prompts several responses from teachers not involved in it. First comes fear ("I'm going to be pressured into doing that"); then comes defensiveness ("I can do it better than they can"), followed quickly by offensiveness ("They'll get what's coming to them"). Often threatened teachers form another camp. The presence of one labeled practice in a school creates a need for a label for everyone else, like it or not. If there is an "open" program, what are the others to be called? "Closed" classrooms? "Traditional" classrooms? "Regular" classrooms?" The reactions of a school staff to classroom labels is much like their reaction to merit pay: if one teacher gets merit pay for excellent performance, what does this say about those who don't get it?

Thus, labeling can intensify competitiveness and antagonism among teachers, creating adversaries where there may have been none before. Labels breed bad feelings about which side is getting the most money, about whether more parents want Brand X or Brand Y, and, of course, about which one is better. Labels produce an atmosphere of inclusiveness and exclusiveness in which there are winners and losers; none of this is healthy for a school.

Furthermore, labels feed the need, particularly among parents, to stereotype: "The teacher runs the traditional classroom; the child runs the open classroom"; "They don't teach the basics in the unstructured mode,' just personal things like creativity and independence." These simplistic definitions stick to classrooms and to teachers who have projected or accepted labels. Few teachers who have donned these "scarlet letters" ever forget the experience.

Given two or three camps, parents tend to collect like iron filings near a magnet around the package they feel corresponds best to their values and life-style. Although few have pure positions on these issues, most feel forced to choose. When classrooms are labeled open or traditional, positions calcify. Although there are many comfortable intermediate positions, labeling tends to make the programs appear both competitive and mutually exclusive.

Hard feelings arise between teachers of different camps. There are frequent arguments in faculty rooms or at PTA meetings over the question, "Who works harder, teachers of open classes or those of traditional classes?" Ripe apples are compared with rotten oranges. Personally, I haven't found a difference in effort between good "open" and good "traditional" teachers or between bad "open" and bad "traditional" teachers.

The extent to which labels can cripple is suggested by a letter I received from a teacher from a western state. She had spent her sabbatical year studying and visiting open classrooms in New England with the intent of returning home to teach this way.

When I returned home I was upset to see how embattled the community was over open classrooms. Few people wanted to talk with me. I was dangerous, tainted. Other teachers, principals, and even parents walked around me for several weeks. I offered to make a report on my year of study but there were no takers. Even several of my close teaching friends would have nothing to do with me.

And the use of labels to describe instruction often generates labels to describe *children* for whom the instruction is seen as appropriate. One school system defined the Open-Education Child: "The child is actively involved in planning the day's work through teacher conferences, through his own initiatives, and through classroom meetings. The child should move about the room to pursue educational activities. The child should be allowed to converse with peers." Teachers in the system presented the curious argument that *only* these Open-Education Children should be placed in open classrooms — a practice that violates the more basic definition of open classrooms as "meeting the needs of each child," whether those needs suggest firm limits or independent activity. The concept of an Open-Education Child also provided in this case a convenient rationale (or rationalization) for excluding difficult children who did not have the prerequisite qualities.

We can ill afford to exhaust the precious energies needed to help children by bickering over ideological labels. More schools should consider taking the position offered by a sensible, sensitive principal in her school's weekly newsletter to parents:

A DECISION: At a recent faculty meeting it was decided that the expressions "open classrooms" and "open education" will be taboo among us next year. These terms have a different meaning for everybody who uses them, and therefore, no real meaning. Instead, we will join with you in defining "good education" for Williams School.

Anne Carr, Principal

Beyond promoting divisiveness, educational labels foster conformity. A teacher who tries to comply with a label is to some degree playing a role, and role playing does not promote examination of teacher or student. A person playing a role is less likely to be fully aware of personal belief and philosophy and is less likely to respond carefully, helpfully, and differentially to children. An effective teacher — regardless of ideology — provides children with the unique set of conditions under which each can learn best and most. Labels constrain the instructional repertoire of a teacher instead of extending and expanding it. If I am not an open-classroom teacher (and if the parents of children in my class do not want their children in an open classroom), it becomes difficult for me to bring in a pair of gerbils and set up a science interest corner, for these have become motifs of the open classroom. If I am an open-classroom teacher, it is difficult for me to provide large-group instruction when necessary, because teachers in an open classroom "don't do that."

Labels interfere with teachers' making full use of all available resources. No teacher who works with a diverse group of children (as all do) can afford to employ only materials, ideas, and methodologies associated with a particular orthodoxy. If behavior modification techniques seem the only way to help Jimmy learn, it is foolish to reject them on the grounds that behavior modification is contrary to the model of open education.

A teacher recently showed me the absurdity of the open-traditional labeling scheme. In her job interview she was told that parents were demanding a second-grade teacher who would run an open classroom. Although she had little idea what an "open classroom" was, she needed a job and accepted the position. Certainly she would run an open classroom, she told the personnel office. I asked her if she would have accepted a "traditional" classroom as readily. "Of course," she said. Whatever they called it, she intended to run her own kind of classroom, with confidence that it would be a productive place for children. She was sure this would be apparent to parents. If you call a moose a duck, it *can* fly!

The difference between labels and no labels in a school, then, is the difference between a teacher fulfilling someone else's expectations (usually only superficially) and a teacher developing authenticity. While labels encourage teachers to imitate an external model, the absence of labels promotes the achievement of more personal classroom goals.

A resourceful friend of mine used to buy all of his clothes in bargain basements. He prided himself on how well-dressed he could be at little expense. He would joke about his "designer clothes," opening his jacket to the inside pocket and saying, "Look, N.L." — no label. It is not easy to choose and wear a suit with no label attesting to its quality. One must make frequent, difficult judgments and have the personal confidence to live with the results. So it is with schools. Removing the labels suggests that the merchandise is uncertified, less desirable, less trustworthy, and dangerously uneven. To live without labels, teachers and parents must have confidence. They must believe that they can make educational judgments based not on cost, not on the words tacked to the classroom door, but on description and observation about how a particular classroom fits a particular child. Labels prevail in schools because they often relieve us of the responsibility for deciding. "It's an open classroom; therefore, I don't want it," a parent can declare. But the absence of labels promotes other questions — "What are the characteristics of this teacher, and of this classroom?" "What does my child need?" — and leads to far more complex and subtle judgments.

Observers in classrooms these days are finding a widening array of hybrid, idiosyncratic teaching practices. Though a few classrooms may appear to be purely open or traditional, more are semiopen or mixed.

Look at a class with desks and rows and elaborate science and social-studies interest areas at the back, whose teacher moves helpfully from child to child. Is this room open or traditional? Is a classroom with no desks and lots of activity centers and a group of twenty-five children seated on the floor receiving group instruction traditional or open?

As personalized, eclectic classrooms have evolved at Angier, labels such as open and traditional have all but vanished. Over the years it has become harder and harder to apply labels to *anyone*. The only labels that fit these classrooms, the only signs that belong on the doors, are the teachers' names. "This is Mrs. Cibley's class." If you want to know more, you can come in and observe for yourself. We cannot label Mrs. Cibley, but we can describe how she teaches math, reading, science, and social studies; what materials she uses, how she groups children for instruction, what limits she sets on children, and how space, time, and subject matter are organized in her class. If you go next door, you will find Mrs. Byers's classroom — and a different constellation of educational practices, unique to Mrs. Byers. More and more the school is characterized by different people, not different ideologies. This is the way teachers come — in their own packages. Teaching is too complex, too contradictory, too personalized to fit any facile description.

An unplanned evaluation of our de-emphasis on labels occurred a couple of years ago. A university researcher sent me a letter similar to this one:

> We should like to observe various types of classrooms. Would you
> please consider your staff members and give us the names of those who
> teach classes of these sorts: individualized instruction, open classroom,
> team teaching, nongrading, etc. Thank you for your assistance.

I wasn't about to undo years of work by placing labels on twenty different teachers. So I did what any reasonable administrator would do — I delegated. I sent the memo to the Visitors' Committee of three teachers and asked them to fill it out. They had no intention of labeling their colleagues either; they went to each teacher and asked for an indication of the category that best fit that teacher's classroom. Not a single teacher felt that any code words described his or her class. A memo went back to the school of education from the Visitors' Committee saying in effect:

> We have a variety of different teachers and instructional practices at
> Angier. Visitors are welcome.

SETTING LIMITS: BALANCING FREEDOM AND RESPONSIBILITY

I have discussed some of the conditions within a school that stimulate diversity of practice and affect staff organization: the encouragement of fantasies about one's ideal job, the opportunity to cooperate with other teachers, the chance to teach children of different ages, and the removal of constraining labels. But ultimately each teacher, child, and parent is more concerned about the instructional conditions *within a classroom* than the organizational conditions within a school. Everyone realizes that the nature of the child's experience with an individual teacher is the crucial element in education.

It is difficult to monitor teachers who are encouraged to be themselves. Incompetence or laziness may hide in the guise of "authenticity." And it is only a small step from "alternative people" and "teacher authenticity" to "anything goes." Institutional anarchy, whimsy, and caprice could quickly follow, and children might suffer. There must be boundary conditions within which teachers function. Perhaps the best way to describe the limits I have set, the parameters within which each teacher makes personal and professional judgments, is to recall my first faculty meeting. Two issues were central: teachers were anxious to know where I stood and what I expected of them; at the same time they wanted me to know that they intended to continue doing as they saw fit. What does a principal say to a staff in a situation like that? Setting limits on adults is difficult, unpleasant, and anxiety producing. Yet an institution as complex and important as a public school — particularly a pluralistic school — cannot function without limits. Teachers find it necessary to set limits on children, principals on teachers, superintendents on principals, school boards on superintendents, and legislatures on school boards. The question is not whether limits will be set, but who will set them and what they will be.

How much teacher diversity and authenticity can the system tolerate? What range of teacher behaviors can be justified as being in the best interest of the children and the school? This is not an abstract philosophical issue but one that comes up daily in letters like these:

Dear Mr. Barth:

I am appalled. I know that braless women walk about Harvard Square — but in an elementary school! And such an alluring woman at that. I am terribly upset that you allow this.

Many other parents feel as I do that by permitting this kind of license, you must condone it. However, we want you to know that we find it unacceptable and we expect you to put a stop to it.

An Outraged Parent

Dear Mr. Barth:

Please mention to the teacher that keeping the well-behaved, quiet children in from recess or after school isn't fair. Punishing the *whole* class isn't fair. If he doesn't know *who's* misbehaving in his class he shouldn't be teaching.

A Concerned Mother

Generally speaking, I deal with teachers as I hope they deal with their students — I trust them until I am given reason not to. Then I am more cautious about trusting them in particular areas. I find this attitude more productive than "I can't trust a teacher until I have ample evidence that trust is deserved." I try to convey to teachers that I expect from them the best each can give most of the time. In turn, in order to provide their best, they can expect me to supply what they need most of the time.

But "best" is a tricky notion. Often what we mean is "Do what I want you to do and do it well." My concern, however, is to encourage the best performance of which children and teachers are capable — on their terms, not mine. For example, I believe that children will have a better year in a classroom with desks in rows than they will if I have to compel the teacher to set up interest areas and remove the desks.

At that first faculty meeting I made a distinction between goals and means that has subsequently proved most useful. In matters of *goals*, the school board, superintendent, principal, parents, and students have considerable, legitimate interest — and say. It is not acceptable for a teacher to quote to me (as one did) John Holt's "Children best learn to read the way they learn to ride a bicycle — without adult intervention." It is not acceptable for a teacher to make unilateral decisions about what shall be taught, be it reading, writing, arithmetic, self-confidence, or independence. Not in a public school system. The determination of goals must come from a consensus within the school community. Fortunately this is not as difficult as it may sound. I have been surprised to find among teachers, central-office administrators, school boards, parents, and principals a widespread agreement on educational goals. If we were to administer a questionnaire with instructions to "check those goals to which you subscribe," most of us would check the same items: precision in written and oral communication; development of basic literacy skills in language and mathematics; independence; creativity; respect for others and property; self-confidence; love of learning.

The quarrels arise more often from the "how" than the "what." Will a child be given instruction in reading with three ability groups, or two, or an individualized program? Shall we use Houghton Mifflin or Bank Street? A phonetic or whole-word approach? Everyone cares and everyone wants to decide — teachers, parents, principals, curriculum coordinators, school boards, and university professors. Means are specific, concrete, visible, tangible. Goals are distant, rhetorical, general, and elusive. For many, means are confused with goals. For many, goals are inferred from means. I recall one teacher who kept a guinea pig in her classroom to provide a stimulus for creative writing. A parent objected, "I don't want my child to become a veterinarian."

I told the teachers at that same first faculty meeting that I felt questions of educational *means* were best determined by classroom teachers.

Teachers are trained and experienced in making these instructional decisions, and they derive enormous professional and personal satisfaction from doing so. But all good teaching is not idiosyncratic. In making decisions about how to teach, I believe teachers should rely on three sources of information: their daily, careful observations of individual children; their own personal and professional philosophy, style, and experience; and the vast body of accumulated literature known as educational research.[3]

Since this, too, is an invitation for autonomy, if not for anarchy, I tried to establish acceptable limits within which teachers might differ. I told the staff that all teachers would enjoy this instructional latitude under two conditions. First, that each teacher respect if not agree with the way his colleagues were teaching, without undermining or belittling. Second, at least twice a year I would expect each to provide, through careful pupil evaluation, written evidence that the teaching methods and materials he or she had chosen were working. Mrs. Jones has to be ready to show that her frequent class trips to the town library are improving second-grade reading skills; Mr. Brown has to be able to demonstrate that the fourth graders, using hand calculators, know more multiplication facts in January than they did in September. Theoretically, every instructional practice must be related to desirable changes in children. In fact, however, we seldom find it necessary to employ these criteria rigidly. Teachers are usually the second (after the children) to know a method is not working.

Thus, no teacher is held responsible for successfully implementing my ideas. On the other hand, no teacher can say, "I want to do it my way, but don't hold me accountable for it." Freedom is paired with accountability, and individuality with responsibility. These are the only uniform instructional limits I have imposed on Angier teachers, although there have been many cases of additional expectations for individual teachers.

By explicitly rejecting undermining of faculty by faculty and by tying instructional responsibility to pupil evaluation, bickering has diminished, teacher performance has improved, and parental confidence has grown. Certainly, there are arguments in the faculty room over how children best learn addition facts or spelling words; no one simply assumes that three reading groups are better than two or better than an individualized reading program. Teachers leave these debates more often stimulated than angered, full of enthusiasm and the confidence that they can return to their classrooms and teach in ways that reflect their own values, philosophies, and personal commitments — and the needs of their students. We have banished the fear that "if you get your way, I lose mine." With this confidence, teachers seldom subvert one another.

A few years ago parents and teachers painted every room in the school with colors chosen by teachers. Some became off-white, others magenta or blue. All were visibly distinct. Teachers have become as proud of the distinctiveness of their unique programs as of their classroom decor. Now they are secure enough to be accountable and secure enough to respect the quite different classrooms of their colleagues. A paper written by one graduate student-observer noted this comfortable diversity.

> I observed teachers and children. In several rooms I talked with teachers about what they were doing, why, and how. Teachers' ideas and feelings about their students, about their curriculum, and about one another were very positive.
>
> The variety of teaching styles was as wide as the range of teachers. Some classrooms were informal, with interest areas, carpets, and lofts; others had three reading groups or desks in rows. Some teachers used individualized programs, others large-group instruction. In each of these very different classrooms, teachers appeared to be industrious, excited, and committed to what they were doing. So were the children.

Over the years, the expectations that teachers respect the educational means employed by others and take responsibility for demonstrating children's progress have been taken seriously and, by and large, fulfilled. By relinquishing my authority to determine instructional means, the school has gained faculty stability and measurable student achievement. It has, I think, been a fair exchange.

Organizing the School: The Final Product

This is the background, the process, and the philosophy that determines each year what and how and with whom each teacher will teach. A few mechanical steps create our final organization. We take the number of teaching positions allocated by the personnel office, the number of children at each grade level, along with individual teacher wishes, and develop three or four organizational plans that work in terms of numbers of children and teachers. Finally, we select one with the most advantages and fewest disadvantages — the plan that does the most for the most.

Ultimately, the most compelling justification for a school organization characterized by diverse teachers, classrooms, instructional styles, and programs rests not with the satisfaction of teachers or parents, nor with administrative expediency, but with opportunities for placement of children into different kinds of classes. In determining the final organization, we attempt to find the plan that comes closest to complying with teacher requests and at the same time provides teachers and classrooms at each age level that differ along dimensions relevant to children's learning styles. In this way fruitful, promising matches can be made at placement time. Through hiring practices, internal reorganization of the existing staff, and encouragement of teacher aspirations we try to ensure that in placing each child we may choose among the following:

(1) A male or female teacher. For some children (perhaps a child without a father or a mother at home) this is a critical factor; for others it makes little difference. We usually have both men and women teaching at each grade level, K-6.

(2) A group of children of the same age, or a group with many older or younger children.

(3) Teachers running self-contained classrooms or teachers cooperating in teams. For some children it seems to be important that they work each day with one, and only one, adult; for others it is important that they work with two different adults (perhaps one for math, one for language).

(4) A more informal, student-centered, material-centered classroom, or a more formal, teacher-directed classroom.

(5) Teachers who have different subject-matter strengths such as language, mathematics, science, and music.

This is how the needs of teachers are balanced against the needs of the students. If we are lucky, one and only one organization emerges that satisfies the needs of both. For instance, one year the final organization looked like this:

ANGIER SCHOOL FACULTY

Grade	Teacher	Organization unit
K	Peggy Newman	Self-contained
K-1	Deborah Horwitz	Self-contained
K-1-2	Sandra Porter-Englehart ⎫	Team
K-1-2	John Roche ⎭	
1	Marian Raedel	Self-contained
2	Marion Shaughnessy	Self-contained
2-3	Richard Hanelin	Self-contained
3	Marjorie Byers ⎫	Team
3	Shirley Cibley ⎭	
3	Bernice Selib	Self-contained
3-4	John McLeod	Self-contained
4-5	Margery Noel	Self-contained
5	Barbara Steele ⎫	Team
5	Richard Salinger ⎭	
5-6	Jeffrey Weisenfreund	Self-contained
6	Helen Jaques ⎫	Team
6	Ruth Elkins ⎭	

In organizing the staff, then, we deliberately and systematically *max-*

imize differences among teachers and classrooms. This is not difficult to do. A principal does not have to mandate differences in teachers. As any principal, parent, or child knows, teachers come that way. The administrator who tries to make a faculty uniform faces a constant struggle; one who expects teachers to differ and organizes the staff in terms of these differences is seldom surprised or disappointed.

So two things may distinguish Angier as a school. First, we have a great diversity of teachers, teaching styles, and philosophies coexisting under one roof. Second, despite these marked differences, we get along well together most of the time.

CHAPTER FOUR

Placement

For every complicated problem, there is a solution that is short, simple, and wrong.

—H. L. Mencken

STAFF ORGANIZATION is one of the productive problems in a pluralistic school. Placement of children in classes is another. Everyone agrees that the correct match between child and teacher is critical to a successful year for both. And everyone agrees that different children seldom learn best under identical circumstances. This is true even within families: the oldest child may well need tender loving care, support, encouragement, and wide latitude, while the youngest might do better with clear, circumscribed limits and a gentle kick in the pants. The conditions under which one third grader thrives — a firm male teacher, lots of small-group work, a great deal of teacher direction — may differ greatly from the optimal learning environment for another third grader, who needs a motherly woman teacher, a highly individualized program, and a great deal of independence.

If we acknowledge that the match between child and teacher is critical and if we recognize that the learning styles of children vary tremendously, then it follows that schools need to provide teachers and classrooms that differ in significant ways. Ultimately, the opportunity to match teaching styles with learning styles is the most compelling argument for a diversity of teachers, classes, instructional styles, and programs within a school.

Schools handle pupil placement in very different ways. Sometimes the principal decides, using a variety of criteria[1]; sometimes the child's present teacher decides; sometimes the child's parent decides; sometimes children, particularly older children, decide. Sometimes teachers draw their class lists out of a hat. Sometimes birth order ("The younger third

51

graders always go to Mr. Jones") determines placement. Sometimes the neighborhood residence of a family determines in which class a child will be placed. Often it is a combination of determinants. Regardless of method, placement presents all schools, uniform or diverse, with some very real problems.

During placement time few principals manage to retain the sense of humor displayed by Victor Atkins, principal of the Cashman Elementary School in Amesbury, Massachusetts:

MEMO TO FACULTY:

From Victor

Here is your tentative class list for next year. Do not go by this list until we have checked it further. Some of the names seem doubtful.

Girls	Boys
Helen Back	Mark Books
Dawn Broke	Ben Down
Molly Coddle	Norman Clature
Dee Duction	Graham Crackers
Rose Early	Stanley Cup
Sally Forth	Ray Dial
Marcia Larts	Eddy Fiss
Beth Lehem	Cliff Hanger
Ruth Lesley	Max Imum
Trudi Liverance	Reg Ister
Lauren Order	Joe Kerr
Sharon Sharalike	Skip Lunch
Polly Syllabic	Jim Nasium
Evelyn Tensions	Nat Ural
Ann Tipathy	Joe Vial
Madelyn Through	Sam Widge
Sue Venir	Andy Work
Girls 17	Boys 17

TOTAL 34

The placement process is least complex when a school offers "apples, apples, and apples"—when classrooms and teachers are purported to be "the same." A principal can sit at home one evening and set up the third grade by shuffling seventy-five cards into equitable piles of children representing boys, girls, leaders, followers, bright, slow. In an hour each child has been placed in a class for the next year and regardless of the assignment, each child will receive the same education—apples. No one can complain, because every child is being treated equally, uniformly, and—supposedly—fairly. This kind of placement provides an administrative solution to an educational problem. It may rest on dubious assumptions—that children learn alike and teachers teach alike—but the process does protect principals and teachers from conflict and parents from anxiety. In many schools that is reason enough to opt for apples only.

In a more pluralistic school, placement presents both greater problems and greater educational opportunities for teachers, children, parents, and administrators. A random placement process is incompatible with an openly diverse staff. When the third grade offers apples, oranges, and pears, when teachers differ in obvious and substantive ways, then *everyone* cares intensely about which child goes to which class. And everyone wants to decide. The more different the teachers and classrooms, the more everyone cares and wants to decide. Placement may take weeks rather than hours, and can involve a cast of hundreds rather than a single principal sitting down with a stack of cards.

Inevitable disagreements about which child should be assigned to which teacher frequently lead to a process best described as participatory bureaucracy; the effort can be remarkably productive. A school where teachers, classrooms, styles, and programs obviously differ encounters difficult, but potentially fruitful, questions: Into which classroom shall each of four hundred children be placed? Who shall decide? On what basis shall these decisions be made? Satisfactory answers demand appreciation and close scrutiny of different teachers and the learning environments they have created, informed guesses about the values and expectations of different parents, and the projection of optimal learning conditions for each child.

Successful placement accomplishes five goals:

It provides a situation in which each child may learn best.

It provides a learning situation in which each parent will have confidence.

It provides a learning situation in which each teacher will have confidence.

It pairs each teacher with children and parents with whom the teacher can succeed.

It provides representative, heterogeneous classes of equal size, each of which can function as a group.

These are goals so rigorous that I doubt it is possible to fully realize all of them each year; but at Angier we have gradually developed a process that allows us to get reasonably close. Let me describe how we have tried to meet these goals — and some of the personal, pedagogical, and political consequences.

Preparing the Ground: A Year-Long Process

Although final decisions are made in May and June, we prepare for placement throughout the year. Basically, our process rests upon two considerations. Under what instructional conditions does each child in a class seem to work best? Which of next year's teachers comes closest to providing those conditions? In order to answer these questions in May, a teacher must carefully observe both children and other teachers from September on.

In the fall I remind teachers that their classes will usually be divided among three receiving teachers for the following year. The question for teachers, therefore, is not whether students will go to Teacher A, B, or C, but who will go where. It is one thing for a teacher to accept and respect different teaching styles and methods and quite a different matter to support another teacher's style at placement time. This is particularly true if one doesn't know much about the other, or doesn't like what is known.

Often, extended classroom observation builds understanding and support. On the other hand, although careful scrutiny of colleagues is important to placement, it does not inevitably happen in a productive and systematic way. Close observation of children is part of most teachers' normal routine; close observation by peers is not. Indeed, peer observation frequently runs counter to the implicit culture of a school. Taboos in education discourage teachers observing other teachers within a school as strongly as principals observing other principals within a district. Therefore, each winter we ask sending teachers to spend at least a half day observing the class of each potential receiving teacher. These visits are impeded by problems of coverage ("Who will take my class while I observe hers?"), by interpersonal tensions ("Will he think I'm snooping or criticizing?"), and by the constant pressure of other more immediate responsibilities ("I'd like to, but I don't have time"). We have tackled these problems by assigning a teacher aide to keep track of who has visited and been visited and who hasn't, and to supply necessary coverage. While these steps don't ensure collegial observation, they do increase its likelihood.

In addition to classroom visits, sending teachers learn about their colleagues at periodic primary and intermediate meetings. We hold each meeting in a different classroom and devote the first half hour to a discussion of the host teacher's style and methods. From the classroom visits and these faculty meetings teachers gradually accumulate a rationale for making placement recommendations. Throughout the year they informally "try on" different kinds of teachers and programs for students and gain a preliminary reading of which fits best. At the same time teachers are able to "update their stereotypes" of one another, so that placement decisions can be based upon current, accurate information about colleagues rather than upon inference and faculty-room innuendo.

Each year placement begins just after spring pupil-progress conferences. Although we attempt to use these valuable half hours to focus on children's progress from January to May, for many parents there is only one item on the agenda: placement. We anticipate this parental anxiety by discussing and sometimes role playing in faculty meetings what seem to be four tough placement questions from parents. These are given below with some appropriate teacher responses.

PARENT: "What do you think of Mrs. Jones's [next year's possible teacher] class?"

TEACHER:

(1) We do a lot of shuffling of staff each year and change who teaches what. It's better to focus on what kind of classroom we think Johnny would do best in, rather than on a specific teacher.

(2) Perhaps you could arrange to visit the classes of next year's possible teachers so you can answer that question yourself.

(3) I have recently spent a half day in that classroom and I find it a comfortable, productive place for children. I'm sure Johnny would do well there [if this is the case].

If a teacher has reservations about Mrs. Jones, it is as difficult not to reveal them as it is important — otherwise the teacher corroborates the parents' fears, all but foreclosing placement in that class. Over the years the faculty has come to grips with the professional ethics and interpersonal consequences of bad-mouthing a colleague, or even of agreeing with or not refuting a parental criticism.

PARENT: "I don't want Johnny placed in Mr. Seymour's class next year. All they do is play around in there."

TEACHER:

(1) I just spent several hours in that class and that was not my impression. Here's what I saw . . .

(2) I understand that you might feel that way, but I strongly disagree.

(3) I suggest you check out that impression with Mr. Seymour. I think you'll find that you're unfairly stereotyping his class.

A mere glance away to avert eye contact, the slightest blink of the eye, conveys implicit agreement with a parent's judgment. Therefore it is crucial not to let these kinds of statements go unrefuted or uncontested.

PARENT: "Will you see that Johnny is placed in Mrs. Brown's classroom next year?"

TEACHER:

(1) If you have strong feelings about your child's placement for next year, you should write the principal a note expressing your thinking and sharing your reasons. Your note will be taken to the placement meeting and carefully considered along with other important information.

(2) Each teacher at the placement meeting represents his or her own views. The teacher cannot be an advocate for the parents' views as well. Parents must be their own advocates.

PARENT: "Where do *you* think Johnny should be placed next year?"

TEACHER:

(1) My experiences this year suggest he will do well in reading if . . . and

in math if . . . [Describes the conditions, but does not name a teacher.]

(2) I feel he is the kind of child who would do very well with any of next year's teachers [if this is the case].

It is important that teachers not convey to parents their own placement recommendation prior to placement meetings because it may be impossible (for reasons of class size, balance, necessity to separate certain children or supply and demand) to make that placement. Parents tend to see statements of preference by teachers as commitments. If a teacher cannot deliver on these "commitments," if parents' expectations are violated, then hard feelings inevitably follow.

Awareness of these poignant, difficult, and sometimes abusive questions, with their great potential for staff divisiveness and parent-school conflict, enables us to anticipate our answers and the consequences of each. Posing and answering these kinds of questions helps teachers throughout the year to respond to parents in ways that support the placement process and one another.

Cultivating the Soil: Parental Involvement

In a highly educated and education-conscious community like Newton we cannot consider placement without considering parents. Nor would we want to. Our placement decisions begin with parents, end with parents, and generally find parents in the middle as well. Concern about parental views always influences and sometimes dominates the placement process. There are many reasons for this. For most parents the choice of their child's teacher for the following year is enormously important. Parents feel, quite legitimately, that for 185 days a year the teacher is crucial to the success and happiness of a child. Parents also are sure that they care more about their own child's welfare than the most caring school can — or should. A school "belongs" to taxpayers; a child "belongs" to mother and father. Therefore parents have a right to be involved in major decisions affecting their children.

There are also clear practical advantages to involving parents in the placement process. Parents who feel they are part of the decision share with the school valuable information about their child. They are more apt to support the teacher and the classroom, and to help the child view school in positive, productive ways. We have found that parental confidence in a child's teacher, or its lack, can have a dramatic effect upon a child's attitude and academic performance. Parents who feel excluded can be destructive. If parents dislike what a teacher is doing, their opposition is inevitably conveyed to children, who may then find themselves the rope in a tug-of-war between the most important adults in their lives. In a situation where parents condemn what the teacher is doing, little learning can occur.

From the teacher's standpoint, a resentful parent can make a school year a torment. As one teacher put it, "It's a little like driving down the turnpike with a hornet in the car. It's only one hornet, but it can sure interfere with where you're trying to go, getting there, and how you feel about the trip!" If Ms. Smith is trying to educate children while some of their parents are persistently trying to educate her, she has her hands full.

A final practical reason for taking parents seriously at placement time is the political reality under which schools operate these days. Shutting parents out at placement time generates midnight phone calls, and midnight phone calls generate intrusion from the central office. Including parents in these decisions may not eliminate appeals to the top (and beyond), but it goes a long way toward keeping important decisions in the school, where they can be resolved on educational rather than political grounds.

These are persuasive reasons for including parents in the placement process. Why not go one step further, then, and turn over the decision to parents entirely? Some schools do this. We have not. The reasons are in part administrative: supply cannot be regulated to meet demand, and classes would be neither balanced nor representative. But the most important reasons are educational. If the parent decides, a match is made between the educational philosophy and values of the parent and what the parent knows of the style and methods of the teacher. At best, this is a match between adult and adult, between parent and teacher. The more important match, however, is between student and teacher.

Many parents are well aware of the two kinds of matches and work hard to distinguish them:

> I'm putting my thoughts on paper so that my placement requests about Barbara are somewhat official. Barbara seems to have done a better job in a more structured classroom than in an informal one. Inasmuch as I have high regard for all of the teachers, I hope this request reflects objectivity rather than a personal preference for predictability and regimentation. Each of my children seem to do better in classrooms where they know what is expected and the schedule has some degree of consistency.

Others do not:

> We prefer our children's school experience to be consistent with our philosophy at home, which is of a conservative leaning. I would, therefore, request that the children be placed in . . .

Some parents can look clearly at their children and objectively perceive their needs. But some can't. What if the parent of a child who needs a great deal of strong adult direction wants him placed in a very informal, student-centered class? What if the parent of a child who needs to be out from under adult domination for a little while each day wants him in a very structured, teacher-directed classroom? In my experience the school that makes placement recommendations on the basis of a year-long, thorough acquaintance with each child and each teacher can best match student and teacher. And reasonable parents will respect a decision they know is based on thoughtful, documented information. Parents who disagree will make their midnight phone calls anyway.

Further, I have found that many parents do not *want* to select their child's teacher. If they take on this responsibility, some conscientious parents feel they have to visit all possible classes, interview parents and children, talk with other teachers in the school as well as with the child — only to make a decision they then have to worry about. This is a task most parents would prefer to bypass if they feel they can trust the school.

When parents choose their children's teachers, complications arise for the school as well. Every parent competes with every other parent to latch onto the "best" teachers. Each fears that unless he demands more, his child may get less. I have seen a mother and father come close to divorce over a disagreement about the kind of classroom in which their child should be placed. These problems are reduced when the schools make the final placement decisions.

Even our careful, thoroughly documented placement recommendations do not always satisfy, however. Each year there are parents who will not accept school-made recommendations. For some, the classroom selected for the child represents a fundamental conflict with their values that they cannot accept. Sometimes these parents accept our data, even supply identical data of their own, yet reach a contradictory decision about who would be the proper teacher for their child. These differences in perception can be very frustrating to the parents, to the teacher, and ultimately to the principal — as this letter, written to me by a teacher after a parent conference, suggests:

> My conferences are going well, but I had a particularly difficult time with Mrs. Boyd simply because she and I see Jim completely differently. I am describing the conversation to you partly to let off steam, but partly because our different views of Jim demand different placements for him for next year.
>
> **Objectively:** Jim, when given a choice of activities, will choose dramatic play. He gets involved, independently, in art projects only to make props for his dramatic play. He is a very active child, but enjoys unstructured activity only. Gym class is too structured for him, and he frequently sits on the side.
>
> **Subjectively — Me:** I see Jim as a very immature child (he is chronologically young, but mentally even younger). I think he chooses dramatic play because this is his need, his stage of development. I do not let him do this all morning — I like him to get a taste of many different kinds of activities — so I assign tasks . . . for short periods of time. He frequently complains that he "doesn't want to" and frequently

asks "When can I play?" I ignore the complaints and see that the task is completed, but I know that these assignments place difficult demands on him . . . so I keep them short. He also has a terrible time in group situations — meetings, movies, etc. — and cried through *Patience* because it was so painful for him to be there. (His mother says he was uncomfortable because this was new for him — and that if he saw it again he'd love it. I disagree. He'd cry again.)

Subjectively — Mrs. Boyd: She sees Jim as a very "channeled" person — he goes to dramatic play for the same reason that he always gives the same answer when she asks what he wants for breakfast. He loves many breakfast foods but is channeled to always give the same answer. He is channeled to dramatic play, even though he is highly motivated and very interested in other classroom activities. The reason he complains when involved in other activities is that he likes to manipulate people, including me. He is, she says, actually very interested and eager to learn. But I've taught him that I can be manipulated. I explained my views and stated that I am not manipulated, but she feels that we (she and I) aren't communicating.

On Jim's thumb-sucking: Mrs. Boyd is very upset that Jim continues to suck his thumb and forbids it, and shames him ("Five-year-olds don't suck their thumbs"). Whenever she is at Angier she comes into my classroom to make sure Jim is not sucking his thumb. She says it's just a bad habit and he must be taught that it's WRONG. According to her, he sucks his thumb at home because it's a bad habit and at school because I don't make him stop. I explained that I see thumb-sucking as a child's way of saying that he feels insecure, unhappy, or bothered about something, that thumb-sucking is a symptom and that the cause must be dealt with, and that forbidding it only adds shame and guilt to the problem, and that in Jim's case, I think he sucks his thumb because he is not quite ready for all the demands that are made on him. She says I'm wrong, that he needs even more demands — because he is mature, but needs channeling.

She asked me what I would do if my child wet his bed at night — wouldn't I tell him he shouldn't — that five-year-olds shouldn't wet their beds? She really thought she had me on that one and was shocked to hear me say NO — that, again, bed-wetting is a symptom — and that I would seek the underlying cause. At that point, Mrs. Boyd gave up on me in the thumb-sucking area and went back to Jim's manipulation of me. I don't force him to complete art projects, she says. He brings home things that aren't completed. At home, he's not allowed to put on just one shoe by himself — he's forced to finish and put on both shoes. I patiently (I hope) explained that completion is not easily defined in children's art projects — that process is often more important than the product — that I wouldn't tell a child (in most cases) that something wasn't "finished" because I would be talking about my standard of finished, not the child's. She insists that Jim doesn't finish and that he must be required to.

Placement for next year: She wants Jim placed in a classroom where demands will be placed on him all day long so that his natural eagerness to learn can be channeled. I think he needs a classroom where he can spend a fair amount of time in dramatic play with building blocks, etc., where he can mature slowly — with teacher's guidance.

Experienced, intelligent, sensitive teachers like this, after a year's experience with a child under classroom conditions, have tremendous insight into that child's needs and learning style. A child's *school* behavior should be paramount for school placement. The school that abdicates placement decisions to parents turns its back on its responsibility to children. If we really believe that what we do matters, we have an obligation to act upon our information and our insights. If we accede to parents' demands, it should be only after we have made our case and they have found it insufficiently compelling. Drawing the line of *who decides* is difficult. The burden rests with the school both to make persuasive recommendations and to offer parents veto power over them when necessary. As we shall see, sometimes we do both; sometimes neither; sometimes one and not the other.

At Angier parents formally join the placement process in early May, when I send a letter inviting them to share the conditions under which they feel their child does best at school:

ANGIER GREENSHEET

May 2

PLACEMENT FOR NEXT YEAR

The faculty, you, and I all feel that the placement of children in classes for next year is a decision of great importance — one that affects your child's life at Angier for ten months. At this time I would like to share with you — particularly with parents new to Angier — the process which we use in placing children in classes for next September.

(1) If you have information about your child and about the kind of learning environment in which he best works and learns which would help us in the placement decision, we want you to share this with us by writing me a note before May 16th. (2) Shortly after all conferences for a grade level have been concluded, the teachers at your child's present grade level, special services (e.g., psychologist, learning disability teachers, resource room teachers, English specialist), and I will meet, compile, and discuss all the information we have about your child, and make assignments. (3) We will then inform you in writing of these decisions. If you have questions about the rationale for the decision, comments, or concerns, I would like you to call me or come and see me within a week.

In making these important decisions we want to consider all possible, relevant information so that placements will be made which will ensure the greatest possible learning for each child. We consider parents' feelings to be a very important factor. However, let me say quite clearly that parents do not choose their child's teacher. This is impossible and undesirable for a number of reasons:

With our small classrooms and large numbers we must have equitable numbers of children — about 25 — working with each teacher. It is not in children's best interests to be in a class much larger than this.

As you know, an important factor which influences the nature and amount of information your child will learn is the composition of his class — the other children he will be working with. We do not feel it is desirable for a child to be in a class predominantly male, female, fast, slow, aggressive, quiet — or in a class which is skewed along any of the many important human characteristics.

There are children who contribute to the learning of other children and children who interfere with the learning of others — that is, there are children in whose best interest it is to be together or separated.

Your child's present teacher has a year's worth of current, rich information and insight concerning the conditions under which your child learns best and most.

In order to maximize children's learning it is essential that equitable, compatible, balanced classes be assembled which reflect what teachers know about the conditions under which your child best functions. You can be sure that throughout the placement process two concerns will be foremost in our minds — that your child will be in a classroom in which he will flourish academically and socially, and that your child will be in a classroom in which you can have confidence.

Roland

We have received as many as three hundred letters from parents of four hundred children, more than one per family, which says a lot about parental interest in these decisions. The number of letters is directly related to the sharpness of classroom differences at a grade level. Where there are visible, dramatic differences — desks in rows and no desks, for instance — there are many letters. Where there is greater apparent similarity, there are fewer letters. As many letters seem to be written to *avoid* a certain classroom as to request placement with a particular teacher.

Parental placement letters serve several functions that help the school negotiate each placement season. The letters let us know in advance what parents are thinking. We may or may not place the child in accordance with the parents' wishes; but whatever our decision, awareness of the values and strong feelings held by parents permits us to anticipate their response and formulate our own. The letters also provide a valuable record, a document to which we can refer before placement (in determining a final organization, for instance), during the placement meetings, and afterward in discussing our decisions with parents. With these heavily loaded decisions there is then no room for misinterpretation, for forgetting who told what to whom and when, or for "here's what you said and here's what I heard" conflicts. If conflicts exist at placement time, it is important that they be conflicts about which classroom will be best for Johnny, not about the decision process itself. As always, in order to focus attention on the content the process must be as flawless as possible.

Inviting parents to communicate with us at placement time serves other important purposes. Most parents want to express their deep concern about their children's education by "doing something" about teacher assignment; writing to the principal provides a constructive, cooperative means for channeling their ideas. In addition, parent letters each year tell us a great deal about children that we don't know (as well as a great deal that we do know), information we use to make placement decisions and to provide better instruction for children on a day-to-day basis.

Parent letters at placement time form a rich and fascinating literature. Because they are central to a discussion of placement in a pluralistic school, let me share several excerpts. (Names of teachers, children, and parents have been changed or eliminated throughout.) The letters vary along almost every conceivable dimension. Some are brief . . . and satisfied:

> This year Alexander has had a fine year with a male teacher, and being on the younger end of the class provided incentive for him. Therefore, as he will be a third grader, we think a third-fourth grade with a male teacher is a good placement for Alexander next year.

Some are lengthy and use the placement letter as a forum to ventilate dissatisfaction with the school:

> From evidence of the past three years it is clear that Judy would be more productive in a more structured classroom. She needs attention and feedback to get a sense of how she is doing in relation to what is expected. A system of notes from the teacher was initiated in response to her unhappiness and lack of productivity. We keep all the notes in a drawer so Judy can refer to them. We would prefer a classroom where such information about progress or lack of progress was part of the classroom routine. From birth Judy has demanded order and routine, which we have learned to provide. With clear expectations and limits she knows how to behave and what to do and can then be more independent.
>
> For the past three years Judy has not had suitable placements. She simply has not performed up to her capabilities. At home she does high-quality work with games, puzzles, drawing, and story writing. Judy does best when she feels accepted and gets feedback that she is doing well. Clearly, she loves a good time and plays vigorously and can be silly. But she needs clear-cut lines between play and work. Learning to get along with other children is not her problem. We feel that it is high time that she concentrate on academics. We would like her in a self-contained classroom with an experienced teacher who is interested in educating.

Parents approach us with different attitudes and levels of confidence. Some are lighthearted and trusting:

It's that time of year again when I'm putting my child's life on the line and pretend that I'm not. Actually, I've grown up a lot. The aura of dignified detachment and sophisticated sublimity I have managed to wrap around my incipient placement panic is becoming normal behavior. From my position of awesome (to me) objectivity you have my total confidence about matters of placement (so long as everything works out perfectly — ha). With that preface, let me tell you what's on my mind.

With possible predictability, but from one point of view unimaginable speed, our baby has arrived at the accepted age for kindergarten. I will spare you a host of details leading to this precarious moment, save for her nursery-school history. In a sentence, she did not fare well at one nursery school with a "find-your-own-way" approach, but was ecstatic in another where accomplishment was more the focus. She enjoyed learning new stories, music, letters, etc. From this we conclude she would do best in a single-grade, self-contained class, rather than a K-1-2. As the baby with two older sibs she gets more than her share of older children.

Naturally, I leave it up to . . .

Some feel less well served:

We would like to see that Bobby is more closely attended to next year. We have looked at other schools and observed what children Bobby's age are doing. They are doing quite a bit better than he is in math and language. We feel a more clear diagnosis of his abilities is in order and that his program can be geared to whatever such a test would indicate. Should a classroom be available which would match his needs, we would like him placed in it.

Some give exacting, implausible conditions:

The following indicate our priorities for next year. We prefer a class where:

(1) Homework is part of the routine and children are taught how to do it.

(2) The teacher is imaginative as well as being strongly in control of what happens in the classroom.

(3) The teacher has a formal attitude about manners and does not permit children to address him or her by a first name. This would follow the standard we set at home for appropriate behavior.

Other expectations are more easily fulfilled:

We would like her put in a class separate from her twin brother.

The way in which parents construct the universe comes through remarkably well in these letters. Some hold to an unchanging philosophy and value system into which they expect their children and the school to fit:

Our thoughts about education haven't changed, so we assume that you know that we prefer a classroom with a structured, traditional environment for both our girls.

Others are more concerned with individual differences than with educational philosophy:

> Regarding placement decisions for next year: my two sons are quite different in personality, and possibly in ability, so obviously I am making inconsistent requests. Sam will probably do better in a more traditional setting. He seems to respond well to a disciplined approach. Jimmy will require a more flexible approach and will respond better in a more relaxed setting.

Some parents, accustomed to thinking in terms of uniform labels rather than diverse learning environments, focus on "kinds of classrooms":

> We think Jenny should be placed in a traditional classroom, not an open one. At home she does better when she knows what she is doing and when she knows that a grown-up is checking on her.

Others are descriptive and avoid labels:

> Dick is most comfortable in a situation where expectations are very clear and where he is not distracted. He has more difficulty with understanding what the instructions are than with the work itself. Having a close relationship with his teacher seems to give him confidence, and he benefits from small-group instruction. Since he only does what is expected of him, he does better with prodding.

Most letters offer both information and a recommendation:

> We are quite worried about Rodney. He seems not to have much self-direction and would flounder in a loose classroom. Clear directions, objectives, and expectations need to be established for him. We hope that a more organized classroom can offer the supports he needs to do his best. Therefore, we request . . .

Parents express very different feelings about the amount of legitimate input they have in the decision-making process. Some insist *they* will make the decisions:

> We are taking this opportunity to let you know what we've decided about Karen's and Jane's placements for next year. We have communicated our thoughts to the children's future teachers. Karen will be in Mrs. Brace's class. Jane will go to . . .

Others have more confidence in the judgment of the staff:

> I have a few thoughts about placement I would like to share. I respect the process you and the staff have evolved and I trust the professionalism you all bring to it. So bear in mind these musings are only meant to be part of the picture.

Some request the same teachers with whom the family has had previous successful experiences:

Sam's older sister had a very good year with Mr. Beard. She worked hard and learned a lot. We prefer his firmness to some of the more relaxed approaches we see developing in the school.

Or the same kind of classroom:

Sandy has blossomed in Miss Totter's caring, informal classroom. We think it essential that she continue in the same milieu. We refuse to accept any other choice for her than . . .

Some parents (and children) think the child should have some say in teacher selection. In most cases the parent's letter speaks for the child's concerns:

We have talked with both Mr. Simon and Jane about their ideas on placement for next year. Perhaps because she is the oldest child in our family, Jane would prefer not to be placed in a mixed-age class where she is among the oldest. She prefers a straight class where the majority of children are her age. This would give her the chance to know more children her own age. We would like to respect her thoughts on this and hope you can work it out.

Harry hopes desperately to be in Mrs. Jones's class, as all his older brothers and sisters have been.

Jim has mentioned several times that he really wants Mrs. Simms in first grade. Since he does better when he has a part of the decision making and feels somewhat in control of his activities, and this choice is important to him, we think that disregarding his feelings would have a lot of negative effects on him next year, both academically and emotionally.

From time to time, however, a child will express his own point of view:

I would like to have either Miss Jason or Ms. Hanks. I want Miss Jason because of the fun things she does. I like the map in the library and the things I see up on the walls about the Revolutionary War. I've thought about being in Miss Jason's sixth grade since I was in fourth grade. I think she would be the best teacher for me. I could do lots of good things in that class.

Professionals who work with children also use this opportunity to make recommendations for classroom placement. Like parental views, these are taken seriously in the process. Most make very specific suggestions:

I am delighted with how well Jamie has progressed this year. He is handling emotional difficulties much more easily. He is more interested in school, and his academic progress has clearly been substantial. He likes his teachers, and the climate of an open classroom seems to be comfortable for him. I recommend that he remain in that same kind of setting next year.

Sincerely,

[Child Psychiatrist]

Carolyn tends to avoid work and runs away from problems. She also has trouble in all areas of language arts. Since she has difficulty transferring information from one form to another (spoken to written, for instance), I think a predictable environment with a highly structured teaching approach is the one I would recommend for her.

Sincerely,

[Learning Disability Teacher]

Some, however, simply give general information to help us make specific decisions:

Dennis Sandleman has been a preschool student in our nursery school for the past two years. He was in a mixed group of older four- and five-year-olds. Our school offers a wide range of activities that include: creative arts, story reading, dramatic play, math experiences, science, reading readiness, and lots of outdoor and indoor physical experiences.

Dennis made thorough use of our program. Quiet games were attractive, as were more boisterous activities. He enjoyed the company of both boys and girls. Math and science problems were easily mastered and he showed superb ability with language in describing his very imaginative art creations.

Dennis enjoyed his friends. He was comfortable sharing and was thoughtful about others' feelings. He was a central figure in dramatic play and could stay involved in activities for a long time.

Dennis was a delightful, outgoing, interested, alive preschooler who brought much joy and energy to all of us.

Sincerely,

[Nursery-School Teacher]

We learn a great deal about our students, our parents, and our program from these letters. Many present requests which make us aware of children's needs:

I have a specific concern about Dianne's placement next year. I feel that it is very important that she be in a class with at least one other black child, and possibly a black teacher as well. She has strong feelings about the darkness of her skin and has gained in many ways from her friendships with other black people in the school.

Some raise good questions for us:

What seems so frustrating is that at Angier most of the stimulating classrooms also seem to be the noisiest. While I appreciate the creative curriculum, I find an additional need for quiet, which supports concentration. Isn't it possible to have both?

Others state a problem and offer interesting solutions:

Would you consider forming a math class to meet the needs of students like Mary who are quick or even gifted in math? This year's one hour each week needs to be expanded into a regular daily class time. Perhaps students from the top two grades who share this need can work together. I think it would ease the transition to the advanced classes in junior high school.

Since there were two mixed-age groups for second grade this year, I assume there will be need for two mixed classes for third graders next year. If that is so, I would like my child in a 3-4 combination and strongly suggest that Kathy Clark be persuaded to teach it. Seems like a good idea, doesn't it?

A rich literature indeed! While there appear to be many patterns and similarities, these placement letters reflect a remarkable diversity of parents and of children's needs as perceived by parents — a diversity I suspect exists in most school communities. The letters suggest that parents are keenly aware of significant and insignificant differences among teachers and among classrooms, and that parents care deeply about the differences they see. The letters suggest that every parent has a unique set of personal and educational values, which form different prescriptions for different children. In our diverse staff there are qualities that appeal to many parents and offend many parents. And finally, the placement letters suggest that many parents are able to communicate precisely their values, observations, and recommendations. These highly literate, sometimes anxious letters may not be representative of what all parents might write, but I am sure the concern and the need for inclusion in the placement process, so evident in these letters, exists among all parents. Parents who do not transmit their strong feelings usually care as deeply about their children as those who do — which raises the problem of how to gain access to their uniquely rich information about their children.

As I reread six years of placement letters — some fifteen hundred documents — I see revealed there many changes over time, developmental stages through which the thinking of parents has gone. Initially many parents responded with *labels* — "open," "traditional," "structured," or with teachers' names. Over the years the responses have become characterized more by descriptions of the classroom styles and teacher qualities so important to parents and to their children. We try to help parents become more descriptive and less like brand-name consumers by abandoning the use of labels ourselves. Repeatedly we ask parents to share with us, not the names of teachers, but the "conditions under which you think your child will do best." Each year we juggle the faculty organization and deliberately wait until after the deadline for parent letters to determine a final organization. We recognize that if no one knows who will be teaching what next year, we all *must* focus on classroom and teacher characteristics, not on individual teachers. If we persistently respond to a label with a question ("What do you mean by structured?")

labels soon lose their value as coin of the realm. Our deliberate diversity has also prompted parents to be descriptive. A pluralistic school, offering a plethora of practices and programs, stimulates parents to be introspective, observant, and sensitive to what they like and don't like, to what they want and don't want for their children.

Over time the number of letters has gradually diminished. Several years ago from the 275 families of about 400 children we received 300 letters; then 200; then 150; now about 125. Fewer parents are making requests; more are leaving the initial recommendations to the school. The question "Who decides?" — at first explosive and polarizing — is now less frequently asked. Decisions have become more cooperative; school and parents take each other's views seriously. More parents are accepting our initial recommendations, not because we have shut them out of the process, but I think because we have included them.

This may be either a good or a bad sign. To the extent that fewer letters suggest parents are accepting our initial placement recommendations out of growing confidence that all the teachers at a given grade level, although markedly different, are good teachers, and if fewer letters suggest that our placement process is usually trustworthy in making successful matches between child and teacher, then we can take heart from a decline in correspondence . . . and enjoy what becomes an administratively easier task of making placement decisions with less parental input. If, on the other hand, a reduction in letters means parents feel that their participation is unwanted, unneeded, and unheeded — that we will make our decisions no matter what parents think — then, of course, a decline in the number of letters becomes a disturbing, unwelcome indicator. I hope the former is the case more often than the latter.

We still deal with one nagging problem of pluralistic schools, the supermarket response to placement. Some parents feel compelled to visit all potential classrooms and pick off the shelf the favored brand. At first "shopping around" was an unpleasant reality for us at placement time, a practice that demeaned teachers and occupied an extraordinary amount of time. The anxiety and emotional overload that is a normal teacher reaction to parental shopping is something a principal must deal with. Here is one principal's response in his school newsletter:

> There is another sore spot for teachers. It is perennial and it is a pain. It is the shopping for next year's teacher. Sometimes I think we make a great error in attempting to honor parental placement requests. We see more of your children in school; we know more or can admit more about a child's learning style because we have experience with them in this school setting. We also know more about our own strengths and our own weaknesses than you will ever know. We try to honor parental requests because we know that if you are happy, there is a 95% chance that the child will be happy in school. That's a goal worth striving for.

But no one likes to be inspected as if in a cattle market, to be bid for or to be rejected. It helps neither ego nor faculty morale. Visitors really are welcome to this school. But when a spring parade of visitors wants to see the teachers in the grade above theirs perform — no one is kidding anybody.

It has got to the point where the teacher "cattle" are inspecting the inspectors and have been known to "perform" outrageously for a parent whose reputation has been labeled "undesirable." In short, some of you — both teacher and parent — are beginning to play games and the whole thing becomes foolish.

We have reduced this problem by baldly stating each year that "the school, not the parents, will decide." We allow parents to visit potential classrooms at placement time, but we don't encourage it. Instead, we continually inform ourselves about ourselves through collegial visits, enabling us to give straight answers to many parents' questions and reducing their need to observe for themselves.

The most satisfying change in the letters has been their increasing acceptance of diversity. Early on, differences *were* seen as Good or Bad. Some classrooms were perceived as offering quality education, others led directly to damnation. Some teachers were competent, others hippy freaks. Primitive, simplistic judgments abounded. The tone has shifted, as this recent letter suggests:

> I have thought a great deal about John's placement for next year. For some children Mrs. Dean's class with its stimulation and emphasis on experience is an excellent place. I am concerned that John would be out of control there much of the time. He seems to need more adult supervision, though some day perhaps he will be able to take on that kind of self-direction. I hope so. At present Miss Reed's class seems more suitable.

Classrooms are seen less as globally good or bad and more as good for some children and bad for others. This is a welcome change and one that enables children to be suitably matched with teachers and allows teachers to be themselves with some measure of security and satisfaction.

Sowing the Seed: Placement Meetings

After each parent letter has been carefully read, the spring parent conferences completed, and the final teacher organization determined, we begin placement meetings. Two or three meetings are held after school each week for several weeks. Each meeting is open ended, allowing sufficient time to discuss important issues fully. As in most such meetings, consensus is reached more easily as darkness approaches. Despite the severe demands on time and emotions placed upon teachers by these meetings, a sending teacher has never been absent from a placement session. They are important, the culmination of one school year and the launching point for the next. Perhaps the best way to capture their flavor is to quote the report of a graduate-student observer.

In early June I observed one of an ongoing series of placement meetings. The principal and teachers met to determine class assignments for the following year. I attended the meeting which placed third-grade children into fourth grade. Roland, the school psychologist, the two coordinators,[2] two L.D. [learning disability] specialists, sending teachers, receiving teachers, and one upper-grade teacher-observer sat around a long table.

Roland opened the meeting by stating the ground rules. Sending teachers (third grade) would do the talking, and lobby if necessary for their choices. Receiving teachers (fourth grade) could not lobby.[3] Any other teacher could attend a placement meeting as an observer. The principal reminded the staff of the two criteria on which they should base their decisions.

(1) Each child should be placed in a classroom which worked best for his or her needs on the basis of
  (a) teacher style
  (b) teacher strengths
  (c) atmosphere of the room.

(2) Each class should be heterogeneous according to
  (a) academic achievement
  (b) social behavior
  (c) sex.

The primary coordinator made columns on a blackboard with receiving teachers' names across the top.[4] It is Roland's practice to have a coordinator run the blackboard in placement meetings. Two of the receiving teachers were requested to assemble permanent record cards in separate piles as the class lists developed.

The formal assignment process then began with Roland asking each teacher in turn around the table to list the "musts."

The definition of a "'must" assignment was given by Roland: whenever a teacher had a strong conviction that the child would benefit greatly by one assignment, and do very poorly in another situation. In this meeting, the definition of a "must" was not challenged. In another meeting which I did not attend, the "must" category was a source of considerable conflict and subsequently the topic of a mid-June meeting of the teachers involved.

The blackboard recorder listed the musts.[5] On the second round, teachers stated their preferences about the other children. The third round dealt with class size and the balance of boys and girls.

During placement decisions we make constant use of important classroom characteristics; for instance, we might place a child without a father at home with a male teacher, or a motherless child with a mothering female. This kind of placement is often made in response to letters such as this:

Concerning Sara's placement in second grade in the fall: I am hoping that she can be in a class with a male teacher, if that is possible.

My husband's job takes him away a good deal of the time. Between travel and late hours he is not often available and when he is, it is difficult for him to be warm with the girls. Since we have moved to Boston, doting grandfathers have not been on tap, so the children have been surrounded by women at home. I realize this is not the school's problem. However, I think her education would be greatly enhanced by having a male teacher.

We might place a child who has always had female teachers with a male teacher and vice versa:

Susan has just completed her third successive year with a male teacher. We feel it might be appropriate at this time for her to have a female teacher.

And there are other reasons as well:

We are concerned about Joanne's being a tomboy. This behavior seems to have intensified this year, which Mr. Edwards has also observed. At this point it might be useful to place Joanne with a female teacher or with a team of women teachers, if that option exists. We don't want her to think of femaleness in a negative way, or neglect her own sense of being a female either. We think knowing some strong female adults could be beneficial to her at this stage in her education.

At each grade level we try to provide teachers with different interests and abilities. Thus, a child fascinated by science might be assigned to a teacher who shares that interest. A child with a Citizen Band license might be placed with a teacher with a similar interest. These kinds of commonalities provide a base for a fruitful teacher-child relationship. Occasionally, we might place a child with an aversion to science with a highly motivating science teacher. Usually, though, we use children's strengths rather than their weaknesses as criteria for placement.

We also have the option of placing children among older, younger, or same-age classmates. This possibility elicits strong responses from parents. Perhaps because the differences are so visible, parents attach more significance to mixed ages than we do. Some parents like mixed-age groups because they give their child a chance for an extended, predictable, stable educational experience. The fourth grader in a 4-5 class can stay in it as a fifth grader:

I would like to recommend that David remain with his present teacher next year. The major reason for this request is the need at this time for David to have as much consistency in adult relationships as possible. Our family is undergoing a divorce and David is subject to the upheavals such procedures usually produce. He has found his teacher this year to be very supportive in the face of his many concerns. We hope he can remain with her.

Others like the flexibility mixed-age grouping can offer. If the child is the youngest in her family and seems to work comfortably with older children, we might place her in the younger part of a cross-age group. Parents recognize the advantages of this kind of placement:

> We would like Paula to be in a K-1-2 next year. She tends to be bossy with youngsters her own age and size and seems to feel good about having older children to look up to and learn from. At home she is comfortable with two older siblings. She is energetic and interested in learning and seems to have plenty to offer to a group of children some of whom would be older than she is.

A youngest child, dominated by his older brothers and sisters, on the other hand, might benefit from an experience with children of the same age or with younger children among whom he could stand in seniority:

> I am writing this note at the request of the parents concerning placement of their son, Denton, for the fall. He will be a first grader. After observing in both the K-1 and straight first-grade classrooms, I would suggest that Denton be in the K-1 for the following reasons:
> (1) Denton has a difficult relationship with an older sibling who does not leave him much room to try things for himself. He is constantly criticized. Therefore, it seems a good idea for him to be the older in a classroom where there is less competition.
> (2) Although Denton is able and popular with other children, he feels pretty insecure. Being helpful with younger children might give him a better idea of his capabilities.
> (3) The K-1 seems to be a very relaxed classroom. Denton needs room to make errors and the freedom to initiate his own questions. He is self-motivated and disciplined so he could manage the responsibility of a more informal classroom.

[Child's Kindergarten Teacher at another school]

Competition is another important factor to consider in multiage groups. A kindergarten child who has tended to select the most able child in his class against whom to compete, might be placed in a straight first grade where competition could be among children of more equal development and ability, or in a K-1-2 where it would be virtually impossible to compete successfully with the most able second graders.

Sending teachers also consider ability and maturity in cross-age group placement. A mathematically gifted first grader might do well with older second or third graders who would challenge him. We occasionally place an older, immature child in a class with younger children. We do not make a routine practice of this; if we did, the upper part of a combined class would soon get a justified reputation as the repository for children with social or academic deficiencies. Even now, parents seem most comfortable when their child is in the younger group of a cross-age class, say the second grade in a 2-3 combination. They seem to feel their child will be intellectually stretched by interaction with older children. On the other hand, many parents are uncomfortable if their child is placed in the older part of a mixed-age group. They worry that the child will be slowed down academically, contributing a great deal of time to helping younger children but missing out on high-level instruction from the teacher:

> I don't want her put in a K-1 classroom as a first grader. I feel she would slide back into kindergarten activities again.

> The classroom situation we want to steer clear of is one where Martha is the older in a mixed-age group. As she is the oldest in a large family and has ample opportunity for responsibilities and taking care of kids younger than she is, we would hope that school would offer her a different situation than her home.

We find the physical size of a child to be an important factor in placement. The preadolescent fifth grader, very large for her age — and self-conscious about it — might be placed in a 5-6 class where she would be among many children of similar size. Similarly, a tiny second grader might be placed in a K-1-2 where his size would not distinguish him from the rest of the class.

Sometimes we exclude certain children from cross-age classes because siblings or a sibling's friends are there. Parents will often alert us to this kind of problem:

> There is a real problem for the children if one of them is placed in a class where his brother's friends are. This makes Sandy worry that his brother will "steal" his friends away from him. It seems best that they are each in a straight-age classroom where the possibilities for this don't exist.

Still, when the match between the classroom and child was the paramount factor, we have successfully placed as many as three siblings in one cross-age class.

Cross-age groups, furthermore, allow us to "promote" most children each year, whatever their level of academic achievement. Retaining (holding back a year) or double promoting (skipping a grade) is justified only by the availability of a more suitable learning environment and peer group elsewhere. Combined classes allow a child to remain with his peers and still receive most of the advantages of retention or double promotion, as many parents recognize:

> This has been a good third-grade year for Sarah with Mrs. Tyson, especially academically. But her young age has made it hard on her to make friends. Therefore, we think it best that she be placed in a 3-4 combination class next year so she can move along with her peers but have the advantage of being with some children who are younger. We think this is better than keeping her another year in third grade.

We have been pleased with the ways Sam's needs have been taken care of at Angier. Up to now he has often felt embarrassed and frustrated by his considerable abilities. We hope his need to be challenged by providing him individualized work can continue. Being on the younger end of a mixed-age class was a good solution for Sam. He felt less different and did not have to cope with the social mismatch of accelerating to a higher grade.

Self-contained and teamed classrooms offer us another kind of flexibility. In a self-contained classroom we might place a child who has difficulty making transitions in time, space, and personnel. The self-contained classroom is often the best setting for the child who has difficulty establishing relationships with adults, or for one who seems to need the continuity and security provided by a single adult. If, the following year, such a teacher teams with a teacher of the next grade — which would permit a two-year placement — all the better:

> I would like to ask that our son Dan continue in the combination grade with Mrs. Leach and Mrs. Josephson. Each year he has had considerable difficulty getting used to his teacher and the new setting in which he finds himself. Eventually, he comes around, the anxiety lessens, and he manages well the rest of the year. The beginning weeks are, however, so difficult that he loses a great deal. I feel it might be best to try to break this pattern by having him return to a familiar setting where he feels accepted and successful.

Teams, especially male/female pairs, are often good for the child with pronounced emotional needs for both a father and a mother. Children with special strengths are often placed in team classrooms, because teaming allows a teacher more opportunity to concentrate on a specialty. A child gifted in writing, for example, might be placed with a team having a particularly inventive literature and composition teacher.

The degree of classroom formality or informality has been our most difficult and controversial issue at placement time. Parents seem to have inordinately strong feelings about open classrooms (both pro and con) and sometimes appear to feel that an entire child-rearing pattern can be destroyed by an incompatible teacher or learning environment. This seems especially true of the parents who are committed to traditional teaching methods. While "liberal" parents who prefer informal classrooms seem able to tolerate more traditional placements for their children, although they may protest a bit, the "conservative" parents frequently find it intolerable if their children are placed in more informal settings. Consequently, we find more letters favoring formal classrooms than informal ones.

With regard to formal and informal classes, even more than in other areas, different adults can take identical data and come up with contradictory conclusions. Take, for example, Bobby, who is very dependent upon frequent adult direction for learning and goes to pieces when given any measure of choice or independence. We might place Bobby in a strongly teacher-directed classroom that provides firm limits and frequent checks. Or we might argue that the child who has been under tight adult control at home and school all his life could gain most from an informal classroom where he might learn to pose some of his own problems, make some choices, and become responsible for them.

We might place Martha, who has severe learning problems, in a quiet, structured, predictable, teacher-directed classroom where she would not be distracted by the complexity of movement, noise, and activity of a more informal class. Yet children in more formal classrooms tend to work in groups, which can rarely accommodate someone with pronounced special needs. We might argue, then, that Martha would fare better in a more informal classroom with much more individualized instruction — exactly what the child with learning disabilities needs. In short, good arguments can be made for placing various kinds of children in either more formal or informal classrooms.

A final classroom characteristic, vague, imprecise, yet often critically important, is teacher personality. When we say "Johnny would do well with Miss Stevens," I think we mean he would do well with a particular adult who is especially motherly, warm, well-organized, and patient. These are not characteristics specified overtly in the placement process; yet personality is clearly a significant influence on teacher recommendations.

No checklist guides placement decisions. The decision to assign a particular child to a particular teacher is determined by a constellation of characteristics of both teacher and child and can be made only after a careful examination of each prospective match. Thus, we go into placement meetings with the conviction that each child will have a better year with one teacher than with the others. It is not "six of one, half a dozen of the other."

Our next job is to balance the classes. Let's return to the graduate student's description of the placement process:

> The group's next task was to go through each list and identify and equitably distribute kids in a variety of ways by using colored chalk. For instance,
>
> (1) kids who act out (white chalk)
> (2) kids who are withdrawn, dependent, or in need of much teacher attention (red)
> (3) kids who are high academic achievers (green squares)
> (4) kids who are leaders (white check marks).
>
> After determining that all the names were on the board, Roland checked the lists with parent requests (letters). The percentage of agreement between teacher choices and parent requests was high. When there was a con-

flict, Roland asked the sending teachers if they wished to change their assignment. In one or two cases, teachers expressed no difficulty in making changes; in others, they were in strong disagreement with parents. Roland listened to their reasons and stated he would "go" with the teachers, but they must be ready to defend with him the decision when a puzzled or angry parent called. A suggestion was made by one of the teachers and accepted that a phone call to a parent prior to formal assignment would be valuable.

Roland then looked at the distribution of minority children and found it as equitable as possible. Finally, Roland and the teachers reviewed the lists to see if any significant factors had been overlooked.

The participants in the meeting seemed comfortable with one another. The atmosphere was businesslike, but not devoid of pleasantries and occasional laughter. I did not hear distress or anger in any of the voices. About halfway through the meeting Roland provided ice cream and cookies. It was my impression that the welcome snack accomplished three purposes: at midafternoon energy levels are low and the food probably made people more comfortable physically; it showed concern on the part of the principal; and it effected the subtle chemistry created by a shared eating experience.

The presence of receiving teachers and observers in addition to sending teachers reflected openness and trust. Although Roland had not planned to include receiving teachers, he readily agreed to their requests to attend the placement meeting. If he had said "no", it would have created unnecessary anxiety among the teachers over what was being said about them. The attendance of receiving teachers forced sending teachers to look even more critically at their choices and be ready to give their reasons in an open forum. Thus, personal prejudices or misconceptions about colleagues could be eliminated as inappropriate professional criteria or surfaced for subsequent examination and resolution. The behavior of teachers in the placement meeting, coupled with a supportive principal, produced a most advantageous model.

The order of the steps was significant, because the "musts" were taken care of first. This eliminated teachers' anxiety about children whose placement they considered most critical. Teacher preferences, the second step, resulted in every child's name being listed quite quickly.

The third round, balancing class size and sex, involved few changes and a low sensitivity impact. The fourth task, identification of various qualities or behavior problems of kids, provided a graphic picture for determining the heterogeneity of each class. Placing the latter task in fourth place eliminated lengthy discussions about each child, since the class lists were close to completion and only a few students needed to be considered for possible changes.

Roland's input about parents' requests was not only a significant part of the process, but it also served to focus on his role as the ultimate decision maker and the person responsible for the success or failure of pupil placement.

This did not run counter to Roland's practice of sharing responsibility, since he indicated a willingness to support the teachers if they had excellent reasons for defending their choices.

I liked the process because it gave teachers control of the content and the principal control over the structure. There was a high level of consistency in the behavior of those present. Roland confined himself to elements in the structure. Teachers spoke in a positive manner, had interchanges with one another either seeking further input or answering challenges. It seemed clear to me that teachers knew their opinions were crucial to the process. They were the experts about their students' learning patterns. Roland's structure of the meeting and his attitude provided clear evidence of his trust in them. Portions of parent request letters which Roland brought to the meeting were read aloud after tentative assignments had been made. There was intense interest on everyone's part. It seemed to me analogous to a report of test results! With each succeeding "match" between placement and request, smiles broadened on teachers' faces. The division of labor and responsibility which led up to this point culminated in a shared experience. Each person had participated. Each step in the process gave evidence of responsibility gladly accepted and truly valued.

The day after the placement meeting I go over the new class lists with receiving teachers who were not at the meeting. Occasionally a teacher will say, "I had Johnny's older brother three years ago and fought with the parents all year. I wouldn't wish another year like that for any of us." Then we move the child. Occasionally a teacher will report prior unsuccessful experiences with a child that make the placement questionable. More often the list is "approved" as it stands. Within a few days a letter goes to the parents of each child, informing them of our placement decisions and asking them to contact me within the week if there are problems:

Dear Parents,

We have placed children in next year's first grades. The psychologist, your child's teacher, and I made these decisions on the basis of careful consideration of all information available to us about each child and about each classroom. We have considered the balance of each class, size of class, parents' feelings, and our own observations of the optimal learning conditions for each child.

We have placed your child into Mrs. Rosenthal's K-1-2 classroom. If for any reason you would like to discuss this placement, please contact me by Monday, June 7th.

With best regards for a restful summer and with anticipation of a fine year,

Sincerely,

Roland S. Barth
Principal

Rain and Sunshine: Reaction to Placement

Each year, predictably enough, announcement of classroom assignments brings fallout from children, teachers, and parents. Although children make placement requests — through their parents and on their own — we do not consider them in the decision-making process. Thus, the final list surprises and disappoints many children. It is quite possible for a placement to satisfy the school and the parents, but violate the wishes (and real needs) of the child. For instance, a child may be placed in a teacher-directed classroom because the parents and teachers feel he needs that setting. But if, as he moves from his desk to his reading group and back again, he can see his friends across the hall building things, writing and producing plays, or preparing an expedition to a nearby woods, there may well be problems. Other children placed in informal classrooms are disappointed at missing out on a "real" learning experience with a rigorous teacher. Many children are upset more by their separation from important friends than by the kind of classroom to which they have been assigned. Although it is a child not an adult who is unhappy, it is no less a problem. Indeed, I have seen youngsters threaten to run away from home over placement decisions. At the very least, it can be argued that how children feel about their new class is important to their relationship with the teacher and therefore critical to the year's success.

Nevertheless, we exclude children from the decision-making process for many reasons. Some argue that elementary-age children are not mature enough to know what is best for them. I'm not certain of that. I *am* sure that the process is already so complex that the addition of yet another variable, even a democratic, child-centered variable, would severely tax our already strained energies. Moreover, the inclusion of children's views in the process would add strains to many households about who gets to choose next year's teacher. There is enough tension already. Finally, I have found that elementary children tend to be *used* in situations where adults disagree about what is best for them. I can envision a teacher saying, "But Susie told me that she wanted Mrs. Brown for her fifth-grade teacher next year, and I think that would be the right placement for her." And the parent responds, "Yes, but that was before I told her that Mr. Smith was also going to teach fifth grade next year. I think Mr. Smith would be just right for her, and now Susie wants him, too." And so on.

I leave it to others to find a way of involving children in the placement process, a goal I heartily endorse. For the moment, we feel fortunate if we can satisfy most of the caring adults most of the time. In schools, adults' concerns tend to prevail over children's, no matter what we wish or say.

Fallout from teachers is far more difficult to deal with. Generally, there is a good distribution of capable teachers and different styles at each grade level. Still, no matter how much we prepare for placement, difficulties surface each year around one or two teachers, into whose classes sending teachers want to place few children. For these sending teachers the problem is not which of several successful environments will be best for "their" children — whether they need apples, oranges, or pears — but rather how to keep each child from getting a lemon. Teachers are "damned if they do and damned if they don't" defend a classroom they dislike to an anguished parent who trusts them and relies on their judgment. Few of us would want to be in their shoes.

For the first few years we hoped these problems would vanish before placement time, and every year we were unpleasantly surprised by their recurrence. More recently I have come to recognize that they *will* exist. Now I try to anticipate *where* they will occur so they may be reckoned with and perhaps settled ahead of time, rather than being allowed to dominate (and sometimes decimate) placement meetings and damage the placement process. One way to anticipate problems is to ask sending teachers to predict approximate numbers of children they will be recommending for each receiving teacher. A little quick arithmetic reveals the discrepancies between supply and demand.

When faced at placement time with a receiving teacher in whom there is little confidence, I have found only a few possible moves — all unsatisfactory — each of which I have employed at one time or another:

(1) Jam twenty-five children in the unwanted class and "tough it out." I have avoided this solution because it makes the staff choose between *not* supporting the decision (in which case you aren't toughing it out) or lying to parents about it by saying, "This is the class in which I have confidence your child will flourish." Either way you destroy teacher integrity and parental confidence in the school, not to mention the productivity of the school experience for the children.

(2) Place fewer children in the class — those whose parents will accept the decision and those whom we feel will not suffer from the placement. This solution means other teachers will have larger classes and runs counter to our placement philosophy of matching child and teacher, but it is less distasteful than the first alternative.

(3) Reorganize the staff so that the teacher in question is teamed with a strikingly good teacher. The new team is easier to sell to sending teachers and to parents, but it amounts to a "forced marriage," promising a less than satisfactory professional relationship and therefore a crippled instructional program.

(4) Transfer the teacher to another school in exchange for a teacher in difficulty there. One system termed this practice "trading lemons." It

may solve the problem in the short run, but a similar problem is sure to reappear in twelve months.

(5) Withdraw the teacher from full-time classroom teaching responsibilities by creating another (nonteaching) position within the school for the teacher. This increases class size even more dramatically for the other teachers and raises year-long questions about why one teacher has an easier load or different job than others. It also tends to reward poor teaching — hardly our aim. Another option, of course, is to dismiss the teacher. In some cases this is a possible alternative; in others it is not. In any event, professional responsibility and due process require at least a year of careful observation and attempts to help the teacher improve. The period between placement and the end of the year is not sufficient.

Lack of confidence in a teacher at placement time may involve the entire staff in strife and antagonism. Yet it also carries with it considerable potential for staff development. I have tried to make use of the annual conflicts, painful as they are, when planning with teachers for the upcoming year. I recall a class to which neither teachers nor parents wanted to send many children. I sat with the teacher for many hours, drawing up and discussing a list of words and phrases teachers and parents had used to describe the class:

open
children not closely supervised
sloppy
little learning
children deciding
without clear guidance and direction
potential for children to avoid learning experiences
open to peer influence
loose
lacking external controls
high stress
unstructured
children left on their own

We then made a second list, containing words and phrases used to describe the other teachers at that grade level:

structured
supervised
formal
clear expectations
disciplined
quiet
orderly
secure

consistent scheduling
external support
children working up to potential
requirements
continuity

A comparison of the two lists provoked much soul-searching and stimulated considerable change the following year. There is much to be said for these kinds of direct, head-on confrontations. Nevertheless, they do not resolve the basic problem for sending teachers, parents, and their children. Over a long period a teacher earns the confidence of a school community through successful experiences of children in the classroom, countless adult interactions, firsthand observations, and the ubiquitous grapevine. Lack of confidence has the same complex basis and cannot be dispelled with a hopeful speech, or even with a year's concerted effort. The problem of teacher fallout remains a knotty one.

The third source of placement fallout is, of course, the parents. When parents receive the letters, we get dozens of frantic phone calls. Conferences with teachers and principal are scheduled. In about 90 percent of the cases what we have done coincides with what parents want us to do. About two or three children in each class, however, perhaps forty or fifty in the school, are assigned to a teacher who at least by reputation violates the parents' values, expectations, and wishes. Sometimes parental reaction is a warranted response to a foul-up on our part:

> I discussed next year's placement for Sandy with her current teacher, Mrs. Grady. We both concurred that the best class for her next year would be Mrs. Green's. This met with my particular approval because my son had been in that class with great success. I am now flabbergasted to receive the placement letter which tells me that Sandy will be in Miss Blue's class next year. I am particularly distressed in that I suggested that we document our strong feelings in a letter. Mrs. Grady felt that this would be unnecessary, since we were in agreement.

These incidents underscore the importance of adequately preparing the staff by anticipating parental questions and providing a clear, consistent process throughout the school. More often, we can predict parents' objections to our decisions. Usually these objections are based upon different interpretations of similar data. The parents in question immediately spring forward as though shot from cannons to protest, demand, cajole, or threaten.

I personally see each of these parents, often in the company — and protection — of the sending teacher, psychologist, or specialist who participated in the placement decision. We state our rationale for the placement decision. We share our observations of the child and our reasons for believing the selected classroom is the one most likely to be successful. We defend our collective best judgment. Cooperative decision making that involves classroom teachers, specialists, the school psychologist, and the principal spreads the burden for the decision and also increases its credibility. Without firsthand insights from other staff members a principal's explanation, based upon little contact with children, would be lame and unconvincing.

At the end of these conferences I sometimes suggest that parents observe the teacher to whom their child has been assigned — not always with the desired results:

> After our conversation last Friday I visited Miss Blue's class; I went, as you suggested, with a "new pair of lenses" on and felt fully prepared to be pleased, or, at the very least, satisfied with what I saw. What I found was a classroom of children, all apparently content, sitting at their desks, which were lined up in three rows. A small group was reading with the teacher; the others were doing some kind of paperwork. The room was certainly not silent, but I would have to describe the atmosphere as subdued. I chatted with Miss Blue for a few minutes while the children got ready to go outside for recess and left the room with a greater sense of unease than I had come in with.
>
> On my way out of the building I stopped in Mrs. Green's room. The class was outside so I did not get to see the kids in action, but my response to the room was a real revelation to me. I was overwhelmed by the richness of materials all around, by the enormous variety of things available to the children. It was as if someone had thrown a pail of cold water in my face and awakened me to what I feel education really is. I want my daughter to have more than simple instructions in the mechanics of reading, writing and arithmetic. I want her to have the experience of learning by trying and experimenting and doing. I want her to be able to learn by interacting with other children as well as with her teacher. I want her to have the fullness that a year of school can offer her and I am afraid she cannot get that from Miss Blue.
>
> At the end of our conversation on Friday you asked me to get back to you after I'd visited Miss Blue's class. I asked if that meant that if I was displeased you would change my daughter's placement, and your response was that if I feel she would have a bad year there, then you would consider a request for a change. I told you then, and I repeat now, that I'm too honest to say she'd have a *bad* year; I'm sure she'd survive as have countless other children. But I'm convinced that she'd not have nearly so good a year as she'd have in a classroom with a teacher or teachers who take a more materials-oriented approach to teaching, and hence I'd like to see her moved. I'm very sorry that I did not make this request in writing before the placements were made, since I feel certain that she'd have been placed with Mrs. Green if I'd requested it. I hope you'll agree about the desirability of placing my daughter in a class that will offer her a rich and growing first-grade experience.

Many parents are concerned by our definition of a poor placement:

Since I spoke to you on Friday I have been feeling quite distressed with the direction of our conversation, and I feel compelled to clarify my interpretation of our discussion.

As I understand it, you feel that a change is warranted in Danny's placement only if you can be assured that he will have a bad year in the straight first grade.

It is your definition of a bad year that causes me such concern. It means nightmares, bed wetting, withdrawal, and no learning. And it is the absence of these symptoms, and no more, which you guarantee Danny in the coming year. This is hardly what I've come to expect (and receive) from Angier.

Our experiences at Angier have always been so positive, so exciting, so reassuring, that I am doubly upset by this placement. It is true that in the straight first grade Danny may not have a year of lying on the rug eating lint, but he will, at least by *my* definition, have a bad year. And it is for this reason that I find his current placement so unacceptable.

These letters raise a difficult and unresolved question: when a parent is dissatisfied with a placement decision, does the burden of proof rest with the school or with the parent? Must we guarantee that the child will have a good year in that class (an impossible assurance, especially without parental support), or is it sufficient that we feel sure the placement won't result in a "bad" year? Should parents be asked to show that the placement decision will result in a bad year for their child? How could they demonstrate this?

With supporting data and reassurance from trusted teachers, about half the initially dissatisfied parents accept the school's recommendation with differing degrees of anxiety, anger, or disappointment. "It doesn't sound right to me," a parent will say, "but Mrs. Cary knows our son and we'll go along with her judgment." In only a dozen or two cases over the years have parents remained obdurate. Even that number has been sufficient to turn a principal prematurely gray. These parents indicate their intention to sell their homes in Newton and move to Tibet — but not before burning down the school — if they don't get their way. With these parents I confer some more. I point out possible negative consequences of their choice. I tell them it is their child whose life is at stake, not mine. If the youngster wakes up with nightmares next November, it will be their problem, not mine.

If after the conferences, the phone calls, the letters, and the hallway discussions parents still demand a change, I usually give in. We know full well that if parents don't respect their child's teacher, they will invariably convey these feelings to the child. I have never seen parents succeed in keeping disdain for a teacher from a child, hard as they may try. Children are astute interpreters of dinnertable questions like, "Did you do *any* work today?" The child, in response, will stop taking the teacher seriously and the basis for an unsatisfactory year is created.

My final step may be to send these parents a brief follow-up letter, which says:

Dear Dr. and Mrs. Jones,

At your demand, we have changed Tammy's placement next year from Mrs. Apple, with whom we think she would do best, to Mrs. Orange, whom you prefer.

Sincerely yours,

cc. Cumulative folder

Some parents who receive this letter reply by saying, "Well, we've talked it over and decided to try it your way." Many parents, of course, want to make the educational decisions for their children and hold the school accountable for making those decisions work. If we make the decision, I am prepared to be responsible for it. If they make the decision, they will be accountable. I am not willing to let parents have it both ways.

Other parents who receive the letter make it obvious that they feel Right Has Triumphed. In any event the process is over, and all of those involved can end one year and begin the next in peace. Generally, we think it makes sense to accede to parents' demands if they are very strong. If we don't change the child's teacher, everyone will be miserable. If we do make the change, the worst that can happen is that the child will not have the best possible year. It seems a reasonable trade.

There is an exception to this general procedure. Sometimes parents request a particular teacher when we have decided to place the child with another teacher who runs a very similar kind of classroom. Highly idiosyncratic demands like these interfere with the placement process without serving legitimate needs. In such cases we make no change, no matter what. These parents say to me, "You aren't listening to us." I reply, "I am listening to you. Here's what you're saying, but I don't agree with you and I will not comply with your demand." Pressed to the wall, my response becomes, "Mr. and Mrs. Samson, as I see it, you have four options: (1) to accept this placement decision — the sooner the better, as far as your child's success in the class is concerned; (2) to transfer your child to another elementary school within the system; (3) to enroll your child in an independent school; (4) to appeal the school's decision to the school committee or to the superintendent."

A few parents have chosen route (4), but without satisfaction. The school committee simply refers the complaint to the superintendent, and the superintendent has never intervened in a school's placement decision.

To my knowledge, no parent has removed a child from school over a placement decision, although several have for other reasons.

What most parents want is reasonable enough, I think. They want the professional educators to listen to their ideas about their children. They want us to share the rationale for our recommendations; they want to be sure we know what we're doing; they want veto power over the final decision. This is what our placement process attempts to provide.

Perhaps six or eight students out of four hundred begin each year in classrooms the staff would not have selected for them — and these children usually do all right. This small concession means that, in most cases, I can say to teachers, "There is not a child in your class whose parents haven't agreed to this placement." Given the built-in problems of deliberate diversity, this is perhaps the biggest gift a principal can bestow upon a teacher. If only one parent is furious about a child's class, that parent will spend the year trying to transform the class, reform the teacher, and make over the learning environment. A difficult time is guaranteed for everyone.

Transplanting: Midyear Switches

Some schools get through the placement process by saying to parents, "Here's where we have placed your child; let's try it and if it doesn't work out, next year we'll move your child," hoping that it will work out or that parents will forget the promise. Other schools reveal teacher assignments only when pupils arrive the first day in September. In either case teachers, parents, principal, and children often become embroiled in a frantic game of musical desks during the opening days of the school year. These whimsical "administrative changes" send unfortunate messages to everyone. Teachers get from parents the message that "you aren't good enough for my children." The principal, by switching children, supports this vote of no confidence. Parents get the message that the school neither knows nor cares which teacher is best for their child, so parents had better intervene. And children get the message that adults and their institutions are enigmatic at best and unreliable at worst.

Despite our painstaking, sometimes painful, placement process, we too find that each year there are parents who want their children reassigned in midyear. They have had an opportunity to see child and teacher work together and have decided the match is not working. We receive perhaps three or four requests for a transfer each year. (I shudder to guess what would happen if we were to employ a *random* placement procedure!) In an extremely diverse school of four hundred pupils, I consider this a positive evaluation of both the faculty and our spring placement decisions.

The small number of transfer requests may also reflect the fact that we make it difficult to move children at midyear. We have developed a detailed process for considering changes, which probably discourages as much as it facilitates transfer. First, we hold an hour-long conference of parents, principal, school psychologist, and classroom teacher at which parents give their reasons for wanting to move their child. It is particularly important that the present teacher attend so that problems are brought into the open. The visibility of the teacher also tends to moderate parents' complaints and provide an opportunity for the teacher to respond to the sources of dissatisfaction. At this conference we spell out the procedure for changing a teacher. We will move a child to a new teacher only if: (1) the current placement is detrimental to the child in ways that are apparent to the principal, the teacher, and the psychologist, as well as to the parents; *and* (2) placement with another teacher predicts more success for the child.

In order for us to assess the child's present placement, the principal and psychologist each observe in the class for two or three hours over several weeks. Records and examples of the child's work are carefully scrutinized. After the observation period we hold a second hour-long conference. In most cases we have found that the child is making reasonable progress in his present class and decide that no change will be made. We may, however, make recommendations to the teacher for specific changes *within* the classroom — such as individualized work in reading, a change of seats, or a new record-keeping system.

There are cases where it is clear that the present class is not working well for the child. He seems to be unhappy and has few friends, a short attention span, and a very distant, perhaps fearful, relationship with the teacher. Then we consider the second criterion: Is there another teacher with whom we might expect *more* success for this child? Children, like adults, tend to carry their problems with them; a change in teacher often means only a new setting for the same difficulties. If another placement does not promise more success, there is no point in moving the child. Kicking a radio may be an accepted electronic solution; it is not an acceptable means of solving educational problems. Instead, we use this opportunity to try to figure out how the child's present classroom might better serve him—through special tutoring, intensive work with a student teacher, or time each week in a resource room to strengthen a fragile ego or build computational skills.

Occasionally (at our instigation or that of the parents) we move a child when it becomes clear that the present placement is not working and another classroom does seem likely to bring more success. A child with newly diagnosed learning disabilities might go to a classroom with an experienced learning disability teacher. In one case we were asked to change an older, very bright fifth-grade child who was working considerably below fifth-grade level. Flaunting normal practice, we moved him to sixth grade, in effect rewarding his low achievement by promoting him. He made a rapid, happy adjustment and had a very productive year. Situations like this suggest that we should continue to consider each request for a change of teacher individually and exhaustively. Fortunately, the number of requests to change teachers remains small. In October we enjoy the fruits of the seeds planted so laboriously in May.

Rotating the Crop: Is Placement Tracking?

Do placement decisions made over successive years constitute tracking? Over a seven-year period does a particular child usually end up in more informal classes? In more teacher-directed classes? In mostly cross-age classes? Or in self-contained classes? Is consistency desirable? Is it necessary? These are second-generation questions that we have begun to ask ourselves.

Each placement decision is made for one year, even when children are placed into classes where they could spend two or sometimes three years. We attempt to take a fresh and flexible look at each match each spring, so that we don't lock a child into a certain kind of class by stereotyping his needs or the predilections of his parents. We have found that children (and teachers) change so quickly that placing a child in a given environment for longer than ten months is neither necessary nor advisable.

Our conscious effort to reduce classroom tracking is reflected more and more in parents' changing attitudes toward placement. There have been several cases during the last few years when parents have insisted that we place children in more formal classes than we would have liked. Because of the constant, visible presence of more informal classrooms within the school, these parents have had the opportunity to observe success in alternative settings. As a result, many parents who were ready to bomb the school at the suggestion that their first grader be placed in an informal class have initiated such a placement for their second grader. An initial match between parent and teacher in this way may eventually lead to an optimal match between child and teacher.

Other parents try out different kinds of classrooms before forming their opinions:

> We want to inform you of our thoughts about placement for Jimmy for fourth grade next year. The history of Jimmy's years at school has been two years in an informal classroom with mixed-age grouping and two years in more traditionally structured classrooms where the classes had children all of one age. In the first type of class he found many difficulties. In the second he has been more comfortable, secure, and has done better work. Therefore, we ask that he be placed in a straight fourth-grade-level class with a more traditional approach to learning.

On the whole, as parents become more familiar with the faculty they become more and more flexible. Rather than asking what kind of education is "best," they now consider the more fruitful question, "What is the best kind of educational program for my child at this time in her development?" Letters demanding "a real, basic education" are gradually being replaced with letters like this one:

> We've been thinking about Lisa's class assignment for next year. We don't know who will be teaching the third grades then, but we do have ideas about the situation she will do best in.
>
> We hope Lisa will be placed in an open, informal class. For the past three years she has been in more traditional environments — which both we and the school favored. But she is changing and growing and we think she is now ready to take on more independent and creative work, where the emphasis is less on teaching and more on her participation and learning.

Despite our attempts to revisit each pupil-teacher match freshly each spring, despite our efforts to dispel labels, and despite the many developmental changes in children, parents, and teachers, some children and some families still have become closely identified with a particular style of classroom. One child year after year will end up in more teacher-directed classrooms, while another usually appears on the rolls of cross-age classes. Sometimes these children come from families with strong, coherent value systems. Sometimes a child seems to succeed only in a certain kind of classroom. I am not troubled by this form of tracking if there are good reasons for a youngster's placement pattern. If there are not good reasons, I would prefer children to experience a range of teachers and teaching styles during their elementary years. Like crops and teachers, children benefit from annual changes in their setting. In any case, a school organized around alternative people rather than alternative ideologies makes tracking less of a problem. Ideologies may fall into tracks; teachers seldom do.

Interestingly, one form of tracking does persist. Children in cross-age groups tend to stay in them. This means that children initially placed in straight-age groups may be denied entrance to a mixed class because of the few "openings," as one industrious and thoughtful parent pointed out:

> I am moved to write by my concern over Sam's first-grade placement and the way in which it came about. I am particularly distressed by what appears to be a kind of "tracking" both in the first-grade and the fifth-grade assignments. I understand that all but two of the girls in Sidney's fourth-grade class are moving on to Mrs. Sazerac's class; that's 83%! And now I learn from the kindergarten teacher that approximately 3/4 of her class have been assigned to the straight first grade and that a primary reason for this situation is that so many of the children already in the K-1 and K-1-2 classes were to be retained in those classes that there was room for only a few new faces coming from other classes. This angers me for two reasons: first, I always had the impression that

among the criteria for placement was the reshuffling of the population at a given grade level; and second, in the case of my own child, it meant that he could not be placed in the class which was the first choice of both his teacher and his parents. While I am pleased that my child is flexible enough that he can do well in almost any kind of classroom, I am not pleased that this means that he is one of the children who gets shifted from his preferred assignment.

At the time that I registered Sam for kindergarten, I suggested that he might do best in a straight kindergarten class, and he has had such a good year that I have never regretted that decision. But I certainly did not intend for his kindergarten placement to preclude his having the option of later going into a class like the K-1-2 which, in effect, is what has happened since those with "squatter's rights" have been favored. At our conference with the kindergarten teacher I told her that the K-1-2 class appealed to me but that I had such confidence in her evaluation that I would go along with any placement so long as she felt it was in Sam's best interest. I did not write a letter expressing a preference since I feel that the parents' role in placement has become too large and since I recognize that a style of teaching which seems good to me may not be the best style for my child. This seems to be particularly true for Sam; apparently the child with whom I cope at home is different from the child the teacher enjoys at school. Thus, when the placement letter came I called the kindergarten teacher to ask for reassurance that in fact placement in the straight first grade was a deliberate decision on her part, only to discover that it was not but was, instead, a placement of convenience.

I have written all this down since I can articulate my thoughts better in writing than verbally, but I'd be happy to talk to you about it. But in the future I think something must be done to restore a balance to the placement process and to avoid the tracking of children in one or the other routes.

Thanks for listening!

No matter how we conduct placement each year, new problems will be posed—by the process, by children, by parents, by teachers, and by our decisions. Like most schoolpeople, we have found that there are few Answers in education anymore. We end up trying to trade unproductive problems for more productive ones, to identify the difficulties that will prod us to examine what we do and why we do it.

Reaping the Harvest: The Fruits of the Process

Placement is an agonizing and exhausting consequence of our decision to accept, and indeed to encourage, a diversity of children, teachers, and parents. Most of the time it is an investment that pays off. Placement is the means by which we can reconcile different educational values and needs of parents, the differing practices of teachers, and the best interests of children. Beginning each school year with a successful match between teacher, child, and parent means that the teacher can use an authentic style, parents can have their children in a learning environment that suits their values, and children can learn unimpeded. An exhaustive placement process enables teachers to live together in a pluralistic institution and teach with responsibility and integrity, at the same time enabling children to live and learn in environments that offer the best chance of promoting their intellectual and personal development.

The placement process has ramifications far broader than determination of next year's class rosters. Two fruitful questions dominate placement: Under what conditions did the child do his very best work this year? Which of next year's possible teachers comes closest to providing those conditions? When a teacher has to think about a child's optimal learning style for future placement, that consideration often affects the current year's instruction in rewarding and productive ways. Assessment of learning is likely to improve when careful observation of students is required. If placement itself were not so critical to student success, the side benefits of the process alone might be worth the costs.

In order to answer our two placement questions, we must look closely and frequently at each child's learning style and at each teacher's instructional style — in short, at our children and at ourselves — rich sources of information to which few schools sufficiently attend. Resolution of the two questions does not guarantee a perfect learning environment for all children; it does, however, begin to make greater use of the information about children and teachers available in schools, so that thoughtfully informed choices can be made about each child's class assignment. Informed choices, however imperfect, are better than uninformed guesses or random assignments.

However powerful and positive an influence our placement process has had, it may find limited applicability in other schools. There are prerequisites that are by no means easily attained. An elementary school must have a critical number of classrooms at each grade level if alternatives are to exist. A small K-6 elementary school, for instance, with one class at each grade level, obviously would not lend itself to this process. Schools must have a minimum population of perhaps three hundred students to ensure two or three different classrooms at a grade level. The different classrooms and their teachers must be varied enough to include apples, oranges, and pears, yet circumscribed enough to discourage lemons. The school community must accept, respect, and to some extent value these differences. Each teacher must care about each child's placement and be ready to translate that caring into action. The staff must be willing to share responsibility for the placement process and the decisions that emerge from it.

While these preconditions may not be present in many schools, it seems to me they are worth developing. When many different kinds of teachers coexist, parents and educators confront competing thoughts and methods and begin to question and refine their own ideas and practices.

Pedagogical questions may replace political issues in the educational forum. When there are alternative teaching styles and an opportunity to match child to teacher, the question "Who decides?" gives way to the more important question "What kind of learning environment is best for Johnny?"

At an open house one September I walked into a classroom and was met by a parent of a fifth grader who could hardly wait to tell me how happy she was finally to have her son in a "good" class — one with homework, desks in rows, and rules for behavior posted on the wall. Looking down the hall toward a more informal fifth-grade class, the mother remarked, "And those poor kids down there. I feel sorry for them." A few minutes later I dropped into the more informal classroom and a husband and wife came to greet me, overjoyed at finding a reading loft, an easy chair, animals, and a highly personal, individualized program for their child. They looked down the hall toward the more formal classroom and moaned, "Those poor kids down there."

That's probably as far as we are going to go. A pluralistic public school can make most people happy with what they have and willing to tolerate what others want. Seldom will many be converted to another way. And placement is the glue that holds it all together — or doesn't.

How Sweet Are the Fruits: Does It Really Matter?

Earlier I commented that in education we tend to take some things, frequently the wrong ones, too seriously, and other things, often the important ones, not seriously enough. The elaborate placement procedure described here suggests that I believe placement one of the "right things" to be taken seriously. We assume that the match between child and teacher is critical, that selection of the right teacher is the most important single decision affecting a child's social and academic growth. It is upon this assumption that the rationale for a genuinely pluralistic school ultimately rests.

Yet sometimes I wonder. I wonder how much it really matters. Each year I see several supposedly misplaced children and, as I have observed, most of them do all right. I wonder if these children would have done any better in our preferred setting? Or might they have done worse? And, not infrequently, a teacher unexpectedly retires or resigns over the summer. The class that had been hand-fitted to one teacher spends the year with another — with no apparent ill effects. How do we know, beyond what our intuitions tell us, that the teacher-child match really does matter?

An abundance of professional literature addresses this question, without really answering it. Studies attempting to justify the match of learning style with teaching style are outnumbered only by studies attempting to measure how much children learn as a function of different classroom characteristics. Some studies try to relate the appropriateness of learning environment to the social class of the students. Some contrast the performance of children in open classrooms with those in traditional classrooms. Some compare children's achievement where behavior modification techniques are employed to student achievement in more child-centered classes. Their results are, at best, ambiguous.

Two of the best studies are those of Vincent Silluzio and Neville Bennett. Because of intense, sometimes controversial interest in cross-age grouping within the Newton schools, Silluzio, director of research there, conducted a three-year study

> designed to determine whether assignment to multigrade classes affects the development of basic skills such as reading, word analysis, mathematics, and listening as well as school attitudes. Children in kindergarten only, kindergarten-grade-one combinations (K-1), and children in grade-one-only classes were given a variety of tests . . . These same children, as first, second, and third graders, were [then] retested . . . In addition, 61 primary grade teachers were interviewed.[6]

Although some differences were observed, Silluzio's most important conclusion was that the assignment really doesn't matter (see Appendix A). A child will perform equally well in a cross-age group or in a straight-age class, and both students and teachers will feel positive, regardless of classroom placement.

A more exhaustive study was conducted by Bennett, professor of education at the University of Lancaster. He asked two questions: Do differing teaching styles result in disparate pupil progress? and Do different types of pupils perform better under certain styles of teaching? He developed and validated a questionnaire classifying teachers into twelve types along a continuum from more informal to more formal. He then chose thirty-seven teachers, representing different teaching styles, and attempted to assess the differential impact of their styles on pupil progress. In the fall and again the following June, he tested children in the thirty-seven classes, using achievement and personality measures. His findings are unlikely to bring joy to partisans of open classrooms:

> The effect of teaching style is statistically and educationally significant in all attainment areas tested. In reading, pupils of formal and mixed teachers progress more than those of informal teachers, the difference being equivalent to some three to five months' difference in performance. In mathematics, formal pupils are superior to both mixed and informal pupils, the difference in progress being some four to five months. In English [composition], formal pupils again out-perform both mixed and informal pupils, the discrepancy in progress . . . being approximately three to five months . . .
>
> Formal and mixed pupils are better at punctuation, and no worse at creative or imaginative writing, than pupils in informal classes.[7]

Bennett's conclusions are clear. It *does* matter into what kind of a class a child is placed. His research unequivocally supports more formal over more informal classrooms. He does not, however, suggest that open classrooms be replaced with traditional ones. He concludes that there are limits to acceptable teacher diversity, and that all classrooms must meet standards, a position with which few would find fault:

> The central factor emerging from this study is that a degree of teacher direction is necessary, and that direction needs to be carefully planned, and the learning experiences provided need to be clearly sequenced and structured.[8]

In education as in other fields, one can find ample research to support almost any position. Speaking from my own experience, I'm not sure if it really does make a significant difference if Johnny is placed next year with Mr. Smith in the younger part of a cross-age group or in Mrs. Jones's more formal, single-grade class. For a few children, it certainly does make a difference; for many, I doubt it does. Most parents *think* it matters, and so do most teachers and most children. Therefore the daily reality is that placement *does* matter to the people most directly affected by it. Whether or not a particular match makes a significant difference to child or teacher, we in the schools must proceed as if it really matters for all children.

A school probably achieves minimum success if it does a child no harm. I don't find this sufficient. Failure to do harm requires that each child be entrusted each year to a caring, sensitive, industrious adult, in short to a decent person. Many parents are beginning to see that personal teacher qualities are more important than other, more visible, philosophic classroom characteristics. As one parent put it:

> We would like Jack to be in a classroom similar to the ones in which he has developed so beautifully during his two years at Angier: one where the teacher is lively, supportive, imaginative, willing to find out each child's needs and strengths and use that information to form a program that is both organized and stimulating.

Perhaps, then, the real importance of the arduous annual placement process lies less in its particular outcome — four hundred teacher-child matches — than in the process itself. Placement provides an annual occasion for all members of the school community to demonstrate their commitment to children. It becomes a time when adults can work together intensely for children, forging bonds of trust, interdependence, confidence, respect, and cooperation. In the long run these bonds may be far more important than whether Johnny will be in Mrs. Jones's or Mr. Smith's class. They really do matter.

CHAPTER FIVE

The Instructional Program

If teachers were invited to experiment with specific aspects of curriculum and then, on the basis of these experiments, a framework were to be developed, curriculum development would acquire a new dynamic.

—Hilda Taba

T HERE COMES in midsummer a week when the garden is at its peak, producing rows of tiny beets, young heads of lettuce, tender rosettes of spinach. And at that moment — the point at which everyone can see what the garden is doing — everyone wants a share. Woodchucks and deer, friends and relatives, gardeners and weeders all want in. This perhaps fanciful metaphor seems to fit curriculum within a school. Curriculum — what is taught and how — is the visible manifestation of the complex workings of a school. Everyone wants a piece of it.

I have commented on the surprising degree of agreement within schools on educational goals. Just as everyone agrees a garden is desirable, few would take exception to Henry Rosovsky's definition of an educated person:

An educated person must be able to think and write clearly and effectively.

An educated person should have a critical appreciation of the ways in which we gain knowledge and understanding of the universe, of society, and of ourselves.

An educated person cannot be provincial in the sense of being ignorant of other cultures and other times.

An educated person is expected to have some understanding of, and experience in thinking about moral and ethical problems.

An educated person is expected to have good manners and high aesthetic and moral standards.

An educated person should have achieved depth in some field of knowledge.[1]

94

But consensus on goals does not produce agreement about means. Instructional means (and evaluation of the effectiveness of means) are the center of the educational battlefield. Officially, curriculum is determined by policy: "Here's the syllabus. Here's what you're supposed to teach. Here's how you're supposed to teach it. We will evaluate how well you are doing." In fact, it is never that simple. The fact that the garden belongs legally to the landowner makes little difference to the gardener — or to the deer. In schools five contenders jostle for control of the curriculum: the "system," usually in the person of curriculum coordinator or supervisor; the school principal; the classroom teacher; students; and parents. They all slug it out, in the best interests of the children, of course.

Curriculum Outlines

Most systems provide teachers with subject-by-subject curriculum guidelines that reflect what someone, sometime, felt children at a given grade level need to know. Some guidelines are hopelessly out of date, some are current; some are so detailed they tell the teacher what color chalk to use; others are broader, more general. Some are political documents to be waved at meetings as testimony that the basics are being taught; others are workable outlines that teachers value and gladly use.

Whatever their quality, curriculum guidelines generate for a school system as many questions as they resolve. I have never seen a set of guidelines that told how to offer a uniform, prescribed curriculum for all children and at the same time respond to the diverse individual needs of teachers and pupils. Nevertheless, guidelines serve a useful function. Education requires careful planning. Useful guidelines provide overall plans, while recognizing that much of what is taught and learned cannot be anticipated. They provide a framework, a coherent set of objectives, which ensures continuity of experience for students as they pass through the grades. Serviceable guidelines help teachers and students organize their experiences without dictating precisely what those experiences should be. Attempts to impose standardization beyond this level have only pedantic interest; complex and rigid guidelines meet with resistance, rejection, and mindless compliance, and insult and assault the potential of most teachers and students.

Good guidelines are taken seriously by schoolpeople. Guidelines are good if teachers have participated in their development, if they include teachers' judgments about what can and should be taught, and if they reflect teachers' knowledge of the ways children learn. Guidelines are good if they offer a sequence through which a child will pursue different subjects — in math, for instance, from addition, to subtraction, to multiplication, to division — rather than providing a catalogue of skills to be learned by all children at a given time. In short, guidelines are good if they are realistic, reflecting the interests and capabilities of both children and teachers.

In one sense, all curriculum guidelines are obsolete the minute they are published, since most teachers continually adapt, refine, add, and omit as they teach. Good curriculum is growing, organic. Teachers follow guidelines as general statements of objectives; but as they follow them, they often supply their own materials, activities, and strategies. In the last analysis, then, the classroom teacher creates the curriculum.

With this realization, each June I ask teachers to prepare their own curriculum outlines for the following year. (Appendix B gives two examples of the results.) These outlines help to focus summer planning, and from them we prepare our orders of books and supplies. I confer with teachers about their plans, offering assistance and occasionally intervening if a teacher's plans are too far out of line with the system's guidelines or at odds with those of the previous or subsequent teacher.

The curriculum outlines are distributed to parents at a September open house, as statements of what teachers intend to do during the school year. Sharing teachers' guidelines each fall lets parents know what is ahead for their children and allows teachers to solicit aid and support from parents to help carry through the plans.

These curriculum guidelines reflect both the system's curriculum goals and each teacher's personal philosophy and style. They embody what the system suggests should be taught and what teachers have learned about children at a particular grade level in a particular school. Unlike system-wide guidelines, teachers' curriculum outlines seldom mesh neatly with one another. Frequently I put on "math lenses" and read sixteen math curricula — an impressive and sometimes unsettling experience. Teacher guidelines are visible, written expressions of the rich, diverse, and highly personalized programs we have fostered. But they don't form anything resembling a coherent blueprint for the elementary years. At best, in fact, they resemble a patchwork quilt; at worst, a random smorgasbord, hardly suitable for solemn presentation at a PTA or school committee meeting. They appear to be capricious and whimsical. They violate traditional expectations (a curriculum is supposed to be nice, neat, tight, uniform, logical, ordered in scope and sequence). And they offer little compelling evidence that anyone is overseeing the school, looking after the continuity of children's experiences as they progress through the grades.

Why then do we continue this practice? Because our guidelines are pretty honest. What teachers say they are doing is, by and large, what they are doing. We prefer messy reality to waving a syllabus and saying, "Here's what we're teaching," when the actual behavior of teachers is quite different (a discrepancy that contributes so much to educators' fear of being "found out"). Impeccable, unified curriculum outlines for a school or a system are often logically beautiful — but functionless. Our outlines have blemishes — but they are useful. They provide an important starting point for curriculum development and coordination. They reveal omissions or redundancies that can be corrected. They bring out disagreements that can be resolved or at least openly discussed. They are, in short, working and workable documents.

Our home-made curriculum guidelines shift the teachers' role. Teachers are expected to be actively creative, rather than passively compliant. In addition to responding to the system's uniform curriculum, teachers develop and implement their own, tailored to their strengths and the needs of their students. While this generates both labor and risks for teachers, most gladly accept the accountability that accompanies writing their own curriculum outlines. With the costs comes a large measure of control over classroom instruction. For most teachers it is a fair trade-off.

I have found that when teachers prepare their own curriculum outlines, crucial issues come to the surface and promote examination of what teachers believe about themselves, about children, and about teaching. The teacher who deliberately decides what to do in the classroom, in light of many alternatives, is more likely to evolve a successful, consistent curriculum than the teacher who is given a package—even if the package is more neatly labeled. Function is sometimes more important than form.

In spite of our untidy methods, the roof has not collapsed. Each year curriculum outlines reveal substantial differences in educational values and instructional means among teachers. Children seem to learn and enjoy learning, and most proceed through the school with little confusion or failure. The roof has not collapsed because teachers know what they are doing, and why, and because they believe in their methods. When this is the case, others are likely to accept and even respect their efforts, no matter how assorted and undignified they may appear on paper.

I have found problems of diversity in curriculum more exciting and productive than problems of uniformity. A teacher-initiated, personalized curriculum is always in the process of becoming. With diversity, we have heated debates, thinking, growth, movement, and change; with an imposed uniform curriculum, what is there to discuss other than "Do we have to do it?"

Ultimately, I suspect, the content of curriculum outlines — system or teacher produced — is less important than whether each teacher can take each child where she finds him in September and proceed as far as both teacher and child together can go until June.

The Informal Curriculum

No matter who writes the yearly curriculum guide, its content never represents all that really goes on in classrooms. There is in every school an informal curriculum, which frequently has as great an effect upon children as the formally stated curriculum. We have tried to use both organized and unexpected extracurricular events to enhance the learning of students.

An example of our planned informal curriculum is the "optional" program. For an hour every Wednesday afternoon adults and children abandon regular activities and rearrange themselves. Teachers (and sometimes children) teach activities such as puppet making, creative writing, exploration of public transportation, use of math calculators, construction of musical instruments, and folk dancing. The groups are small and the range of choices as broad as we can make them. Children sign up for an activity for six weeks; then "courses," instructors, and students are scrambled again.

This program often provides opportunities for students to engage in totally new activities with children of other ages with whom they normally have little contact. It allows children to make choices, and to live with the consequences for several weeks. Optionals encourage teachers to try out ideas and share interests that they feel may not fit into the usual program, although these ideas and approaches often cross-pollinate and do find their way into regular classroom time. Adults not usually considered teachers — parents, custodians, principals, husbands, wives, and friends — also instruct children. Although none of these activities appears in a curriculum guide, all inject vitality, variety, and substance into the curriculum.

Unanticipated important happenings also become content for the informal curriculum. Once a fire killed five members of one school family. This event was too important for the community to be ignored. So we attempted to help children deal with it. The day after the fire we wrote to parents:

Dear Parents:

We write to you at a time when all of us in the Angier community are shocked and saddened by the death of Mr. Harold Santorn and four of his children. We are painfully aware of the great loss with which Mrs. Santorn and her daughter Julie must somehow deal.

It is important at this time that we think hard about how children can best be helped to deal with loss by death or separation. Let us share some thoughts with you and invite you to do the same with us, and with one another.

Angier children will react in many different ways to the Santorn deaths. Those who knew Harold, Jamie, Ben, or Debby may share the family's grief. Many more will, for a time, be fearful for their parents' safety as well as their own, wondering "Who would take care of *me* if *my* parents died?" or "Will I die in a fire?" Because by now your child is probably aware of the tragedy, it would probably be helpful to talk about it with him, answering his questions. This could provide an opportunity for you to address some of your child's perplexing questions.

All children will, of course, have to deal with loss at some time. In fact, most children first worry seriously about death, loss, and abandonment sometime between the ages of four and seven, regardless of whether they have had any relevant personal experiences. How a family answers a child's questions about the meaning of death depends on their particular religious or philosophical beliefs. We think, however, there are some issues concerning loss common to people of all ages and all beliefs, and thus calling for similar treatment.

First, it is important to remember that a child's *feelings* at a time of loss are similar to an adult's even though his thoughts may be different. Like an adult, a child feels sadness, emptiness, pain, and anger, when he loses someone important to him, and he needs to be offered a chance to talk about it, and needs to be allowed to express his feelings with tears, and action, and words. Reassuring physical contact — everything from an extra touch to being held, depending on the child's wishes — can be especially helpful. Also, children need to know that adults grieve too. They can learn this by having parents share their feelings at a time of loss, perhaps by telling their children when they are sad, for example. Children sense when adults are sad or angry anyway, but it helps them if adults can say so, and say why. Finally, children need to know that grieving can take a long time, and may not begin until long after the loss.

Although it may seem kindest to try to protect a child from the knowledge of an anticipated loss (for example, the expected death of a terminally ill relative or an imminent divorce in the family), it probably isn't. Most people, including children, can deal best with loss if they have some chance to prepare for it, and full experiencing of it when it comes.

We urge you, therefore, to share your feelings with your children, and to encourage them to express theirs, both concerning the loss about which we grieve together now, and any future loss they may face. This is no easy task, especially since it must often be done by adults who are grieving too, but it is an important one.

Sincerely,

Nancy Lankford, School Psychologist
Roland Barth, Principal

Attempts to make sense of personal tragedy and triumph, of national crises and successes, all so much a part of children's and adults' experience, are important to a real curriculum. What is taken seriously in schools must extend far beyond printed curriculum guides.

Connections for Teachers, Connections for Children

In a school characterized by varieties of teachers and diverse programs, visitors frequently ask, "Do children have problems adjusting from one teacher to the next, from one type of classroom to another, from one method of teaching to another?" Despite the patchwork-quilt quality of our curriculum outlines, children do not seem confused. Our primary problem — and the primary problem of most elementary schools — is helping children make connections among ideas and people and among different elements of the curriculum. It is not sufficient to say that each teacher takes each child where she finds him in September and goes as far as they can together by June. Where does she find him? How does she find him? How long does it take to find him? Where does she take him? How does she take him there? How is where one teacher takes a child related to where another teacher takes the same child? What are the implications for one teacher of the previous teacher and the subsequent teacher? In college, even in high school, the connection-making burden falls on the student. In elementary schools, the adults must initiate the process and help the child learn to make connections independently. We cannot assume that the efforts of twenty-five or thirty adults who instruct a child during the elementary-school years will magically fall into place within the child's head, ultimately making sense.

I have found the most important factor in enhancing the quality of children's connections to be the quality of connections among their teachers. To the extent cooperative, frank interpersonal relationships exist within the staff, the right hand knows and cares what the left hand is doing and what both hands do makes sense to children. Although connections for children are made partially through articulated curriculum outlines, the greatest continuity comes from adults related by bonds of respect, interdependence, trust, communication, and caring. Without these bonds curriculum development is another rhetorical, futile exercise of form with little substance.

When teachers work comfortably and confidently together, integration of subject matter is frequently self-initiated and self-sustaining, dependent upon neither principal nor curriculum coordinator. When a school faculty begins to enjoy trusting, interdependent relationships, alliances form that cut across classes and subjects. Recently I discovered the librarian, art teacher, music teacher, and a fifth-grade classroom teacher teaching a unit on musical instruments. The librarian organized the research, the art teacher supervised the creation of musical instruments in the art room, the music room became the concert center, and the classroom teacher took over planning and coordination. My part consisted of accepting an invitation to come and observe! Had I tactfully tried to impose this kind of cooperation, even planned with painstaking care, it would have fallen flat. Imposed curriculum coordination engenders, at best, subservient behavior among teachers. At worst, it creates friction, resistance, and an increased desire to be left alone.

For me the important question has not been how to articulate and integrate curriculum but rather how to provide conditions within the school that will promote the personal and professional cooperation of the staff. Faculty trust, interdependence, and mutual respect come slowly and often with difficulty, but they are qualities worth working for.

We attempt to foster communication in several ways. I have mentioned the placement-time practice of teachers observing in classrooms at the next higher grade level, and the primary and intermediate staff meetings held in different classrooms twice a month to allow the host teacher to share methods, philosophy, and curriculum. In addition, each year I appoint from the faculty a coordinator in each subject area to serve as liaison between the school and the central administration, between teachers and the principal, and among teachers. The language-arts coordinator, for instance, in addition to full-time teaching responsibilities, keeps abreast of each teacher's written curriculum through frequent conferences, classroom visits, and familiarity with individual curriculum outlines. The coordinator asks, "How does this teacher's writing program relate to what others are doing?" She supplies teachers with language-arts materials and books, serves as a resource person (particularly for teachers new to the school), and helps plan and conduct staff meetings in language arts. She oversees a small budget with which she purchases materials for common use. She distributes proofreading checklists for children's written work and instructs teachers in their use. She leads discussions of phonic and linguistic approaches to reading and talks about the appropriateness of each for different children. And she learns a lot about the tenuous position of being both a classroom teacher/colleague and a facilitator and limit setter for other teachers. The simultaneous work of a half dozen faculty curriculum coordinators — more than a third of the staff — ensures that most teachers talk with other teachers about children and subject matter. Teachers cooperate with the curriculum coordinator because the curriculum coordinator is a teacher.

Our basic objective is to keep teachers in touch with one another and with themselves — to establish a basis for staff satisfaction and development that leads to caring about children. This is a crucial task. When a child has a nightmare about school, it seldom concerns whether desks are in rows, circles, or absent; whether the children use gerbils or workbooks; whether students learned to factor numbers by one method last year and a different method this year; or whether the reading book is from the same series. Only principals have nightmares about that sort of thing. Children's nightmares about school are dominated by the quality of their relationships with teachers and other children. If these relationships are characterized by ridicule, shame, punishment, failure, or fear, children have nightmares; if these relationships are marked by helpfulness, support, success, and understanding, they usually do not. If the school can provide the latter qualities with consistency, scope, and sequence as children move from teacher to teacher, subject to subject, and grade to grade, we have done much of our job. At that point our patchwork quilt provides not confusion but a protective cover for children in the school.

Discipline

A personalized, child-centered curriculum notwithstanding, we find many children who have their *own* ideas about what they will and won't do, and how. Year after year national polls find discipline one of the major concerns of parents. Polls of teachers reach similar conclusions. Parents and teachers agree that order and discipline are the foundations of teaching and learning. Again we find little agreement about means. Some parents criticize schools for providing insufficient discipline; others attack schools for disciplining students excessively in ways that violate civil and personal rights. Some teachers complain that the problem lies with overpermissive (or overrigid) parents.

All schools have rules. And teachers and administrators are far more committed to enforcing those rules than the "spare-the-rod" critics would suppose. Administrators and teachers live in close daily contact with large numbers of students and the simple instinct of self-preservation, if nothing else, makes them at least as concerned about school discipline as parents. Discipline in schools does not break down because schoolpeople like disorder, but because schools do not have enough effective ways to say to a child, "If you do that again, _____ will happen." Enforcement of rules is, without question, a major school problem. Ten to forty percent of the nation's high-school students are absent each day without cause, many of them "habitually absent" or truant. Despite the rhetoric, despite the legal mandates for compulsory public education, many schools have become de facto voluntary. To suspend a child because he is cutting school — that is, to punish him for not coming to school by forbidding him to come to school — is a perfect example of the bizarre and impotent institutional logic under which schoolpeople must function.

What about the student who hurts another or destroys property? What do we say, "If you do that again, I'll tell your parents"? Many parents cannot be contacted. When parents do come to school, the conference is often an occasion for parents to criticize the school. "I take care of him at home without your help," parents say, "it's your job to handle him at school without mine." In the old days students who hurt others or damaged property were spanked at home or paddled at school. This may have provided some deterrent, but in practice it flirted with abuse. To-day many states have wisely removed corporal punishment as a possible completion to "If you do that again, . . . "

Unfortunately, the only all-purpose response to seriously disruptive behavior seems to be suspension. On first inspection it seems logical. All other responses appear to have been declared illegal, immoral, or ineffective. Suspension temporarily solves the problem for harried administrators, teachers who want peace and quiet, and students who prefer to learn. It does little, however, to solve the long-term problem. The suspended student reappears in one day or three and, predictably, reacts with more anger, resentment, and disobedience.

Increasingly, suspension is being put to dubious use. Students have not had access to due process; a number of them come from minority groups.[2] In some schools suspension seems to be used as a tool to clear out an undesirable element.

Abuse of suspension has led to pressure from civil liberties advocates. As a result, the courts have established that students are entitled to virtually the same due process rights as an accused felon. The Newton *Rules and Regulations* now contain the following clauses:

> Sec. 12   Principals shall have authority to suspend (as provided by State law and subject to an appeal by the parent, guardian or custodian to the Superintendent) any pupil from school whose continued attendance is deemed by the principal to be prejudicial to the good order of the school because of, but not limited to, such behavior as: acts of violence or assault upon another person; interference with another's civil rights; stealing and/or willful destruction of property; disruption of the school; persistent or excessive truancy; and repeated disregard of the duly constituted authority of the school.
>
> Prior to any action on suspension, the principal must give the student an informal hearing at which he must notify the pupil of the charges against him and afford the child a chance to defend himself.
>
> If, after the conclusion of the informal hearing, the principal suspends the pupil, then the principal shall immediately, in writing, inform the parent, guardian or custodian and the Superintendent of such suspension and the reason therefor.
>
> No pupil shall be permanently excluded from school except by the Committee after written statement of the reason therefor to the parent, guardian or custodian of such pupil and an opportunity for the pupil and his parent, guardian or custodian to be heard by the School Committee.[3]

Although few would contest the right of a student to due process, many administrators find compliance difficult, if not impossible. Hearings, elaborate record keeping, letters and copies of letters, meetings, and conferences before, during, and after suspension all demand hours of labor from a principal. When a day's work is required to respond to a three-second rock thrown through a window, the backlog of cases accumulates faster than it can be dispensed. The principal's office becomes a miniature version of the circuit court. Once this happens, schools stop according due process or stop suspending students. In the former case, there is legal trouble; in the latter, "If you do that again, . . ." is reduced to a meaningless threat. Neither suspension nor nonsuspension is a solution for school or student.

At the elementary level, discipline is a less serious problem than it is at the secondary level. Students are physically smaller and weaker than the adults around them, making control by fear and force possible, if not desirable. Further, younger children are less prone than adolescents to strike out against others. And many parents of elementary-school children still believe in the school and in their progeny. Nevertheless, discipline is a major problem in elementary schools; a large part of the problem is the very limited repertoire of responses to misbehavior and the unpredictability with which these meager responses are employed.

At Angier we have developed three parallel sets of student rules and three different kinds of consequences when they are violated. Each classroom teacher establishes rules for students in that class. Regulations vary: in some rooms there are rules on how to write headings and make margins; in others, on when to talk, move about, sharpen pencils, go to the bathroom, and chew gum. There is great variation from class to class. Like tidy, uniform curriculum guides, consistent, uniform school rules connote logic and respectability. But I have found no good reason for school-wide policies governing behavior in different classrooms. Like college students moving from one professor to the next, children move from teacher to teacher, adapting readily to different behavioral expectations. Rules governing children's behavior are as intimately related to teaching style as choice of seating arrangement or textbooks. Classes cannot reflect the different values and philosophies of teachers if everyone is expected to comply with uniform procedures and rules. Furthermore, when teachers set their own expectations for children, both teachers and children take the expectations seriously. Teachers handle violations with consistency and care. Most become very resourceful in finding their own completions to the phrase, "If you do that again, . . ." Although I frequently confer with teachers about rules and about their classroom reward and punishment systems, responses to infractions do *not* include referral to higher authority. Children are not sent to the principal's office for breaking classroom rules. As with curriculum, teachers assume responsibility for their own classroom rules. They make them — and then make them work — or they revise them so that they function better.

The second set of formally stated expectations for children governs behavior in common areas — halls, assemblies, playgrounds — places where children and teachers from many classrooms must live together. In these situations I find diversity neither workable nor acceptable. When some are allowed to throw snowballs and others are not, when some are permitted to run while others must walk, there is no order. When a problem arises, teachers and I meet to determine whether a school-wide policy is necessary. As with the relationship between the higher and lower courts, we issue overriding policies in as few cases as possible:

RULES FOR CHILDREN'S BEHAVIOR IN ASSEMBLIES

No food of any kind (including gum) is permitted.

At all times children are to sit on the floor (no standing up or lying down).

Children are to remain at all times with their class (no wandering around).

No roughhousing.

No talking during presentations.

Children may respond to presentations at appropriate times and in appropriate ways. Boos and whistles are not appropriate.

RULES FOR SNOWBALLS

Throwing snowballs is permitted only in the area of the playground behind the backstop, nowhere else. Those who venture into this "combat zone" do so at their own risk.

These uniform policies are usually successful if they are few in number and if teachers are instrumental in identifying the need and determining and enforcing the policy.

The third level of discipline is for children who repeatedly violate either classroom rules or the rules of common areas. These are children who cannot control themselves and for whom teachers, alone or in concert, cannot provide effective control. In these situations principal, psychologist, and parents must become involved to provide the child with more and different kinds of adult help and control.

We attempt to work with habitually disturbed and disturbing children in a manner that simulates the legal and judicial system of the larger society. Initially the child may be referred to the psychologist for observation and testing. This probably tells us a great deal about the child's difficulties, but it does little to ameliorate them. The second step is to hold a conference with the classroom teacher, psychologist, principal, parents, and child at which the teacher describes and documents the child's behavior — not with labels such as "naughty" or "disrespectful," but with examples of specific incidents. The teacher runs through the saga: "On September 10, Johnny hit Billy with a baseball bat — four stitches. On October 15, Johnny set fire to the wastebasket in the classroom — fire department. On October 21, Johnny pushed Suzie's desk over — broken toe. On October 26, Johnny left the room without permission and ran outside."

Usually a child who gets to the conference stage has violated many rules of acceptable behavior. In the meeting we identify one or two of the most serious infractions, generally those related to the safety of the child and other children. We tell both Johnny and his parents that from now on Johnny will be expected to obey two rules: (1) no hurting others, and (2) no carrying or lighting matches. If (or more often, when) he violates one of these rules again, a specific consequence will follow. Consequences, like rules, are tailored for each child. After the first infraction, A will happen; after the second, B; and so on, leading up to the bottom line — suspension. We ask parents to accept the process, and to pledge their support as well. Most do. I follow the meeting by sending a letter to parents, teacher, and child. For example:

Dear Mr. and Mrs. Smith:

I want to summarize what we said in our conference last week. Because of several recent incidents we have established two rules for Johnny's behavior while in school:

(1) He will not hurt other children;

(2) He will not carry or light matches.

His teacher will inform you whenever one of these rules has been breached. If there are any further incidents we will proceed along these steps:

(1) After the first incident Johnny will have a conference with his teacher and me.

(2) If there is a second incident we will ask you both to come in and have another conference with his teacher and me.

(3) If there is another incident, we will immediately call you and ask that you take Johnny home for the remainder of that day. If the incident occurs after lunch, we will ask you to keep Johnny home the following day as well.

(4) Should there be other incidents, step (3) will be repeated.

In addition to this procedure, Johnny will be rewarded upon completion of days during which he does not break these two rules. As you know, Johnny has been referred to our school psychologist for her evaluation. She will be calling you soon to discuss this with you.

We hope these steps will help make Johnny's year a productive and constructive one.

Sincerely,

The conference and letter summarize what the school expects of the child and what the school will do if the expectations are not met. This counteracts the tendency for participants in unpleasant conferences to come away hearing and believing what each wants to hear and believe. Through the conference and letter we sharpen for the child what is expected of him, laying out tangible, possible ways in which he must take responsibility for changes in his behavior. We convey to the child that the teacher, administrator, and parents *care* about him (as well as caring about those who may be the object of his misbehavior). We provide the teacher with the support needed to simultaneously manage the child and continue to teach the entire class. And, finally, the conference and letter outline a procedure that complies with the system's, the state's, and the federal government's legal definition of due process.

We use a carrot as well as a stick. Children with severe problems may not alter their behavior in response to a pull *or* a push, but many move in response to both together. We sometimes use simple behavior modification techniques: a child may get points for *not* breaking a rule, first for an hour, then a morning, then a day, then a week. Points can be converted into toys, fruit, or special privileges.

After the conference and letter, a child's behavior generally improves — for about a day. Then it regresses to its former condition. At this point it becomes essential that teachers conscientiously keep records and predictably supply consequences. The procedure outlined in the letter shifts the burden from the teacher to the child, who must live with the consequences of his own behavior. Punishment is not a question of the teacher being "mean" to the child; it is the inevitable, predictable consequence for the child of violating rules of the school community.

When, after a few days, Johnny reaches level (3) — and children usually do — I ask the parents to keep him home for a day. Legally this constitutes "suspension," although we try not to use this ominous term. Our intent is to convey to Johnny: "We are removing your privilege of attending school for one day because you have broken a rule three times. We care about you; these rules constitute the conditions under which you may attend school." To the parent we give the message: "You must assume responsibility for your child all day tomorrow as we discussed at our conference. We think the action will help convince Johnny that these rules are important." And to the teacher this action says: "You will not be expected to deal alone with this child's problems indefinitely. Others — psychologist, principal, parents — will help."

After one or two days at home we have found a remarkable change in most children's behavior. Rule violations are dramatically reduced, for many reasons. First, the child has learned the school will do what it says it will do. Second, rewards for compliance may have become desirable and the one or two rules not impossibly difficult to obey. Third, parents get angry when they must stay home from work or find a sitter. They introduce their own rewards and punishments, which work in concert with the school's. And finally, if the school is a reasonably humane, exciting place, the child discovers that staying away from school is not as pleasant as it might have seemed. All of these factors, taken together, are capable of modifying most children's behavior. When one or two "behaviors" have been brought into line, we sometimes introduce one or two more, such as leaving the classroom only with permission. We have found that this elaborate process, this dramatic display of concern, consistency, and consequences, often brings *many* elements of a child's behavior into line, not only the one or two that were first singled out. Knowing that "if you do that again, *something* will happen" is a powerful force for changing behavior.

There have been very few situations where children did not respond to this program, where behavior showed little or no change. Some were removed by parents from the school and placed elsewhere; some entered residential, custodial institutions. In a sense, the process worked in these cases too, because documented misbehavior and repeated suspension brought the severity of the problems to the attention of the child, the parents, the school, and community agencies.

While we implicitly expect all students, not just Johnny, to refrain from assault and arson, I find no useful purpose in inundating all students with all possible rules. Only when a rule has been violated repeatedly do we make it explicit — and then only for students who appear to need it displayed in neon lights. Most students most of the time function without a catalogue of rules hanging over their heads — and most exercise at least as much self-control and responsibility as they would if they lived each day under an explicit code of behavior.

Clear expectations and carefully laid out consequences for misbehavior both maintain order in school and teach children about the limits of socially acceptable behavior. A process for children modeled after the adult legal system establishes "discipline," allowing teachers to continue class instruction unimpeded, and at the same time constitutes an important part of the curriculum. Learning to live within the constraints of the school society is as important a preparation for life in a larger society as is knowledge of the multiplication tables. For many children it is a more difficult lesson.

CHAPTER SIX

Parents

Such fathers as commit their sons to tutors and teachers and themselves never witness or overhear their instructions deserve rebuke, for they fall far short of their obligation. They ought themselves to undertake examination of their children and not place their trust in the disposition of a wage earner; even the latter will bestow greater care on the children if they know that they will periodically be called to account. Here the witty saying of the hostler is apt: "Nothing fattens the horse so much as the king's eye."

—Plutarch

JUST AS TEACHERS, central office, principal, and children jostle for influence over what children will do in school, so do parents. Involvement of parents in public schools is an old phenomenon and a new one. Rural parents used to take turns lodging the local schoolmaster, chopping wood for the stove to keep the schoolroom warm, and carrying water for the bucket to keep the schoolchildren cool. In more recent times PTAs, open houses, and school fairs have become fixtures of the educational scene.

As human-service industries have burgeoned, citizens have organized to ensure for themselves a fair share of these services. "Citizen participation" has become a strong force in all corners of our society — law, medicine, politics, consumerism — and especially the public schools, considered by some the most accessible and responsive public institution. Parents of schoolchildren have shifted from indirect to more direct involvement in schools. They are demanding that *their* schools become more accountable to them. In particular, parents seek influence over the curriculum — what is taught and how it is conveyed.

Parents' motives are straightforward. Many wish to be involved in the instructional program because they are proud of their neighborhood and school and because they derive satisfaction from giving and helping. Many enjoy sharing what they know about being a doctor or a telephone repairman. And, as placement letters reveal, many parents want to become involved in the school in order to make what is taught there more congruent with their own values. For some, this means addressing teachers by first names; for others, it means stress on explicit rules for behavior. Many parents seek involvement in the curriculum in order to

109

reform content and methodology: the state capitals are a waste of time, but the U.S. involvement in Vietnam is worthy of study; sex education should not be taught, or should be taught only as "plumbing," or should be taught with attention to both plumbing and feelings. At the base of much parent involvement is the desire somehow to increase their child's achievement — make the underachiever an achiever, the achiever a superachiever, and the superachiever a happy, well-adjusted Merit Scholar.

Most parents care about their children's education. Nevertheless, the programs of many schools are handicapped by meager parent involvement, often apathy. The problem for principal and teachers in such schools is to get parents involved at any time, in any way. If parents attend a parent-teacher conference once a year, the school — and the parents — may feel satisfied.

From the vantage point of other school principals, however, parent involvement in schools is substantial and might be considered in three categories: help, critical examination, and adversary action. There are hundreds of examples of parents' voluntary efforts that support, supplement, and complement the efforts of school personnel and enrich the life of the school.[1] I have seen parents raise money through fairs, raffles, and bake sales, using the revenue to augment the library collection, buy a rug for the office, or hold a year-end luncheon for teachers. Parents organize, edit, publish, and distribute the school newsletter. (For an example see Appendix C.) Parents recruit and train volunteers to staff the school library or teach a course in the school's optional program. They identify people, places, and events in the community that can bring creative arts into the school or take children into the community.

One group of particularly imaginative parents in our school sent out a questionnaire and organized a resource file — a catalogue of parental interests, skills, and abilities from which teachers could draw to supplement their curriculum:

PARENT RESOURCE FILE

Please answer with "Mr." and/or "Mrs." where appropriate.

_____ (1) I am willing to explain my trade, occupation or profession to a class or group of children. (For example: CPA, dairyman, cleanser, carpenter, chemist, architect, dress shop owner, grocery store owner, dentist, engineer, auto dealer, insurance agent, doctor.)

_____ (2) I have lived, traveled or vacationed in the following places and can share my knowledge, experiences, artifacts, slides and pictures with a class.

_____ (3) I am willing to share the knowledge and experience gained through community involvement or volunteer activities.

(For example: ecology, politics, conservation, improved housing policies, save-a-historical building.)

_____ (4) My knowledge of a sport is such that I am willing to share it with a class or group of children. (For example: tennis, golf, volleyball, horseshoes, jogging, hiking, mountain climbing, surfing, scuba diving, boccie, sailing, canoeing, camping.)

_____ (5) I have taught a course in or studied the following subjects and would be willing to present this material to a class or group of children.

_____ (6) I can share my knowledge of the following hobbies, crafts, skills. (For example: sewing, embroidery, candle making, cooking, jellies, pastries, bread, bouillabaisse, foreign and colonial foods, leather work and tooling, block printing, crocheting.)

_____ (7) I have a special interest that I would be willing to share with a class or group of children. (For example: astronomy, archaeology, a sculptor, an artist, a composer, a period of history, birds, flowers, entomology, coins, stamps, rocks.)

_____ (8) I am willing to have a small group of children come to my home to:

(a) observe my collection of antiques, Christmas tree ornaments, butterflies, models, records, rocks, etc.

(b) work with me on a special project such as weaving, cooking, wood carving, sculpting, etc.

_____ (9) I am willing to give a short talk, lead a discussion or a six-week course as part of the Optional Program on the following subjects.

_____ (10) I am unable to participate in the parent resource program.

_____ (11) I am able to help as a volunteer parent in the classroom

(a) with reading_____math_____science_____social studies_____art_____music_____gym_____general

(b) with field trips_____

(c) as room mother_____

_____ (12) I am willing to help as a volunteer in the library.

The room mother who faithfully accompanies every first-grade field trip, the mother who spends a hundred hours sewing costumes for a Gilbert and Sullivan production, the father who stands in the rain all Saturday afternoon selling hot dogs to raise funds — these parents are all more the rule than the exception. The extraordinary energy and dedication with which so many parents engage in a wide variety of school-helping activities does not go unnoticed. Each school has its own examples of the constructive, imaginative work parents do to augment the curriculum and staff of the school. This form of parental involvement in schools is welcomed and valued by schoolpeople. Indeed, many schools could not function very well without parents.

Parents also participate in schools as questioners, examiners, seekers of change in curriculum and structure. PTA groups often examine a particular subject-matter area: basic skills and sex education are especially popular these days. Parent-teacher meetings provide an opportunity — or a mandate — for school personnel to describe a particular aspect of the school program and respond to parents' questions and suggestions. Frequently schools or parents establish committees to monitor a part of the school program, such as the English curriculum (see Appendix C) or the school safety program. An ambitious parent group can devise and circulate questionnaires to assess community satisfaction with a school's instructional program; an example from our own school is given in Appendix D.

Parents who examine and question school programs are often instrumental in bringing school and home closer together and thereby improving children's instruction. They are also often frustrated — less by what they examine and question than by limitations on their ability to change what they find wanting. These limitations are a source of hard feelings between schoolpeople and parents. Many teachers and administrators are reluctant to give parents access to the operations of the school because they fear parents will not like what they see and demand changes. Don Davies, director of the Institute for Responsive Education at Boston University, observes that many schools have reacted to this fear with "window dressing activities — those that are designed to provide the appearance of an open and responsive school or school system with lots of citizen involvement, but without much reality."[2] Many schools are trying to have it both ways — allowing and even encouraging parents to examine and question, while at the same time reserving for themselves control over change. Alienation and disillusionment inevitably follow, unless the limits on parental decision making are specified in advance. If parents are told the parameters of their influence and know the probable outcome of their involvement, they can decide whether or not to participate. This procedure is honest, although it tends to make control rather than curriculum the issue that parents question and examine. Nevertheless, I prefer to have parents take me to task for being direct and autocratic rather than for being indirect and deceitful — frequently the choices for a school administrator.

Another alternative more easily expressed than fulfilled is to change school practice in response to parents' recommendations. In actuality there is no such thing as "the parents." Parents are not a homogeneous bloc with a single set of values or desires. In fact, I have found parents to be of as many minds as bodies. Some parents want snowballs allowed on school property, others want them banished; some want ability groups, others deplore them. To comply with the demands of a few parents (usually those who are shouting the loudest) often means violating the wishes of other parents (and many teachers) and pitting parent against parent in the process. As I suggested earlier, I find a more successful course is for schoolpeople to make policies in light of broad parental views and then to implement those policies with sensitivity to the highly differentiated needs of each parent. The balance of power in implementing policy varies with the kind of policy. I believe some decisions are best handled by the principal (for instance, the formal evaluation of teachers); some issues are best determined by teachers (choice of instructional methods); some by parents (whether their child will participate in a sex-education program); and some can be resolved jointly (the creation of a day-care center within the school).

While this decision-making model satisfies both logic and me, it does not necessarily resolve the issue for parents. Although involving parents in the school as critic/examiners has the potential for cooperative and collaborative efforts, there will always be tensions over how much access to how much of the school parents should have, and how much decision-making control they ought to exercise. When all is said and done, most schoolpeople feel "enough" is too much, and most parents feel that "enough" is too little. This fundamental discrepancy frequently leads to a third form of parental participation — adversary involvement. Adversarial parents criticize, judge, and attack what the school is doing and attempt to bring about change by any means possible. The number of adversary parents varies according to the health of the school and the nature of the community. I have seen entire school communities provoked to the point of insurrection by insensitive, ineffective educators. More typically, a group of parents dissatisfied with the direction the school is taking or unhappy with a particular teacher, administrator, or program attempts to exorcise the demon from their children's school with a zeal reminiscent of the Spanish Inquisition. I remember a slip I made in a faculty meeting called during a community controversy over a proposed urban-suburban classroom exchange program. "Don't worry about our parents," I assured the teachers, "their bite is worse than their bark." Neither the staff nor I found my words very reassuring!

Sometimes adversarial parents are fueled by their own difficult relationships with their children. And sometimes the school serves as a readily available whipping boy for parents whose children have difficulties or whose children's performance is short of what the parents would like.

Adversarial parents, in addition to being angry and outraged, often feel powerless, unable to effect change. This sense of helplessness increases their anger and pushes them to employ whatever power they think they can command. I once received a copy of a letter from an outraged parent addressed to the governor of Massachusetts, with a carbon to the president of the United States. Neither was of much help in settling the issue. More often, such a letter goes to the superintendent or the school committee:

> Too many teachers at Angier are not teaching reading, writing, math, spelling and science sufficiently. Today my daughter is spending the day at a private school. I will not be surprised when the headmaster there tells me she is behind the second-grade children there. My daughter has had a distressingly small amount of supervised teaching in her three years at Angier. I believe in public education, I want my children to go to their neighborhood school, but I cannot allow their academic potential to be wasted . . . I feel that they should pay triple attention to their primary responsibility — teaching academic subjects. They are currently doing a miserable job. I resent the time and effort I've had to spend calling attention to my children's academic status and needs. (This year, my daughter spent the first two months turning pages in books she could not read; it was not until *I* discovered it that the teacher realized. On the other hand, my son's abilities were grossly underrealized — despite a specific letter from the psychologist and several pleas on my part that he be given appropriate work. It was *April* before he was given work appropriate to his ability.)
>
> P.S. I expect that my name, though not necessarily what I said, will be confidential.

Ironically, most adversary parental involvement is over this kind of issue. It is ironic because a child's achievement is seldom enhanced by badgering parental pressure. I think it is possible for parents to contribute to their child's academic success by providing the kind of home whose characteristics appear to be related to school achievement:

> The high achiever's home has been found to be characterized by a strong, warm, and empathetic relationship between parents and children, as well as by good communication among family members. It has also been found that mothers of high achievers gave them good verbal stimulation in early childhood, praised them for small accomplishments, and were attentive in responding to their questions and requests for help. High achievers have also reported that their family life featured the sharing of ideas, recreational pursuits, and confidence. They have described their parents as affectionate, approving and trusting, and encouraging without being pressuring. Both hostility and extreme dependence have been generally absent; the children have usually accepted their parents' standards, but within a democratic atmosphere. Most important in these homes has been the role of the father as a respected, effective, and "instrumental" leader. The mothers have been loving but not necessarily demanding or overprotective.
>
> The underachiever's family environment has been found to be quite different from that of the high achiever. It is typically characterized by rejection, physical punishment, varying degrees of indifference, ambiguity,

parental conflict, sterility in affection, and meager communication. The father is often verbally unrewarding and indifferent.[3]

If these are indeed some of the determinants of academic achievement, it is evident that the school can have only a limited impact on a child's capacity for learning. This is not so obvious, however, to many parents.

No one can blame parents for wanting their children to learn more, for wanting them to have easier access to the advantages of this world. But one can, in many cases, question their methods. Some of my best friends are parents. My parents are parents; my wife is a parent; even I am a parent. It is nevertheless true that we parents as a group often behave in a primitive, insensitive, inconsistent, and frequently outrageous fashion when it comes to getting what we want for our progeny. Our efforts can be nonproductive or counterproductive in ways that led one principal I know to label a parent as "severely gifted." Another principal, in response to a parent who told him she paid taxes and his salary so that he had jolly well better do as she wanted, computed her portion of his salary — 32¢ — and keeps it in an envelope in his desk, ready for their next encounter. I have seldom seen a case in which angry *ad hominem* arguments between home and school have done anything but exacerbate a problem. Out of frustration or from concern for their youngsters, many parents show school personnel little of the respect, responsibility, and accountability they expect and demand in return.

In his study, *Elementary Principals and Their Schools,* Gerald Becker found that most principals considered working with parents "one of their most difficult problems."[4] No doubt many parents think working with the principal is one of *their* most difficult problems. A principal who has been burned a few times in encounters with belligerent parents tends to become cautious, conservative, and perhaps distant when dealing with all parents. Similarly many parents, shut out or once rebuffed by a callous administrator, begin to see all administrators as adversaries.

It is an unfortunate fact of school life that rapport and trust between parent and principal is extremely tenuous. Indeed, the relationship between parents and schoolpeople appears to be full of conflicts. Parents fear that unless they gain access to the school and to the important decisions educators are making that affect their children, their offspring will be shortchanged, or even abused. Teachers and principals fear that if parents are let in the door they will intrude into and even take over important educational decisions, placing schoolpeople still more in the position of being accountable for decisions made by others.[5] Perennial issues concerning hiring, evaluating, and reappointing teachers, judgments about what shall be taught at what grade level in what manner, determinations of acceptable behavioral and academic expectations for children, all provide regular occasions for tension, fear, struggle, and sometimes conflict between parents and schoolpeople.

Whether we want to or not, principals and teachers must take parents' involvement in schools seriously. First, we have no choice. The political reality is that schoolpeople will implement important decisions affecting personnel, budget, and program only so long as parents accept those decisions. Responsiveness and accountability to parents is the price we pay for some measure of local responsibility.

Secondly, faced with the ever increasing reality of school life that there is more to be done than hands to do it, it is clear that we *need* parents to keep schools going. With parent participation schools have libraries, newsletters, and field trips; without parents many schools would have none of these services.

Concern for the welfare of children, of course, is the most important reason schools must take parents seriously. To the extent that schoolpeople and parents — the caring adults with whom children spend most of their waking hours — can work in concert, they can frequently have a greater influence on children than either can working alone, and certainly much greater than if they are working at cross-purposes. The placement and discipline processes I have discussed illustrate this point. Most principals have observed the differential effects of parents on children as we attempt to discipline disruptive youngsters or provide needed extra help with the multiplication tables — without parent involvement, against the wishes of parents, or in alliance with parents.

One might expect that sharing a preoccupation with the same children would form a common bond, bringing principal, teacher, and parents together. Unfortunately, this bond seldom develops naturally or spontaneously. We schoolpeople need help in finding ways to work cooperatively with parents; and parents badly need assistance in translating their basic concerns into actions that will improve the situation for their children, the school, and themselves. A major task confronting schoolpeople and parents is somehow to transform a relationship commonly characterized by indifference, anxiety, fear, and anger into one of mutuality, cooperation, trust, and support. Indeed, the reform most critical to student success in school may well *not* involve new curricula, testing, minimum competencies, budget reforms, or control, but rather the forging of a productive coalition of parents and school practitioners.

Parents and schoolpeople must continuously seek to apportion responsibilities so that parents can provide what they alone can best give — love, acceptance, support, consistent discipline, and values; so that schools can offer what they and only they can best maintain — a learning climate that is orderly, caring, flexible, and appropriate to the styles and needs of each child. Only then will parent and practitioner together begin to build a fourth form of relationship, one that remains elusive for many schools — a cooperative colleagueship in the education of children.

CHAPTER SEVEN

Pupil Evaluation

May 4, 1950

Dear Mrs. Barth:

I am writing in regard to Roland's report card. In transcribing from my grade book to Roland's permanent record sheet I made an error on his citizenship grade. The mark should be C instead of B. I have had to speak to Roland quite a number of times this six weeks period and I had him marked down in citizenship but as stated before I made an error in transcribing.

Roland has the ability to be an A student both in academics and citizenship if he would settle down. I am sorry that it was necessary for me to write you.

Sincerely yours,

[My Seventh-Grade Homeroom Teacher]

WE EDUCATORS have made too many promises we could not keep. Despite the impressive rhetoric of our behavioral objectives and curriculum guides, only some students have acquired only some literacy skills. Other recipients of high-school diplomas are unable to read or write. Now parents are seeking a mechanism to guarantee that their children will learn the basic skills of reading, writing, and computing necessary for future schooling and the world of work. A four-star constellation is rising in the educational skies: back to basics, standardized testing, minimum competency, and accountability.

The Four Stars

BACK TO BASICS

In times of economic unpredictability, high unemployment, and inflation, the natural tendency of a society is to become conservative—to identify the essentials and pare away everything else. Many citizens today want to forgo new libraries and wider streets, preferring to retain only skeletal services, such as fire and police protection and garbage pickup. They also want to cut away at schools, snipping the so-called frills of art, music, and social studies, and keeping only the basics of

117

reading, writing, and arithmethic. Their battle cry is BACK TO BASICS. Their root assumption is that these educational staples were once taught and learned, but now are not; their objective is a return to the conditions under which they were educated. "After all," they argue, "we didn't turn out so badly."

The back-to-basics movement has placed already defensive educators in an even more embattled position. We have responded in three ways. Some have maintained, "We have always taught the basics and will continue to do so," a response that infuriates critics who feel they have ample evidence to the contrary. Another response has been, "Let's move ahead to the basics," a reply that denies the good of the good old days but offers some hope for rapprochement. And a few educators have declared, "Yes, we have been negligent in our responsibilities. Education has gone astray. Let's go back to the basics."

In the battle for basics the primary weapons have become the concepts of minimum competency and accountability. If someone can determine which specific literacy skills "all third graders *must* learn before June," teachers, principals, and children can be held accountable for the development of these skills. To accomplish that goal, the schools will be forced to attend to the basics. Accountability can be turned to many uses. If students do not achieve minimum competencies, teachers and administrators can be dismissed, like factory workers whose efforts on the assembly line do not measure up to quality-control standards. Children who do not achieve the defined basic skills will not be promoted; high-school students will receive a "certificate of attendance" but not a diploma. The standardized test is the logical instrument for gauging minimum competency, since it supposedly is objective—a written examination that can be administered to students throughout the school district, the state, or the nation. The current phenomenal growth rate of the testing industry corresponds with the growth of the back-to-basics movement.

The logic of the back-to-basics movement, of minimum competencies, and of educational effectiveness judged by standardized tests appears persuasive and irrefutable. Legions of disillusioned parents, taxpayers, and educational critics have found it so. For myself, I find the logic both myopic and specious—the logic of those outside the school looking in, advanced by those with insufficient understanding of how schools function and children learn.

STANDARDIZED TESTING

There are several holes in the apparently well-knit fabric of the back-to-basics movement. First, there are problems with the means of measurement. Standardized tests have long been the largely uncontested measure of pupil success, and frequently the indirect measure of teacher efficacy. No longer. The debate on standardized testing has begun. Among the searching questions being asked by the National Consortium of Testing are the following:

Standardized testing has profound implications for public policy. Many major education studies (for example, the Coleman and Jencks reports) have been, and are, basing their conclusions to a large extent on standardized test results. These studies often have serious effects on educational policy decisions at a national level. To what extent has their reliance on test results skewed those crucial decisions?

How appropriate is the industrial model of determining efficiency to the process of education and its evaluation?

Tests are widely distributed as diagnostic tools; however, we don't yet know that they are actually used diagnostically. To what extent are tests that are intended for diagnosis actually used for that purpose, and to what effect? If it is found that they are so used, how well or appropriately do they serve the need for diagnosis?

There are many unintended consequences of testing for children, such as ego deflation, inappropriate peer comparisons, and the like. To what extent do these consequences occur?

Standardized achievement tests are often said to be the "best available" measure regardless of their purported faults. What do they measure, and how do they compare to other measures of the same skills?

How accurately does the content of standardized achievement tests reflect the knowledge, skills, and information students should have within content areas; that is, does the content area or coverage of the tests actually match the objectives of education?

What other measures—alternatives to the standardized tests—are now available to educators? Where are they being used? What evidence do we have of their effectiveness? For what? For whom? Are there additional alternatives that should be developed? If so, how can we stimulate their development and use?

The accountability movement has often linked funding of educational programs to standardized test results. Is that a reasonable practice? What are its effects on children, teachers, and educational institutions?

Federal and state governments have used standardized test results to determine educational need. How reasonable is this practice? What are its effects?

Achievement test scores are widely reported publicly as measures of school effectiveness. How reasonable are test reporting practices? How knowledgeable is the public about the meaning of such scores? What are appropriate ways, if any, to report test results, and how might these ways be encouraged?

Criticism of testing has been particularly strong as it relates to children under the age of nine. Are there negative aspects of testing that more strongly affect young children than older ones?

Test publishers claim that standardized tests are habitually misused by the education community, particularly by teachers and administrators. Is this true, and if so, in what ways? How can test publishers and the education profession reduce such "misuse"?

What mechanisms can and should be developed for making the industry accountable to the public on a continuing basis?

Testing and curriculum are inextricably linked in theory, and, in practice, standardized tests seem to have strong influence on curriculum decisions. What effects do tests actually have on curriculum, and are these effects legitimate and desirable?

Many point to a lack of congruence between the assumptions about child development that are implicit in the content, substance, and score-reporting of standardized tests, and the growing body of knowledge about child development and curriculum. Can evaluation procedures be designed that build on this body of knowledge?

There is substantial evidence that standardized achievement testing — whether by the nature of testing procedures or by the nature of the tests themselves — enables society to discriminate against minority groups in the allocation of educational resources and in access to employment. What reforms are needed to prevent such discrimination?[1]

We schoolpeople contribute to the testing hysteria by our actions. We give students elaborate preparation for testing, construct our curriculum to anticipate test items, flaunt scores at PTA meetings, wave them around in parent conferences and promotion discussions, and employ them in forming ability groups. We compare children's achievement-test scores with IQ or aptitude-test scores, giving rise to the curious concepts of "overachiever" and "underachiever." Overachievement means that the achievement test score is higher than the IQ test score; underachievement means merely that the achievement test score is below the IQ test score. In placing this enormous weight upon the scores from two tests administered once a year, we can easily draw unwarranted inferences from dubious premises. But most of us do it anyway, giving credence to the present belief in the infallibility of testing:

Dear Mr. Barth:

Sam's scores on the Secondary School Admission Test arrived today and were as follows:

Reading Comprehension - 280 - 53%ile
Verbal - 255 - 30%ile
Quantitative - 250 - 26%ile

Needless to say, Mrs. Simpson and I are very concerned about these scores. We have discussed Sam's education and his poor performance on other nationwide tests with you in the past. With an IQ of 130, he is obviously a very bright child; he performs near the top of his class at Angier, according to his teachers. As you know, we have had great concerns over the lack of basic skills and vigorous academic challenge at Angier. (You may recall our feelings with our older son were similar and have been reinforced by his experience at private school. He has per-

formed to the best of his capacity but has found himself at an extraordinary disadvantage because of his lack of adequate preparation in
grade school.)

A discrepancy between "ability" and "achievement" test scores offers a
Rorschach from which anyone can conclude anything.

Another common practice, frequently mandated by law, is to publish
and compare test results of different schools in a district — and then attribute differences to the quality of their educational programs. This
drives schoolpeople to distraction. Most studies conclude that income
level and educational background of parents, not student or school effort, are the major determinants of test scores.[2] In Newton, for instance,
there is an almost perfect correlation between the scores of the twenty-
two different elementary schools and the income and educational level of
their respective communities. Drawing other inferences from these
school-by-school scores is unreliable and dangerous. Norm-referenced
standardized tests may be useful in comparing one school district with
another, but if they are used to compare smaller units such as individual
schools, classrooms, and, most of all, students, they become increasingly
less reliable.

My experience with standardized tests leads me to conclude that fewer
are better. Standardized achievement and IQ test scores should not be
administered unless they can be shown to serve the best interests of
children. To the extent that standardized tests provide accurate, reliable
diagnostic data — "item analyses" — they may be useful to teachers in their
efforts to tailor instruction to the needs of individual children. Few tests
do this, however, and even fewer teachers use scores in this way. I see little indication that the standardized tests most commonly employed
reveal information about pupils that help their teachers teach them more
or better. As Joseph Featherstone has put it, "Children and teachers do
not get any heavier for being weighed."[3] Michael Patton, director of the
Minnesota Center for Social Research, states it less kindly: "People who
say norm-referenced, standardized tests can be used for diagnostic
testing are out-and-out lying."[4]

Standardized testing actually serves the needs of adults in the management of education. Tests help in making decisions about funding education, ability grouping, labeling, sorting, and promoting or retaining
students. And, ultimately, they promote standardization of curriculum.
When standardized tests become the yardstick against which teachers
and pupils are measured, they soon become the tail that wags the dog.
For instance, one reason writing is not emphasized in schools as much as
reading and mathematics is because it cannot as easily be tested.
Teachers organize instruction to prepare their students for tests. When
standardized tests become the means of comparing schools, principals,
teachers, and children, they also promote competition — and the prob-

lems associated with the push to excel at any price. Recently, one state's supreme court issued a restraining order postponing the administration of a standardized reading test to 700,000 city public school students in grades 2-9. It turned out that the tests had been mailed early to the schools, and both principals and teachers were charged with copying the tests and coaching students in the correct answers. Schools in another city, under a new accountability system, recorded impressive gains in student performance between fall and spring. According to teachers, the gains were achieved by elaborate preparations for the spring tests through drills in class, notes home to parents, and practice with actual test questions. There must be better determinants of educational practice than standardized tests.

In Newton, at the request of the principals' organization, group IQ test scores now reside not in the schools but in the central office, where they are used for research purposes. Although available to parents and teachers, they are rarely consulted. It has been my practice to place student achievement scores in the bottom drawer of a filing cabinet and leave them there. I have found these scores useful primarily as a barometer for parent and central-office confidence in the school. When parents complain about the conditions of the school building — lights, floors, heat — it is usually a symptom of more basic dissatisfaction with personnel and program. And when numerous parents demand to see their children's scores, or the central office wants to talk about them, we can reasonably infer that our clients outside the school lack confidence in what we are doing. Conversely, to the extent that they do not mention test scores, despite their public appearance in local newspapers, I assume that those outside the school have confidence in us.

Minimum Competency

The concept of minimum competency raises as much havoc with student-centered instruction as do standardized tests. Embedded in the concept is the notion of children as identical units, items on the factory assembly line, which move at the same rate and whose important qualities are readily observable and measurable. However, as anyone who has taught school knows, children are not identical, they seldom move anywhere at the same rate, and it is extremely difficult to measure accurately their most important qualities, let alone ensure that they all *have* them.

Legislatures and school boards that demand — and schools that guarantee — minimum competencies from all children not only demean children by reducing them to objects, but deceive both parents and themselves. With guns to their heads, schools have been trapped into promising what they cannot deliver, forcing principals, teachers, and students to engage in cover-ups. Logically pursuing an illogical path has consequences for all parties to the educational enterprise. For instance, taxpayers in one city filed a class-action suit against the school board for allegedly failing to provide quality education because the board established a seventh-grade reading level as minimum for high-school graduation. As one citizen put it, "We're paying for twelve years of schooling, but we're only getting seven."

Let's examine a list of minimum competencies in geometry for sixth graders, devised by one school system:

Understand more complex spatial relationships;

Classify shapes in space (three-dimensional shapes) and in the plane (two-dimensional shapes) according to their attributes;

Discover patterns and identify properties of two-dimensional and three-dimensional figures;

Develop concepts of symmetry related to point-, line-, plane-, rotational, and translational symmetry;

Identify the symmetries of figures in the plane and of objects in space;

Understand and use words such as "slide," "turn," and "flip" in describing motions of figures in the plane and in space;

Develop and use the concept of coordinates;

Understand, represent, and use concepts such as "vertical," "horizontal," "perpendicular," "parallel," "angle," "triangle," and "polygon";

Understand the concept of congruency;

Identify relationships between similar figures and apply measurement skills in scale drawings.

A reasonable enough list. Yet what does it mean? What does it mean to say that by June all sixth graders will be competent in these skills? Some sixth graders *enter* in September with these competencies, and more; others have some but not all of them. By June most students will have more skills than they had in September. But some—the child with a reversal problem, or another with no depth perception, another with a reading disability, another with no sense of dimensionality—will not have developed competence in all these skills, nor is it reasonable to expect competence. Of the others who have developed "competency," what does that mean? What degree of competency is "minimum competency"?

A more useful conception recognizes the range of students' abilities and disabilities and acknowledges the disparate rate with which children acquire new skills. One realistic model has been suggested by Jim Short, former director of mathematics for the Newton public schools. Short suggests four levels of student competence in a skill: (1) *exposure*—children who are exposed to a topic, say the concept of geometrical congruence, are familiar with the language and have some sense of the meaning, but little consistent ability to use the language or the concept; (2) *control*—children who are able to control the skill of congruence know the language, understand the meaning of the concept, and can correctly solve problems that employ the skill about 50 percent of the time; (3) *mastery*—children who have achieved mastery of a skill can successfully complete problems perhaps 80 percent of the time; (4) *maintenance*—children who have achieved mastery of a concept periodically engage in activities that call for its use.

The Alternative Public School in Cambridge, Massachusetts, uses a similar gradation when assessing a child's skill development:

Code: _____ No exposure to date

x _____ Exposure

xx _____ Partial mastery

xxx _____ Mastery

LEVEL B

GEOMETRY AND SPACE

_____ Can identify regular polygons, e.g., hexagon, rhombus, trapezoid, and others.

Understands concept of perimeter of polygon:

_____ regular (including rectangle and square)

_____ irregular.

_____ Can measure perimeter of polygons.

_____ Understands concept of area of rectangle and square.

_____ Can measure area of rectangle and square.

_____ Can identify spheres, cones, cylinders, pyramids.

Understands concept of:

_____ rays

_____ union of rays as an angle

_____ right angle

_____ relationship of points and lines

_____ parallel lines

_____ perpendicular lines.

Can draw:

_____ rays

_____ union of rays as an angle

_____ right angle

_____ points on a line

_____ parallel lines

_____ perpendicular lines.

Can distinguish between kinds of triangle—isosceles,

_____ equilateral, and right.

Can express tenths, hundredths, thousandths in decimal

_____ notation, e.g., $1/10 = .1$.

_____ Can solve word problems involving fractions.

_____ Can use fractions in measurement.

_____ Understands fractions as ratios.[5]

Evaluation based on *degree* fits the realities of children, teachers, and the instructional process. While the concept of minimum competency offers a straitjacket, suggesting success or failure, the four stages imply development as children move toward competence in a skill. The four-fold model recognizes that students move at different rates through the stages, that it is unnecessary for all children to be at the same stage, and that it is unreasonable to expect all children to achieve 100-percent skill mastery.

Accountability

The quality of children important to measure in schools is increment of growth over time, not absolute level of achievement. We in the schools cannot — and should not — guarantee that by June all children within a class will know everything on the curriculum guidelines — or 80 percent or 50 percent of it. Education is a human enterprise, subject more to the laws of human nature than to those of computer technology. Educators may guarantee that all children in a class will *receive instruction* in a predetermined set of skills; we cannot guarantee that every child will master them by a predetermined time. Many parents control the hour at which a child goes to bed at night, but much as they might like to, these parents cannot control the hour that a child goes to sleep. Similarly, we in the schools can control to some extent what is taught, but we cannot ensure what is learned. Competency, like sleep, is determined by factors largely beyond our control. The degree to which any student achieves rests largely with the learner himself. We can influence the progress, using the carrots of grades, stars, candies, or dollar bills, or the sticks of retention, staying after school, and failure. These gimmicks, while effective from time to time, serve the adult need to control students better than they serve the student development of competency in the basic skills. Somehow we must learn to accept this realization — and relax a bit.

Those who ask the schools to concentrate their efforts on testable reading, writing, and number skills have lost sight of the breadth of human potential. They have a narrow conception of the richness of human life and of the capacity of schools to develop that potential. Schools must assume accountability for teaching — *in addition to* the basics — qualities such as resourcefulness, logic, self-control, independence, and creativity that will have at least as much payoff in life as the multiplication tables. Because schools are not able to develop all of these capacities in all students — because these characteristics are difficult to measure — is no reason to eliminate them from the curriculum.

Further, an expanded program not restricted to the basics is a powerful means by which children acquire fundamental skills. They may learn as much arithmetic from playing store as from filling out workbook pages, as much about writing from creating invitations to a birthday party as from copying a prescribed paragraph from the board, and as much about reading from sitting in a subway car on a field trip reading overhead advertisements as from a basic text. To eliminate the frills of playing store, holding birthday parties, and taking field trips is to limit acquisition of the basics. To ask "What can be eliminated so that schools can devote all their energies to the basics?" is unnecessarily to restrict and unbalance the diet, on the one hand, and to water down the "meat and potatoes" on the other. The appropriate educational question is not "What is basic?" but "What experiences for children in this class are likely to be most effective in developing reading, writing, and arithmetic skills and other important personal and intellectual qualities?" This is a question that teachers who know and work with students can answer better than legislatures or school committees. And this is the question for which schoolpeople must assume accountability.

To move back to the basics by holding teachers, principals, and children accountable for student attainment of arbitrary standards of performance as determined by standardized tests is a dangerous enterprise. The good that may come from this endeavor may be far outweighed by the bad. It is more important for children to learn to do a few things well and to care about their accomplishments and themselves than for them to be expected to master many arbitrarily chosen subjects. Children who engage in the never ending production of worksheets, workbooks, and homework assignments with one eye on the clock and the other on the paper of the student at the adjoining desk may develop little lasting competence. We live in a climate of decreasing resources and declining student enrollments. Still, we need not yield to a decline in human values or a decrease in common sense. Attempts to ensure development of the mind should not give way to mindlessness. I should like to suggest another method—more humane and, I believe, more effective—to promote and evaluate pupil competency.

Pupil Evaluation

Acknowledging the diversity of teachers and children has advantages—and costs. Angier teachers pay for their instructional responsibility with a commitment to extensive pupil evaluation. Twice a year we ask teachers to demonstrate, in a systematic and careful way, that their students are making progress. Although this process takes many hours of time and concentrated effort, most teachers assume accountability and readily pay the price for their diverse programs and idiosyncratic teaching styles. Without a commitment to evaluation rooted in instructional responsibility, I doubt that we could expect teachers to develop and implement a comprehensive individual pupil-evaluation system.

In schools everybody evaluates everybody and everything. Constant, intense association seems to compel informal, periodic judgments about the adequacy and effectiveness of people and programs. Ultimately, program evaluation is synonymous with pupil evaluation. There is no such thing as an effective program from which students learn very little or an ineffective program from which they learn a great deal. While evaluation of students by teachers is perhaps the most systematic and visible form of assessment, it constitutes only a portion of the judgments that continually take place within a school. Indeed, as teachers are evaluating children, the principal is evaluating teachers' evaluations of children (and therefore evaluating teachers), parents are evaluating teachers' evaluations of children, children are evaluating teachers and themselves, and teachers are evaluating themselves and what they have and have not been able to do for each child. Schools turn wheels within wheels within wheels.

The first formal scrutiny of children at Angier usually comes prior to the initial year of school during extensive prekindergarten screening. Our interview with parents and hour-long individual observation of each child fulfills a state law requiring that entering students be screened for possible learning disabilities, provides data so that kindergarteners can be placed in the most suitable classes, and gives kindergarten teachers information about each child with which to make instructional decisions during the first weeks of school. And, not the least important, the kindergarten screening is also a welcome to new parents conveying to them the teachers' immediate concern for their children.

Subsequent formal assessment of children occurs twice each year. Newton has had a system-wide report card, which looks like most others: columns for teachers to check "excellent," "satisfactory," or "needs improvement" in math, language, science, social-studies skills, and personal qualities such as "cooperation" and "finishes on time."

In Newton any elementary school may devise a different method for evaluating children. The school must petition the school committee for permission to use an alternative procedure, show that the proposed evaluation system will work better for that particular school than the official report card, and establish that the new system is acceptable to parents. Under this liberal policy Angier and more than half of the schools in Newton have developed unique reporting systems—an imaginative and all-too-rare example of a school bureaucracy accepting and legitimizing diversity among different schools within a district and acknowledging that a good evaluation system reflects and enhances the philosophy and values of a school.

In evaluating children, as in most everything else, teachers would like to do it their own ways. Some prefer grades, some report cards, some checklists, some reports without a conference or conferences without a report. I have not permitted faculty diversity in pupil evaluation. In the areas of curriculum, methodology, and the appearance of classrooms, diversity brings cross-fertilization, discussion, healthy debate, and staff development. But pupil evaluation must be uniform. Like placement, evaluation needs a coherent, agreed-upon policy; for a major purpose of pupil evaluation is to examine and report a child's personal and academic growth at school over the years. A longitudinal examination of student development is impossible if every year teachers employ different criteria, different measures, and different reporting systems.

The manner in which a school reports to parents is both medium and message. The parent-teacher conference is a moment of truth, an occasion where mutual trust and respect is established — or not. The objective of our pupil-evaluation system is to give a full and honest report of the progress of children in relation to their own ability, to their past performance, to the achievement of others in school, and occasionally (if parents request it and if we have the information) to national norms as measured by standardized tests.

Children, parents, teachers, and administrators are all responsible for a student's education and must all be involved in its evaluation. Evaluation brings to the surface the child's strengths and weaknesses and often shapes decisions about how to build on the former to overcome the latter. Pupils are involved throughout the process, partly so adults may know their views, but primarily so pupils can develop independently the ability to assess their own performances. Most children see evaluation as something that descends from adults, the sky, or some combination of the two. When we manage to convert this perception to a sense of evaluation as realistic self-appraisal, we have added another important element to the school's informal curriculum.

The Process

The evaluation process we have developed at Angier is described in this memo from the principal to the faculty:

Here is the procedure we will use this year:

(1) As soon as possible, but before Thanksgiving vacation, write a draft of one evaluation of one of your present students in the manner you feel would be most effective for you and for your students and their parents.

(2) Each evaluation should include information on the child's progress in Language, Math, Science, Social Studies, and Social Development.

(3) Share this with Roland, and "negotiate" if necessary.

(4) Shirley [the teacher/chairperson of the evaluation committee] will see you about scheduling your parent conferences.

(5) Conferences may begin on December 1st and must be completed by February 13th.

(6) As last year, there will be one half-hour conference in the winter and one in the spring, each accompanied by a written evaluation.

(7) Before sharing your evaluation with parents, make sure you have discussed it carefully with each child. The child may also be present at the conference if you wish.

(8) Make sure you put the original in the cumulative folder and give the carbon to parents.

(9) Art, Music, and P.E. [physical education] teachers will write five evaluations per class. Specialists, try and select children (1) about whom something has not been written in recent years, and (2) about whom you have considerable to say.

(10) Before any typing is done, homeroom teachers will assemble each child's entire evaluation and give it to Roland to read.

(11) Teachers may hand evaluations to Roland as a group or in smaller pieces, whichever you prefer.

(12) Janice and Peggy will be doing the typing.

(13) Conferences are an excellent occasion to show examples of children's work to parents. You may want to begin collecting examples of "early work" against which to compare "later work."

In addition to addressing progress in the "meat and potatoes" — mathematics, language and social development — reports may include whatever else the teacher feels is timely, appropriate, and important. The only people who read *all* of your reports are you, me, and the typist. Don't worry about making each one a unique piece of literature. If you have a good word, a good phrase, or a good sentence which accurately describes more than one child's behavior, use it and repeat it. Generally children are different and your reports will reflect these differences.

In addition to these written statements, any teacher may use checklists, scales, or other helpful devices which convey to parents what and how the child is doing in school. Checklists are not acceptable as a substitute for written anecdotal statements.

One copy of each anecdotal report on each child goes home with the parent, and the original becomes part of the child's folder. The two reports written on each child each year replace written annotations on cumulative record cards normally filled in by each teacher for each child each June. This saves a lot of time and effort and makes sense in light of recent legislation giving parents access to their children's cumulative records. In effect, parents always know what we are saying about their children in the cumulative folders. We are not keeping two sets of books.

This complex process takes place just before each formal parent conference. The request for a written evaluation of each child's work is a deceptively simple-sounding task. As any teacher knows, writing a precise, comprehensive description of twenty-five children's progress is an exacting, difficult, and time-consuming assignment. These written statements, so central to pupil evaluation, require a six-step process that begins long before the report is drafted. Teachers must first observe the children's behavior. They must then keep records, organize and store the data, and, finally, retrieve the information and translate it into prose. Only then is the teacher ready for the parent conference. These steps are all crucial to successful evaluation. Few teachers are adequately prepared for them.

Preparing for Evaluation

Adults make too many decisions affecting children on the basis of whim or pressure from those around them. Parents tend to do this — and so do teachers. How much of what a teacher does each day reflects the immediate needs, interests, and abilities of children? And how much springs from a teacher's preferences and needs or the system's educational prescriptions? Although instruction, of course, is a result of all these factors, I find insufficient weight is given to children and the messages they convey. School has become increasingly adult centered as principals, parents, central office, and school committees have placed more and more demands upon teachers, leaving them little time or reason to read children's messages. To some extent, the rich information children offer is not available to adults because we do not attend to it. When we do *look* at children, we often see little. We don't know what behaviors to attend to, how to focus our attention, or how to interpret what we see. Productive observation is inhibited, children are deprived of "representation" in the determination of instructional decisions, and teachers are deprived of data that could make classroom experiences more relevant, valuable, and, as we say so often in schools, meaningful.

Because teachers are not generally taught this kind of careful evaluation in college as part of their professional preparation, and because the normal order of things rarely allows them to pick up such skills on the job, we held a series of in-service workshops intended to sharpen observational skills and refine teachers' capacities to translate what they observe into thoughtful and communicative pupil-progress reports.

The first workshop was a warm-up, a general discussion among teachers on the topic of observation. From this meeting each of us emerged with his own set of notes. Here are mine:

Some things to consider when observing children and recording their behavior:

(1) Ethics of observing children without their knowing it.

(2) Difference between looking at something and observing it.

(3) If the observer is the teacher, how do you keep from participating?

(4) Why am I observing?

(5) What do I want to do with what I am observing?

(6) Dual role of an observer/teacher is that of helping and judging. How do you balance the two?

(7) Observing and evaluating. Implicit in an evaluation is the notion that you are going to change behavior. Why should the behavior change?

(8) Words which need sorting out: looking at/observing; record keeping; evaluating/judging.

(9) Problems involved in observing: How do you have time to observe while teaching? How do you record what you observe while teaching?

During the discussion each teacher was given a class list of the workshop participants.[6] For development of observation skills each was assigned responsibility for observing and recording the behavior of one member of "the class," while at the same time engaging in the discussion. This assignment simulated classroom conditions in which the teacher must simultaneously teach and observe.

One participant's observation of another:

Susan said very little during the discussion. She spoke three times with Sally, but never shared with the group her ideas or questions. Yet her facial expression and her eyes following the discussion from one speaker to the next suggested that she was interested in the group's deliberations. Perhaps she felt uncomfortable about sharing her ideas — or lack of ideas — before twenty-five others. She may well have behaved differently as a member of a smaller group.

When observations were shared, it turned out that Susan did not participate because she felt self-conscious about being observed and having her behavior recorded, and because she was preoccupied with her own task of observing the person beside her. This exercise made concrete many of the abstract considerations of observation. The problems inherent in teacher observation emerged, then, both from direct experience and from abstract discussion, each reinforcing the other.

Doubts about the reliability of observations led to the second workshop on observational skills.[7] An objective of this workshop was to sharpen the awareness that one observes behavior through different lenses and can choose the focus and change it depending on the information sought. A second objective was to help teachers distinguish between observed behavior (fact) and conclusions drawn from observed behavior (inference) — an area of considerable confusion in writing reports.

At this session four teachers sat on a rug in the middle of the faculty room and worked on an activity using mathematics blocks. One was designated the leader, another was blindfolded. The rest of the faculty observed this activity with no specific instructions.

After ten minutes the activity was halted and the observers discussed the difficulty of the assignment. Most agreed they were looking at rather than observing the interaction. In order to observe, they recognized, it was necessary to put on selective lenses that would help determine who would be observed. Should they attend to everyone in the group? any pair of members? the leader and a member? the blindfolded member and the leader? In order to observe productively it was clear that one must determine ahead of time which behaviors will be attended to. In observing behavior related to the task, should they note how the task was chosen? who decided what the group would do next? who took the initiative? how successfully the task was completed? how criteria for "success" were established? To appreciate behavior related to the materials (that is, the blocks) should they concentrate on the materials used? by whom? how? whether or not they are rejected? how? In observing personal interactions should they try to perceive how much the "observees" interact? with whom? whether verbally or nonverbally? by initiating? by responding? with what tone of interaction? Finally, can one determine from behavior how people are feeling? whether the observee is committed to the task? what his feelings are about the others? about his role in the group? about being observed by a large group? about being blindfolded?

After this interlude the block activity resumed with observers taking notes on their (now) selective observations. After another ten minutes teachers were asked to categorize their observations as *facts* or *inferences*. Examples of facts were verbal or nonverbal communications, body gestures, facial expressions, sounds, side comments, and the time relation of one behavior to another. We found that inferences—interpretations based upon observed facts—could be made during or after the observation period, and we determined that each should have at least one example of observed behavior to support it. The more observed data support an inference, the more credibility the inference earns. Whereas observed facts might be prefaced by saying, "I see that . . . " or "I hear that . . . ," inferences might be prefaced by saying "I conclude that . . ."

Here is an example of one observer's sorting of fact and inference:

Fact	Inference
Sally yawned	Sally was tired
Sally's eyes were closed much of the time	
Robin kept looking up at those who were observing him	Robin felt embarrassed
Sandra [the designated leader] told the players when it was time to take turns with the blocks	Sandra dominates in group situations

By the third workshop the staff had developed working definitions of observation and had practiced observing one another. Now they were ready to turn to keeping records and organizing data. To give everyone a common case to consider, we developed "David Hypothetical," complete with assorted observations and data. The data on David were similar to those teachers accumulate about most children:

DAVID HYPOTHETICAL

(1) Moved to Angier this September from Waltham.

(2) When D. is losing in a game, particularly if there is no other player losing more drastically than he, he often decides he no longer wants to play.

(3) Reading comprehension quite good for his age. Can retell a story accurately and makes good inferences from what he reads.

(4) Absent 7 consecutive days and 2 others out of 24 in this record period.

(5) Completes math assignments quickly. There are often errors, most of which he can discover when asked to go over his papers.

(6) Both teacher and lunch attendant have encouraged D. to join outdoor games several times when he has been standing on the sidelines. Once in the game he participates fully.

(7) Is the youngest of three children and only son.

(8) Some trouble decoding unfamiliar words without clues from context of story or illustrations.

(9) Other children appear quite willing for D. to work or play with them though they do not often actively seek him out to do so, and vice versa. The one exception is Sam, a boy who lives near D., and who frequently invites D. to join him.

(10) Understands arithmetic concepts very quickly. Some gaps in his number facts knowledge.

(11) Often holds head very close to book or other materials.

(12) Father is an attorney.

(13) Almost always spends a part of each day doing some solitary activity and occasionally asks to go to the library for time alone.

(14) D. is somewhat taller and heavier than most of his classmates and his large motor coordination is well developed.

(15) Always listens very attentively when a story is being read and twice brought books from home to be read aloud.

This data sheet was cut up with scissors to make a pack of "cards" for each teacher. In addition to the cards, teachers received additional miscellaneous anecdotal information about David:

David H.

9/28-10/2   Brought in book on dinosaurs: got out two other dino-

saur books from library. Wrote story on dinosaurs —
ideas very interesting, handwriting hard to read, occasionally reverses letter or mixes upper and lower case
letters. Worked daily in phonics skills workbook but
only after I reminded him. Parents in for Open House:
they asked "How is he doing?" in tone which made me
think they expected bad news. He chose cooking for
Wednesday optional.

10/5-10/9   D. is listened to when he contributes in a group discussion. Did more of that this week than before. Began
original film strip on dinosaurs with Sam. Absent Thurs.
and Fri. Looked forward eagerly to cooking optional.

10/12-10/16   Absent all week. Flu.

10/19-10/22   Came in each day with report from news to discuss with
me. Says he watches TV news and discusses it with
(holiday 10/23) parents. Absent Tues. Wandered around on Wed. for
some time before choosing an activity. Spent a lot of
time with Dienes blocks this week. He is one of first children to grasp new concept when using the blocks.

10/26-10/30   Excited about Halloween and especially about making
masks in Tuesday art class. (D. rarely chooses art activities within the classroom.) Wed. - built an elaborate
relief map habitat for his toy dinosaurs alone. Absent
Thurs. Trouble settling down to work on Fri. Mother in
to pick him up one day and asked when conferences
would be, to find out "how he's doing this year."

Participated during One Week

	David	Amy	John
Reading in group	M T W Th F		
Silent reading	M T W Th F		
Work in reading skills workbook	M Th F		
Creative writing	W		
Handwriting skills sheets	—		
Writing to convey information (reports, journals, etc.)	M T W Th		
Science - water project	—		
Science - other	M T W Th F (dinosaurs)		
Dienes blocks	M W F		
Math facts worksheets	T Th		

Math group meetings   T Th F

Painting/drawing   —

Makes musical
  instrument   —

Works on Newton map   T W

Finishes Newton map   —

Joins free discussion
  group   M T W Th F

Talks in discussion
  group   T F

Then each teacher was asked to

pick an age for David from five to eleven that is a familiar age level for you. Of course, his age will influence your interpretation of the data. Read and think about all the information on David. Try to picture him and become familiar with him as you would if he were a real student in your class about whom you were going to write a report.

Teachers are, of course, frequently bombarded with too much raw information about children and consequently have difficulty making use of it. We deliberately inundated the staff with data about David H. so that they would have to develop strategies for handling it. The staff suggested many different ways of arranging the data, then sorted the cards and information into categories such as:

high certainty	or	low certainty
a strength	or	a weakness
academic development	or	social development
to be used in report	or	not to be used in report
parents will be pleased	or	parents will be upset
inference	or	fact

We observed, talked about observing, collected data, and organized it in different ways. In the fourth workshop teachers took the assembled and organized data and from it wrote a report. In many ways this is the most difficult step for teachers — selecting from the vast array of information about a child available to them, organizing it, and translating the data into anecdotal prose. These were their instructions:

(1) Review the data presented on our imaginary child, David Hypothetical.

(2) Organize it in a way you find useful.

(3) Write a report to his parents based on these data. You do not need to incorporate all the data in the report; just decide what you feel is most relevant.

For your own information, jot down your organization scheme so you can examine it closely later. Perhaps you will outline rather formally, or you may fit the data into a preexisting structure that you like to use for all your reports, or whatever. Your categories might be subject matter areas, or strengths and weaknesses, or certainties, likelihoods, and speculations, or any others *you* find useful. The point is to be aware of and record the way you go about organizing the data so you can think about it later, can perhaps try out another organizational scheme and see if it works better, maybe get ideas about alternative ways of getting the material organized from some colleagues.

Here is an example of a report prepared about David Hypothetical for his parents:

David has made a good adjustment to Angier since his move in the fall. His classmates, especially Sam, are quite pleased to have David work and play with them. They listen carefully to him when he contributes to group discussions.

I have noticed that there are times in the day when David prefers to be alone. Occasionally he asks to go to the library where he can be by himself. At lunch recess he often stands on the sidelines and needs encouragement before joining a game. Once involved in a game it appears important to David that he do better than the other players. Being larger than most, and well coordinated, he usually finds great success in physical activities.

In math, David grasps new concepts quickly whether presented through manipulative materials or more abstract means. He completes most assignments quickly, although he often makes several errors which he is capable of correcting himself when he goes over his paper. These errors often seem related to gaps in his number facts. The school can loan a set of flash cards and I feel practice at home would be of great help to him. I feel his work will improve even more when and if he can learn to work more slowly and carefully, without worrying about how he is doing in relation to others in the class. (He's doing fine!)

David's reading comprehension is quite good for his age. He can retell a story accurately and draws good inferences from what he reads. His listening skills are also well developed; he attends carefully when a story is being read and has brought books from home to be read aloud to the class. David has experienced some difficulty decoding unfamiliar words in the absence of clues from the context or illustrations. His handwriting is frequently difficult to read. He occasionally reverses letters or mixes upper and lower case letters. I have noticed that he holds his books and other materials very close to his eyes. It may be that he has difficulty seeing clearly. I suggest you have his eyes tested for the possible use of glasses.

In social studies and science David is fascinated by dinosaurs. He brings books in from home and takes others from the library. His written stories about dinosaurs are imaginative and engaging. He built by himself an elaborate relief map habitat for his toy dinosaurs. Currently, he and Sam are making an original film strip about dinosaurs.

David rarely chooses art activities within the class, preferring to participate in the art room, which he does with enthusiasm. He was particularly excited about the Halloween mask project.

This has been a year of great progress for David. We look forward to seeing him in the fall.

After each teacher had written a report on David, we talked again:

(1) How much of the recorded data did you use in your report on David? On what basis did you decide to include or exclude certain data?

(2) What information do you wish you'd had that was missing? What might you have learned from it?

(3) Have you distinguished carefully between observation and inference in the report?

(4) Are your inferences stated with the degree of certainty or tentativeness you believe they deserve?

(5) What can you state with the highest degree of certainty from the data given? What would be your wildest speculation based on this data?

(6) If you were David's teacher, would you have any concerns about him? What? Did you write about them in the report? Why or why not? If not, would you communicate them to his parents verbally? Why or why not? What would be your next move with respect to each of these concerns?

We give teachers many guidelines for report writing. We ask them to follow generalizations ("Jane is a strong reader") with two or three specifics that have led to this conclusion ("She reads very rapidly; she takes many books out of the library; she is confident reading aloud"). I encourage teachers to report baldly and honestly all problems and weaknesses they observe in children. Many are understandably reluctant to talk about problems because they fear they may be held accountable by administrators or parents, who can be quick to attach blame to the teacher who identifies a child's problem. A teacher might say, "Johnny is having difficulty controlling his temper." Often the parent will respond, "He's never had that problem at home. You must be doing something to provoke him." Despite the risks involved, we have found that parents can come to accept negative statements about their children if they are made objectively and backed with substantiating data. On the other hand, if we do not mention a child's reading problem when both teacher and parent know he has a difficulty, parents' basic confidence in school and teacher is eroded.

To promote trust and soften parental distress, I ask that each statement about a child's weakness be accompanied by one or two specifics conveying what the teacher is doing to address the problem:

Johnny has difficulty attending for very long to a task.	I have moved his seat to a quiet corner of the room. I'm giving him very short assign-

> ments and gradually increas-
> ing their length as he becomes
> successful in completing each
> one.

This has been a highly successful strategy. Most parents *know* their child is weak in particular areas; what they want to know is what the school is doing about it. Further, for teachers to make some intelligible statement about how they are handling a child's problem, they must first have identified the area of difficulty, given the specific problem some thought, and taken steps toward a remedy. Evaluations can shape teachers, just as teachers shape evaluations.

I also encourage teachers to follow statements about children's problems with thoughts about what parents might do to help. (Appendix E gives one school system's set of suggestions.) Parents are almost always concerned about their children's problems and want to do something to help. If teachers do not give them direction, many parents will take the matter into their own hands and do whatever seems right to them — get a tutor for the child, take him to a psychiatrist, curtail television privileges, or worry loudly at the dinner table. Frequently these attempts are neither helpful nor appropriate; they exacerbate the problem rather than provide a solution. If the teacher makes suggestions to the parents, it is more likely that the parents' input will be helpful and coordinated with the efforts of the school. At the very least, teacher suggestions ensure that parent and school are in communication. That in itself goes a long way toward solving many children's problems.

By the end of our workshop we had developed a clear, simple, effective formula for writing a report: explicit separation of fact, inference, and opinion; generalizations followed by specifics; statements of problems followed by teacher responses and suggestions for parents. We developed some examples, following the formula:

STEVEN

Steven has a perceptive mind that is quick, logical, and analytical. (generalization)

He developed a unique strategy for finding the number of beans in a jar using a balance. (specific)

He was able to play a complex chip-trading game . . . which he had never seen before . . . almost immediately. He then taught others the game. (specific)

Steven writes well. (generalization)

His poem about winter was sensitive, imaginative, and full of feeling. (specific)

His understanding and use of punctuation — periods, commas, quotation marks — is consistently accurate, even in poetry. (specific)

Steven has had difficulty getting along comfortably with many of the other boys in the class. (problem)

I have spoken to him about the importance of allowing other children, perhaps less able than he, to work without being criticized or ridiculed by him. (what is being done about problem)

We have changed his desk and some of the members of his reading group. (what is being done about problem)

Helping Steven learn to work cooperatively, positively, and without criticizing others, is something which his parents can help reinforce at home. (what parents can do)

SUSAN

Susan is a very artistic and visual child. (generalization)

Her art work is expressive, colorful, and imaginative. (specific)

The mural which she designed and completed after our trip to the farm showed an accurate recall of the field trip, a fascination with animals, and a lovely sense of humor. (specific)

Susan is working hard in reading, but with only limited success and interest. (generalization and problem)

She rarely takes books out of the library or reads for pleasure in the classroom. (specific)

She has difficulty attacking strange or new words. (specific)

She is quick to give up without attempting to sound them out. (specific)

I have found some high-interest-level books which she enjoys and can read with little difficulty. (what is being done about problem)

I think as her confidence and interest in reading builds up she will be able to move to more difficult material. (opinion, prognosis)

It would be helpful if Susan could read aloud to her parents at home each evening with these books so that reading will soon become for her a regular, comfortable part of each day. (what parents can do to help)

Susan has been a very constructive, valuable member of the class. (generalization)

She takes responsibility for arranging the chairs each morning and at the end of the day. (specific)

Children frequently appoint or elect her when a class spokesman is needed. (specific)

She has formed a committee to decide which playground materials the class would like to order for the spring. (specific)

Once we had the basic formula well in hand, we turned to small but significant issues of syntax. We collected past pupil reports from cumulative folders and examined excerpts. We found that the use of connecting words such as "however," "but," "when," and "although," was critical to the meaning of a statement, each changing the implications of the whole. We made these into exercises, looking at the changes wrought by word substitution:

John frequently reads alone (when
                              but
                              however
                              although)
the rest of the children read together in small groups.

This close examination of excerpts illustrated some of the real dangers involved in trying to record observations and conclusions that both reflect actual behavior and can be shown to parents with confidence (or even turned over to a court if necessary). So useful were some insights gained from these exercises that they were distributed in memo form for ready reference:

Some opinions are written as though they were facts. This leaves the writer in a very vulnerable position if challenged and doesn't really provide useful data for the reader:

"a lovely child with many hang-ups"

"still has a tendency to be sneaky, but not seriously so"

"needs to be accepted for himself rather than trying to fit him into an all-American boy role"

"as he gains maturity . . . he will be able to step forth into new fields with boldness and forthrightness"

Opinions can, however, be stated as opinions and substantiated with observable behavioral data:

"continues to have problems in peer relationships. She does not have close friends in the grade and she complains of others 'making fun' of her. Very likely this stems, at least in part, from the fact that she is a slower learner than her classmates"

"seems more relaxed and happier. For example, an arithmetic paper with errors marked, returned to him, no longer causes him to stamp his feet and cry"

Some comments would be more valuable, and perhaps less risky, if expanded:

"social relationships in unstructured groups pose some problems" (what kind of problems? how manifest? what observed behavior led to this conclusion?)

"has trouble dealing with frustration" (under what circumstances? what happens — withdrawal, tantrum?)

"grade-level performance in all language areas"

It is very important to note in the record significant events or conditions in a child's life such as:

Health data - e.g., handicaps, medications, serious illness, or accident during the year.

Family status - e.g., births, deaths, or major illnesses of family members
during year; separation, divorce, or remarriage of parents.

Special services - e.g., reading help, psychological evaluation, speech
therapy, private psychotherapy.

After these pupil-evaluation workshops, teachers were prepared to
write pupil-progress reports. As batches came to me in draft form, I read
them carefully and frequently conferred with teachers about individual
children, suggesting changes in language if I thought a statement might
be inaccurate, excessive, or inflammatory. (Parents once threatened to
sue if the word "passive" was not removed from their son's report.)
Reading over the reports also gave me a chance to learn a great deal in a
short time about the progress and problems of the children in the
school—and those of their teachers. Finally the drafts were typed, with a
carbon for the parents. Here are two examples of recent pupil evaluations.

ANGIER SCHOOL

PROGRESS REPORT

Child: Peggy

Grade: Kindergarten   Teacher: Mrs. Fontaine

Peggy is a reserved but friendly child who appears to enjoy the
kindergarten room. In September Peggy had difficulty in separating from
her mother, often insisting on a prolonged leavetaking, and this lasted for a
month or two. Peggy seldom cried, or if she did it was for only a brief
period of time and then she became engrossed in what we were doing.
However, she remained at a distance from the other children. This reserve
is lessening, I am happy to say, and Peggy is enjoying more the companion-
ship of her peers. Peggy tends to be adult oriented, so this is real social
progress for her. When Peggy was ill recently the other children missed her.

Peggy is a very able little girl. She has demonstrated ability in each of the
disciplines—language arts, math, science, social studies, art, and music. I
would like to see Peggy less concerned with having things just right. Often
her enjoyment is spoiled because of this. An example is when she cried at
her birthday party because she had to settle for a broken gingerbread
cookie. Peggy seems to need to know that materials as well as adults will be
there for her when she wants them. She is also very concerned about doing
a perfect job. I hope to help her relax about the finished product and enjoy
the process. Her very strong abilities should easily take care of the finished
product!

Peggy came to school knowing all the capital letters and all the lower
case, with some h,l,u,d hesitation. Her fine motor skills are well developed.
Early in the school year she did some beautiful drawings of horses, a real
interest of hers. Another well-developed skill is her auditory discrimination. She was one of the first to learn initial consonant sounds and apply
this knowledge in our group meetings. Her choice of words to demonstrate
initial sounds was excellent. I have started working with Peggy in a small

group on linguistic patterns and very soon she will be reading in a preprimer.

Peggy's math skills are excellent. She came to school able to identify numerals up to 20, and able to order numerals from 1 to 10. She has enjoyed the chip-trading game, where she learned the base 3 trading operation quickly. She has demonstrated skill in attribute work and pattern work with color cubes. When I introduced a wooden number puzzle consisting of 12 parts, Peggy was able to put it together easily, using the numerals as well as the shapes as clues.

Science activities have also held her interest. She is able to make intelligent estimates, witnessed when we were working with measurement in water play and when we did a unit on sink and float. "Heavy things sink," she said, after trying out several objects. She enjoyed coloring many "Parts of the Bird" pictures when we studied birds. Peggy should enjoy watching the chick-hatching process, which we are just starting with our incubating eggs. She has a keen sense of observation and is able to integrate this into her other experiences.

Peggy does not enjoy dramatic play and will never choose this as an activity. She stayed away from the hospital corner the entire time it was in operation. She also avoids messy activities. I trust she will feel more relaxed in both these areas as the year progresses.

It is a pleasure having Peggy in the classroom and I look forward to witnessing a continuation of the already excellent progress Peggy has made.

PROGRESS REPORT

Child: Debby
Grade: 5   Teacher: Mr. Burns

Personal and Social Development

Debby has shown a very positive attitude and seems to be enjoying her work. She is always willing and able to help out another student, academically. Debby takes pride in her work and her study habits have shown increased improvements since early fall.

Debby has shown she feels better about herself and daily work by a more evidenced relaxed attitude in both of her teachers' rooms.

Reading and Language

Debby's diagnostic reading tests show that her reading and comprehension skills are above grade level.

Her weekly spelling and her spelling in all of her writing is superior. Debby's original poems in her own book are sensitive and show a wide variation of theme running from whimsy to serious thoughts. She is very capable of diversity as the title of her book would intend: *Different Kinds of Poems for Different Kinds of Moods.*

Debby's written work in the language skills areas shows a high degree of competence.

The entire class looks forward to hearing a poem or a story written by Debby.

Social Studies

Debby's work on the Japan unit was excellent. Her oral reports to the class were informative and very well organized. The class enjoyed her slides and her explanation of them was very clear and interesting. Research was conducted in a self-motivated fashion.

Math

Debby has produced fine work in math this term. In the unit on symmetry Debby displayed a good understanding of the material presented. She shows interest in her work, asking questions when she doesn't understand. Debby needs to review basic facts in order to gain speed and accuracy in all types of computation. She is presently learning to add and subtract unlike fractions.

Science

Debby has become a more independent worker in science. She displays a good understanding of concepts presented, and is able to use these concepts to solve problems. She works well in small groups, which she seems to prefer to individual work in science. Debby has finished a unit in buoyancy and is working with density now.

In this age of forms, mimeographs, and xeroxes, parents rarely receive a single-spaced, typed document about their unique child. While many parents don't like all of what they read, most respect the teacher's insight and thoroughness in accumulating and sharing information. Most reports are written carefully, read carefully, and retained carefully by parents.

PARENT CONFERENCES

Parent-teacher conferences revolve around these progress reports, although many go off in other directions (such as placement) according to the agenda of teacher or parent. Conferences are short (usually a half hour) and infrequent (twice a year). Consequently, teacher and parent must make the most of the opportunity by preparing for the conference and getting down to important issues right away.[8] Parent conferences and pupil-progress reports both must offer more than vague, bland banalities. By failing to convey detailed, accurate, substantiated information about students to parents, many schools encourage a lack of parental confidence. If a teacher cannot convey to a parent that she knows a great deal about a child, if parents think a teacher is unaware of a child's problems, isn't doing anything about them, or — worse — doesn't care about them, then each half-hour conference serves only to generate a negative view of teacher and school. This credibility gap, in turn, promotes demands for more seemingly reliable measures of progress, such as grades or standardized test scores.

After several years of workshops geared to developing a thoughtful evaluation process, I think we have learned how to convey to parents a thorough and honest picture of what we see and think. Still, there are those — in school and out — who would rather we use letters, grades, and percentages — which, they feel, tell them more clearly how each child is doing. Grades are real to them, entities they can relate to their own experiences. Parents think they know what an A means. They are less sure about a statement that "Johnny is a good reader; he takes many books out of the library, reads aloud with confidence and fluency" and what it means in terms of how Johnny is *really* doing. Some teachers also would prefer to return to the ease and reputed objectivity of grades and letters. Generally, though, we have found that a teacher who can sit down for a half hour with a parent, showing with precision and documentation that he knows the child's strengths but is also aware of weaknesses and what to do about them, can establish that the student is growing, learning, and improving. When this happens, a satisfying evaluation and a productive parent conference has taken place. I believe this kind of evaluation, more than PTA meetings, newsletters, standardized test scores, or public-relations promotions, fosters parental trust in teachers and in the school. Standardized tests can compare a student's ability or achievement with that of other students. But this is not sufficient. If we give parents anecdotal statements rich in information and documentation about their child's progress, letter grades (and standardized test scores) pale in comparison.

Information assembled and shared at evaluation conferences is as valuable to teachers as to parents. Pupil evaluation can become a powerful instrument of staff development. A teacher expected to collect, organize, and discuss what she knows about children builds an accurate, detailed picture of each child that has far greater instructional usefulness than an unrelated assortment of anecdotes, grades, checks, and bits and pieces of information that may well have been previously used to characterize the child. The teacher who can intelligently appraise what children are doing today can prepare an effective lesson tomorrow. While the skills of observation, record keeping, report writing, and communicating with parents are formally exercised only twice a year, they are used by teachers each day throughout the year.

Written reports and parent-teacher conferences have payoffs for children as well as for parents and teachers. For most children a letter grade, a percent, or a score (my own C in citizenship, for instance) connotes an arbitrary judgment, a mathematical manipulation shrouded in mystery and abstraction. Although many parents may feel they know what these symbols connote, their precise meaning is unclear to most students — and to most teachers.

Written descriptions of a child's behavior help remove evaluation from the realm of mystery. Young children learn better from the specific than from abstractions. Verbal portraits, which attempt to describe their behavior, are more concrete than symbols intended to represent that behavior. Written statements documented with observed facts enable children to make connections between what they do and adults' appraisals of what they do. Indeed, many teachers write evaluations relying heavily upon records, logs, and collections of papers that children maintain. Consequently, the evaluation process teaches most children that they can be instrumental in determining what teachers write about them — that evaluations are not pulled out of the air. Written evaluations not only characterize a child's behavior more accurately than symbols, they may also promote change and improvement in that behavior. That is probably the most important function of pupil evaluation.

We have found this process successful in conveying to parents what their children are doing in school and how well they are doing it. Where children have weaknesses, are performing below what adults expect of them, or are experiencing difficulty, we seldom attempt to fix accountability or determine whose fault it is. All parties to the child's education — teachers, administrators, parents, and students — discuss, affix, and assume responsibility. When these parties work cooperatively together, the issue changes from determining accountability to determining a remedy — who is going to do what about addressing the problem. And in the education of children, remedy is ultimately far more important than accountability.

There is much debate these days about what constitutes the best form of pupil evaluation. There are advocates for standardized tests, alternatives to standardized tests, criterion-referenced tests, and norm-referenced tests — all displaying evidence and high feeling. My own belief is that this is not a public-policy decision to be resolved by legislatures, the courts, or the advocates or critics of testing, but rather an educational decision best made by each school. Because evaluating pupils is a school function, closely tied to instructional responsibilities, the best pupil-evaluation system is the one developed and implemented by principals, teachers, and parents. Only under such a system does the evaluation of children complement the prevailing values, objectives, methodology, and philosophy of the school. Just as I feel that pluralistic schools can be more effective and creative than uniform schools, so pluralistic evaluation systems, each consistent with a particular school philosophy, are more effective and creative than uniform national, state, or local evaluation systems.

CHAPTER EIGHT

Staff Development

Roland has never offered help in the classic sense. He will
help you identify the difficulties, he'll listen to you for
hours, and he'll support you when you hit a chuckhole,
but he does not attempt to solve the problem for you. He
does attempt to provide you with resources, to tell you
what other people might help, what other places you might
go, and he asks you to come back at some point and tell him
how you worked it out.

—A teacher

THE PROFESSIONAL LIFE of most teachers is arid, infertile,
and poorly cultivated. In *School Teacher*, his searching
sociological study, Dan Lortie found three dominant
characteristics among teachers: conservatism—a preference for the
familiar, the comfortable, and the secure; presentism—a tendency to live
from day to day, with little long-range sense of a personal or professional
future; and individualism—a quality of loneliness and isolation, even
from colleagues across the hall.[1] These qualities are antithetical to personal and professional growth. They work against the professional
vitality of each practitioner, even as they erode the effectiveness of
schools.

Those who want to improve schools, reformers from without and
within, run headlong into this teacher ethos, which they term "resistance
to change." They try to coax, subvert, and cajole. Then they try to barrel
over, burrow under, or work around teachers—all with little success.
These reformers view conservatism, presentism, and isolation as teacher
problems to be overcome. I see these characteristics more as symptom
than as problem, the inevitable response of teachers to an unhealthy
school environment. Those who want to change schools by changing
teachers would do better to address the debilitating conditions under
which teachers work rather than the teachers themselves.

If we have learned anything about educational change over the past
twenty years, it is that change imposed upon schools from without does
not work; at best it promotes momentary compliance, which vanishes
with the departure of the change agent. On the other hand, change that
emerges from within the school, especially from individual teachers, is
authentic. The person invested in the change is intrinsic to the situation,

146

committed to both the change and making it work. Changes emanating from classrooms persist as long as the teacher is committed to the idea, which is usually as long as the idea is productive for teacher and students.

Probably nothing within a school has more impact on children, in terms of skills development, self-confidence, and classroom behavior, than the personal and professional growth of teachers. When teachers individually and collectively examine, question, reflect on their ideals, and develop new practices that lead toward those ideals, the school and its inhabitants are alive. When teachers stop growing, so do their students.

In one sense, there is no such thing as staff development or teacher training. When a system deliberately sets out to foster learning in staff members by committing everyone to workshops, little may happen — except that everyone is satisfied that they are going through the motions of doing their job. In another sense, *everything* that happens with teachers in a school has potential for promoting teachers' personal and professional growth. Staff development is least effective when planned, premeditated, and deliberate. It is most fruitful when it is an incidental outcome of other school functions thoughtfully fulfilled.

In that context everything we have discussed to this point can be considered staff development. Expecting teachers to give their best most of the time, and providing them with responsibility and resources to deliver that best, is staff development. Living each day with colleagues diverse in style, method, and philosophy, is staff development. Learning both to tolerate and to respect these differences is staff development. Examining and questioning one's own practices and those of others, and becoming interested, not jealous or frightened, when someone has an exciting new idea is staff development. Providing opportunities for teachers to fantasize about their professional goals at organization time and daring them to realize these dreams is staff development. Working closely each day with another teacher on a team is staff development. Eliminating constraining educational labels and extending the repertoire of instructional ideas and materials available to teachers is staff development. Expecting teachers to assume a large measure of instructional responsibility and develop their own curriculum outlines is staff development.

The placement process too is an important instrument of staff development. When teachers observe in other classrooms and respond to the questions, "Under what conditions does a child learn best?" and "Which of next year's possible classes comes closest to providing these conditions?" they engage in staff development. The hard talks about why parents have strong feelings about placing children in a class offer opportunities for growth. And developing skills to observe children's behavior, keeping records, organizing data, writing reports, and learning to hold effective parent conferences is staff development.

All these activities can powerfully advance the personal and professional growth of schoolpeople. But none of them has staff development as a raison d'être. This is why I find that "in-service training" of teachers, on-the-job professional development, has much greater power and pay-off than "pre-service training." These and other contexts for growth are available to the practicing teacher; few are available to the student preparing to teach. The opportunities emerge organically from the job, and the learning they generate is immediately applicable to the teacher's work. In-service professional development is more effective than pre-service professional development because it develops out of the richness of actual school experiences rather than an abstract conceptualization of those experiences.

Immediacy, however, does not make on-the-job staff development either easy or inevitable. Growth-producing experiences must pierce the shell of tension and isolation that surrounds a great many classroom teachers. Like most administrators, I frequently walk through schools with a superintendent or school board member. Inevitably, it seems, when we enter a classroom the teacher's response is friendly — a smile, a handshake, and an invitation to come in and sit down. Yet this outward pleasure is often belied by body language conveying anxiety, if not panic; by tense facial expressions; unnatural laughs; quick, fierce glances at the children; and apologies for noise, the mess, the heat, or the cold. Why are teachers anxious and fearful when principal or superintendent visits their classrooms? I think the answer to that question reveals a good deal about schools, teachers, administrators, the relationship among them, and the possibilities for teacher growth.

The tense response suggests to me that teachers live under a cloud of preoccupation with the discrepancy between performance and expectation, between "what I am doing" and "what they want and expect me to do." The fear comes from the belief that the administrator is there to judge, evaluate, punish, or even dismiss a teacher because of this discrepancy. Teachers, often unsure of what is expected of them and the extent to which they are complying, know only that it is impossible to accomplish all that is expected. Even if teachers are following the curriculum guide to the letter, and if all the children are in the right book and on the right page, they know many children in the class are not doing everything expected of them. Teachers know that the class is not working for some children as it should and that there may be no way to make it work. In short, the anxiety-laden responses to visitors (and the unfortunate classroom practices that spring from fear) are the predictable outcome of saddling teachers with the impossible task of making someone else's ideas and methods work for all students.

As principal, one of my personal goals is to be able to walk through the school at any time, with any guest, and enter any classroom largely unnoticed by children and teacher. I delight in being ignored, because this response suggests a busy, committed teacher, less concerned about what the outsider thinks than whether the activity is going well for as many children as possible. I value this response because it suggests that teachers know what they have planned, and why. They know it works most of the time for them and for the class—and that sometimes it doesn't. When it does not work, they know it is a problem between teacher and child, not between teacher and superior. I find that teachers who respond to visitors with friendly indifference are generally confident and competent. They have personal and professional authenticity. For these teachers the discrepancy that matters is not between "what I am doing" and "what they want me to do," but rather between "what I am doing" and "what I want to be able to do." Teachers who are intent on making professional behavior consistent with their beliefs about children and learning are seldom preoccupied with conformity to the expectations of others. Conversely, the teacher who is unclear on important questions finds that somebody will happily impose external clarity. An instructional vacuum—an empty teacher—is quickly filled by other teachers, parents, principals, school committees, and superintendents. The response of teachers to visitors is a telling indicator of the underlying dynamic operating within a school or school system. It is a response that has powerful implications for staff development.

Joseph Featherstone has observed that "American teachers . . . have the worst of two worlds: they are constantly being harassed by the administration and they are lonely in their work."[2] The best of both worlds, on the other hand, is available to the teacher supported by both the administration and a network of collegial relationships. These are conditions conducive to the development of practitioners and to the vitality of a school. They are difficult conditions to provide. But there are ways. I have seen school practices contribute effectively to administrative and collegial support networks and begin to erode the debilitating conditions Lortie and Featherstone have documented. In such schools teachers have no need to flinch when visitors walk through the door.

Promoting Interdependence

If a collection of independent, isolated teachers is to coalesce into a faculty, suspicion and competition among them must give way to a sense of joint venture. This can only be encouraged by providing ample means, opportunities, and occasions for teachers to talk and work with one another. Nothing engenders a feeling of inclusion, nothing increases participation more than advance knowledge of who's doing what; nothing infuriates and isolates more than activities that simply turn up, without prior notice or invitation.

One device would seem too simple to be effective, but we have found it a powerful means for bringing teachers together. This is an in-school weekly periodical (known in our case as ITEMS) to which everyone contributes—provided the contributor's name is signed—and which everyone reads. ITEMS offers an immediate, easy way for teacher, principal, custodian, or secretary to communicate with all other staff members. It also provides a common record of who said what to whom and when. Its spirit and richness is suggested by a look at one issue:

ITEMS

Item:On May 16th we expect a number of visitors from Newton junior high schools and on May 21st from the senior high schools. The procedure will be the same as it has been in the past for all visitors.

Roland

Item:Tuesday, May 8th, we will have a faculty meeting from 1-3 concerning sex education, particularly the implications for all of us of a number of children's books in this area now available in the school.

Marge Hartl and Helen Jaques

Item:There will be a parent-faculty meeting Tuesday afternoon, May 1st, from 1-3 at Louise Freedman's house. If you would like to attend, please see me. The topic is discipline—so your comments are welcome!

Roland

Item:Wednesday, May 2nd, is the next brown bag lunch, from 12 to 1.

Barbara

Item:Is anyone missing a reel, "Behind the Scenes at the Supermarket?" Please see Ann.

Item:The first 4 language arts workshops will be on the "synectics" materials. The school will pay the cost and we are to have 2 people in attendance. I shall be going as part of the language arts summer program. If you are interested please see me. The dates are May 8, May 22, June 19. This should be a great experience.

Nicki

Item:The video tape recorder is being stored in the little room off of Nancy Lankford's office. You *must* sign up in advance to use it. Please do not use it unless you feel comfortable with operating it. It consists of $2,000 worth of equipment—let's be careful!!

Nancy K.

Item: Plea to teachers from Anita Bamel: Now that the nice weather is here and kids are spending more time outdoors, please ask them to confine their noisy activities to places away from the building. Their sitting and playing and shrieking on the grills next to the building creates a major distraction for learning disabled kids trying to learn. The same holds true for girls using the basement girls' room as a social hall. Please ask your kids to cooperate. Thank you.

Anita

Item:The deadline for the following is April 26, Friday:
1) Summer pay (green sheet)
2) Visiting day (yellow sheet).

Ann

Item: All teachers planning a personal day in June should fill in "Plan to be absent" form before May 4th.

Ann

Item:You may count on holding evening parent conferences on the dates previously announced—May 9, 13, 23, 31 and June 6. In the event the custodial situation has not been favorably resolved by May 9 we will hold evening parent conferences in parents' homes—that is, if you can find a parent willing to let you hold 4 to 5 conferences in one evening in their home. I don't anticipate difficulties in making and arranging these, but should they arise we can pursue the church, etc.

Roland

Item: There are a couple of dozen small 48-star American flags in the office. If you can think of a use for them, see Nancy.

This simple, dittoed sheet, rarely more than a page long, serves many functions. It alerts teachers to activities, workshops, and meetings taking place within the school, the community, the system, or the area. No one is left out because the word didn't get far enough along the grapevine:

Item: On Monday, March 7th, from 3:00-4:00 p.m., Paulette Cherniak [a graduate student] will be demonstrating creative movement techniques for classroom use with a group of primary children. You are cordially invited to observe and join in the question/discussion period. The demonstration will be about 40 minutes with 20 minutes for discussion. If you are interested please leave a note in my box.

Sheila

It legitimizes sharing by providing a ready marketplace for teachers to offer ideas and materials to others:

Item:I have access to lots of lovely fabric samples. If you can use any, please let me know.

Debby

Item: I have 12 snails to give away (also a fish tank filter and heater to lend, but no fish tank). Let me know by noon Thursday if you want some snails.

Joan

Item:We have two students who have been trained to operate the "ditto machine" each day. If you have any materials to be run off, they *must* be in the box located in the inner office room by 8:15 a.m. Otherwise they will be done on the following day.

Ruth

ITEMS also provides a simple, small-scale mechanism for teachers to try out ideas and float trial balloons with colleagues:

Item: Several faculty members have indicated a desire to learn more about recent library acquisitions — in addition to the few books introduced to the class during the library period. Irene and I would very much like to share with you information about recent children's books. The problem is, of course, time. Would you be interested in attending a monthly half hour meeting — perhaps at 8 A.M. or 1 P.M. on Thursdays? Any other suggestions? (Please use the tear-off sheet on the bottom of the page to indicate your interest.)

Barbara and Irene,

YES, I WOULD BE INTERESTED IN ATTENDING A MONTHLY MEETING TO HEAR ABOUT NEW BOOKS IN THE LIBRARY. MY PREFERENCE IS

8 A.M._____   1 P.M._____Other_____

_____
Teacher's name

ITEMS offers a means for the central office to communicate with the staff, and a way for teacher/coordinators to organize activities without spending valuable time canvassing corridors:

Item: From the superintendent: As you know, there is a paper shortage which will probably become more acute as time goes on. I am sure you have already thought of many ways to save not only paper, but supplies which are either wholly or in part derived from paper. I should like to remind you to:

(1) Reexamine your orders with a view to reducing them as much as possible;

(2) Use both sides of the paper and wherever possible use other materials — e.g., blackboards;

(3) Encourage your students to use all paper supplies with great care for their conservation;

(4) Hold mimeographing and duplicating to the lowest possible minimum.

All of this will entail many changes in the habits of most of us — which may turn out to be a good thing. If you have thought of creative ways to save paper please let me know so that we can share them. Thank you.

Item: The next primary meeting will be Oct. 21st at Meadowbrook from 1:30-3:30. Mrs. Barbara Durant from the Division will be talking about math activities for learning disabled children in the primary grades.

John R.

Item: New arrivals in supply room: manila folders, blunt scissors, pencil sharpeners (first come, first served), pointed scissors (upper grades, 3-6), mucilage, and tissues (K-2). Thanks.

Jeffrey

Item: We are out of coffee and funds. Please bring your own instant coffee and label your name on it with masking tape. Sugar and milk for the coffee will be provided. We'll keep the coffee pot filled with hot water to be used for coffee, tea, or soup.

Faculty Room Committee

ITEMS is used to call meetings and to handle "administrivia," saving faculty meetings for more substantive issues:

Item: Re. late slips, beginning Tuesday the late slip procedure will no longer apply. It's sufficient that each teacher keep a careful record on the attendance sheets of children coming to school after 8:45. When it's clear that a child has been late frequently, please include this data as part of the biannual pupil evaluations. We would appreciate it if you would go over this change with your students prior to Tuesday.

Roland

Finally, it allows us to express staff solidarity, through congratulations, appreciation, and humor:

Item: By all accounts the Open House last night was an extremely successful evening. Congratulations to you all for knowing what you're doing, doing it, and being so able to convey what you're doing to parents.

Roland

Item: Thanks, Anita, for the glorious cheesecake.

An Anonymous Consumer

Item: Our heartfelt thanks to Peggy for the cheerfulness, cooperation, and expertise with which she handled the coordination, typing, and distribution of our pupil evaluations. A yeoman job well done, Peggy.

Shirley

Item: Kathy O'Kelly, a graduate student at Harvard, will be "shadowing" me all day on Monday, April 11th, to see what a principal does—or doesn't.

Roland

The in-school weekly periodical, a mundane enough practice, develops a life of its own and provides a vehicle that can change as well as reflect the school. A lively staff newsletter generates a sense of "us," enhancing the quality of life in the school. Simple, inexpensive practices like newsletters, if conscientiously pursued, frequently have far-reaching effects upon schools and the professional and personal lives of their inhabitants. They are often more important to staff development than a series of glittering workshops run by high-priced outside consultants.

Promoting Resourcefulness

Another seemingly mundane area of school life is the budget. But control of spending is control of people and classrooms and therefore is not to be taken lightly. Each year the Newton school system allocates about

$40 per child for instructional purposes, about $1,000 for a class, or $16,000 for a school of four hundred pupils. Although this amount represents only about 10 percent of a school's actual budget (salaries, building maintenance, and heating costs command the lion's share), it is a considerable sum. In Newton this account is entrusted to each principal, an excellent example of an uncommon delegation of authority from central office to local school. More typical is the case of a principal in another district who, supporting his teachers' desire to brighten their classrooms, requested funds to purchase paint. The assistant superintendent told him that colors other than the prevailing institutional green would distract children and cause their reading scores to fall. Request refused.

Principals responsible for instructional funds often make unilateral decisions about what books and materials to buy, or they wait and see who asks for money and then selectively purchase what they consider worthwhile materials (perhaps math textbooks) and refuse funds for other uses (perhaps field trips). This frequently leads to a game of "He has it; let's see if I can get it out of him," the burden resting upon each teacher to figure out which lever to pull to win the jackpot. Many principals, being accountable for how funds are spent and responsible for maintaining continuity, deploy monies on behalf of uniformity. They approve, for instance, only reading textbooks by the same publisher. Even so, selectively giving and withholding requires a rationale that will justify decisions to outraged teachers who guessed wrong.

I have chosen to divide the pie in a different way. The central office conveys to me responsibility for the $16,000 allocated to our school. From it I first take what is needed to purchase equipment and materials for the whole school—a new mimeograph machine, a movie projector, classroom materials for the supply closet. A committee of teachers determines these school-wide expenditures; I sign the purchase orders. The remaining money I parcel out according to a formula: $400 to each experienced classroom teacher, teacher's aide, and the principal; $500 to each teacher new to the school; and $500 to each specialist—art, music, library, physical education. How this money is spent is up to the teacher; it can go for texts, games, food, teachers' workshop tuition, testing materials, or field trips. Four hundred dollars—about $10 a week for an entire class—is not very much to spend on 25 students for 185 days. But it is $400 more than many teachers see.

Teachers can draw from their "account" by making requisitions through the district purchasing department (frequently getting good prices but having to wait several weeks for delivery) or by paying cash and submitting a receipt (trading greater expense for immediate delivery). They are reimbursed by the school secretary through a revolving petty-cash fund. The latter practice gives teachers immediate control over materials and supplies, permitting them to introduce new materials tomorrow on the basis of what they observe children doing today.[3]

Although I read and sign each expenditure request because I'm ultimately responsible (and, I confess, because I'm curious to see what teachers are buying), I have never questioned—let alone rejected—a teacher's purchase, even for such frivolous-sounding items as 1,000 tongue depressors for $14.95. (A few weeks later I found the tongue depressors being used by first graders in constructing their own abacuses, and subsequently in building a suspension bridge.) Some teachers make mistakes in spending, but I've never seen the same mistake twice.

Keeping track of separate accounts for two dozen teachers and translating each purchase into a code acceptable to the central office is a nuisance. Still, I have found compensating advantages in this system for myself, for teachers, and for pupils. When each teacher has a personal budget, the principal does not have to justify countless decisions about who got money for what and why. When teachers control the money, they have no illusion that the principal has an unlimited Swiss bank account. When the money runs out, that's it. The budget system has freed me from an imperial role I have always disliked. Rather than judging requests and funding only those I deem valuable, I now enjoy parading in front of teachers possible uses for *their* funds:

> Item:We have received from the federal government two surplus type-writers (all caps) in good working order as part of the swords into plowshares program (they have been used to type induction orders!). If anyone would like one of these machines for classroom use, see Roland. Price: $15 from your account.

When representatives from book companies come to the school, I tell them truthfully that I have only $400. Then, I announce in ITEMS that a salesperson will be in the building to demonstrate, for instance, a new math series for primary grades. Interested teachers come, checkbook in hand. I no longer function as middleman. The salesperson must convince teachers, the direct consumers, that their product is valuable for children. This places these important decisions in the hands of those most qualified to make them.

We have found that teachers entrusted with an instructional budget behave as they do with their personal budgets—they become highly resourceful, responsible, and frugal. With the "system's" funds they are only too willing to buy fancy sets of textbooks without regard to cost. With their "own" funds, they weigh carefully the cost of each potential purchase against the anticipated advantages for their students. A set of texts for an entire class (which can cost over $400) has not been purchased in five years. Usually teachers buy five or six copies for the class. With $178 saved by not purchasing science texts, a resourceful teacher can handsomely furnish an entire science interest area for a classroom. Given a limited but personally controlled budget, many teachers find imaginative ways of scrounging or constructing needed classroom materials without spending a dime. As one anonymous teacher put it,

We have done so much
for so long
with so little,
We are now qualified
to do anything
with nothing.

I remember a kindergarten teacher whose students accidentally broke an expensive 'unbreakable" phonograph record. The next day the pieces appeared in a box as a puzzle, which delighted children tried to assemble. Before teachers controlled their own budgets, $40 bus trips to local places of interest were common. Now the students travel by public transportation — at 10¢ a pupil — and learn something about public services along the way. When hiring a sixty-passenger bus is necessary for a field trip, you can be sure two classes of children will be on board, not a single class of twenty-five. Teachers have too many other uses for "their" money to waste any of it. Only occasionally does scrounging and resourcefulness exceed acceptable limits:

Item:The milk company is unhappy about losing many of its cases. It seems that frequently fewer are picked up than were left off. They inform us that we will now be charged for any missing cases. Nuf said.
Roland

No more free cubbies!

Another welcome, if unanticipated, consequence of teachers' controlling their own budgets has been a dramatic cross-fertilization of ideas among the staff. Instructional responsibility, backed by purchasing power, fosters experimentation, discussion, and cooperation by bringing into the school a constant flow of widely assorted new materials, books, and activities, all of which are cheaper if shared. A box of geoblocks costs about $40. Although well worth the price, they represent a sizable fraction of a year's budget. However, if three fourth-grade teachers each contribute $13, their students can use geoblocks about as often as if the blocks "belonged" to one class. When teachers purchase materials together, they have a sense of common ownership that leads to discussion of different uses of the materials and classroom visits to observe children and other teachers using them. "Borrowing," often a contentious practice when teachers are isolated, becomes legitimate, commonplace, and necessary when everyone is trying to stretch budgets:

Item:Teachers, could you *please* lend me your staplers next week. It's most important for a project we are doing. I shall be around on Fri-

day to collect them. (They should be marked with your name.)
Thank you.

Anne DeSalvo

A teacher aide keeps track of teachers' purchases and sends a statement to teachers every month or so, informing them of the balance in their account. Some teachers exhaust their entire budget by February and must borrow from others to get through the year. They repay their loan the following year — learning something about planning from the process. A few underspend, and the surplus reverts to the principal for school-wide items. The librarian, who feels her allocation is insufficient to meet her goals for the library program, annually engages in fund raising. She advises her colleagues that a tithe, 10 percent of their annual budgets, represents a reasonable contribution. Teachers usually chip in, but many give only after securing a blood oath that *their* funds will go toward the library's collection on trains or dinosaurs or other pet classroom projects. Other staff find other ways of hustling the funds they need for their class:

Item:The PTA Budget Committee will be meeting on Tuesday evening, Sept. 19th, at 7:30. If you would like to come, you are welcome. I urge any of you who will be needing funds for different projects this year to attend. You are your own best advocate.

Roland

Students eagerly participate in class efforts to get the most for the least. For instance, two classes operated a store to help finance a field trip to Philadelphia (which would otherwise have consumed the entire year's budget). The physical education instructor and his students sold school sweatshirts to finance new equipment. One class planned and constructed an elaborate seven-foot reading loft at a total cost of $65 for supplies. These kinds of activities make teachers and students both interdependent and instrumental in running their lives, qualities notoriously absent from many schools.

The school system that fills a classroom with expensive manufactured materials deprives both teachers and students of the opportunity, responsibility, and excitement that comes from identifying needs and securing resources. Foraging materials from trash piles on the way to school or discovering new uses for such old standbys as sand, wood, water, leather, and cardboard promotes a kind of motivation and learning the glossiest multimedia package cannot provide.

To get the instructional materials they need, then, most teachers negotiate this sequence of steps: check other teachers to see if any have and might be willing to lend what is needed; check the curriculum director in the central office to see if the materials might be loaned or purchased by the director; find another teacher willing to share in purchasing the needed materials in exchange for partial use of them; construct the materials from inexpensive available components; encourage students to find the materials at home or in the local library; see if the PTA will contribute funds. Only as a last resort, when many of these steps have been exhausted, do teachers purchase materials from their accounts.

This budget system has had ripple effects that extend far beyond its modest nature. I have found the money I allocate to teachers worth far more than its market value. Teachers' need for instructional materials is immediate, urgent, and specific; the school system's provision of instructional materials is slow and often irrelevant to the need. Money in teachers' hands brings into classrooms what is needed when it is needed. Furthermore, money has symbolic importance for teachers. Money is power, stored energy. Teachers feel the power of being able to get the things they need. Being entrusted with money is a vote of confidence — a confidence I have had no cause to question over the years. In addition to the vote of confidence for teachers, the feeling of importance and instrumentality that accompanies it, and the responsibility and resourcefulness it promotes, the budget system has had a subtle yet extraordinarily pervasive effect upon the professional and personal interdependence of the faculty. Like words in ITEMS, dollars in the budget provide a means of communication and exchange that has brought teachers and good ideas closer together. As one teacher put it: "It helps people sometimes just to give them what they want or think they want." The budget is another common school matter, with uncommon possibilities for the professional development of a faculty.

Promoting Responsibility

It is impossible for one person to run an institution as complex as a public elementary school. The person who attempts to do it all may get control, consistency, and uniformity, but he pays for these successes with ineffectiveness and exhaustion. When the faculty participates fully in operating a school, the results are also mixed: frequent disagreement and a lot of careful juggling are the price of considerable effectiveness and some measure of sanity.

An effective administrator makes sure that *someone* is attending to all the important areas of school life — himself or someone else. I favor someone else. Every principal has strengths and weaknesses and encounters tasks that seem crucial and those that do not. A principal can usually find others who like the things he can't stand, who are strong where he is weak. He can ensure that the administration of the school employs the abilities of all the available personnel. I am convinced that involving many others in the decisions of a school, while time-consuming and tedious, is in everyone's best interest — the administrator's, the faculty's, and the children's.

I have delegated responsibility to teachers for important aspects of school operation by revitalizing those tired old workhorses, the committee and the coordinator. At Angier we have a large and fluctuating number of committees ranging from Audiovisual to Pupil Evaluation to Sex Education to Visitors. This is hardly unusual. Most schools have many committees, generally composed of reluctant members — reluctant because committees tend to be overused and underutilized. Often membership is a frustrating exercise in attending meetings and engaging in unending talk, which turns to conflict whenever a decision must be made. Even if consensus is reached, those who appointed the committee often disregard the hard-fought conclusion, thereby promoting further disappointment and anger.

None of this is inevitable. I have found that committees can encourage collegiality and address important problems of a school — under certain conditions. First, there must be a need or an unsolved problem to generate the committee's existence. A committee on school rules is unnecessary when school rules exist (or don't exist) and are being followed; a committee on student safety is necessary when three children have been injured in automobile and bicycle accidents. Second, committee members should be entrusted with complete responsibility for analyzing the problem and determining its solution. If a committee is going to have a different level of authority such as "recommending to the principal," this should be carefully spelled out before the first meeting and before people agree to serve. If the solution to a problem will require money, the committee should command some funds with no strings attached. Third, committees should be small — one, two, or three members at most. We have found adequate "representation" of a staff of twenty-four requires a committee of twenty-four, so our committees no longer pretend to be representative. Teachers should not be shanghaied onto committees; selection should be made from those who know and care about the problem and are willing to translate their concern into work. If no one cares that much, the need for the committee is questionable. Fourth, teachers should serve on no more than two or three committees. This is easy if committees are transient, abolished when the work is done, and reconstituted only if a problem reemerges. Standing committees generally engage in a lot of standing around. And, finally, if the principal is a member of a committee he must keep his ears open and his mouth shut.

I have found that teachers are quite willing to work on a school problem through the committee structure if a committee is small enough so that each member has an opportunity to influence its deliberations and if members feel the ultimate decision rests with them and not with outside authorities. When responsibility is real, teachers work hard to make real decisions and assume accountability for their decisions, keeping colleagues advised of committee progress:

Item: As a result of our last meeting, the policy for visitors will be as follows:

(1) Visitors are welcome;

(2) Visitors may come five days a week, with permission in advance;

(3) Morning and afternoon;

(4) Up to ten a day.

Visitors Committee

Item: Re. Fire Drill, October 17, 9:20 A.M. It went well. It became apparent about 25 seconds into the drill that there were several classes confused about where to go once outside. This was caused because the children were not in their homerooms. It might help the special teachers (music, art, library, etc.) if homeroom teachers could review fire drill procedures for rooms their children regularly visit. Special teachers will also have to review this procedure. Congratulations to the kindergarten class caught on the stairs—and to those teachers who helped to straighten out the confusion in the front of the building. In spite of the problems, the time was well within reasonable limits.

Dick Salinger, Fire Marshal [and teacher]

Committees hold open meetings, check out possible solutions with the full faculty, and frequently put alternatives to a vote. The faculty in turn usually accepts and supports decisions made by committees. After all, the effectiveness of each committee depends upon staff acceptance and support. Imaginative solutions to problems frequently emerge. The visitors committee, for instance, wrote a little manual for visitors to the school and trained student guides to conduct tours. This set a welcome tone, eased demands upon secretary and principal, and provided each visitor with a staff list, a map of the school, and a student guide with whom to talk.

In addition to serving on committees, many teachers assume specific school-wide responsibilities as coordinators. The subject-matter coordinators in language arts, math, science, and social studies mediate between the school and the central office, ensure continuity in curriculum, and work toward reducing redundancies and omissions. With a small but personally managed budget and focused responsibility, each coordinator can have considerable influence over a subject-matter area. The primary and intermediate coordinators serve as de facto assistant principals with many planned and ad hoc responsibilities. They assist in the organization of the staff, help with scheduling, chair placement meetings, and hold meetings of their own twice a month with primary or intermediate teachers. And they meet each week with the principal to plan the agenda for faculty meetings.

In the curious society of schools it is often taboo for one teacher to help another. Helping somehow suggests that one is better than the other, that one is competent, the other incompetent. Further, when teachers see each other as competitors, cooperation and mutual aid make no sense at all. Formally appointing coordinators, without saying exactly what they are to do, makes it easy and legitimate for one teacher to help another. It also allows coordinators to do what they feel is most needed. One experienced teacher/coordinator spoke of her strong feelings about offering assistance to teachers new to the school:

> The question of inheritance raised memories of my first few days at school five years ago. There was not one single thing in my room— nothing—although there had been a first grade the previous year. There was nothing usable in the materials that were left. I was handed new Ginn readers, no curriculum guides; as I had never taught I could have used some. I followed the basal reader guide and read it nightly and learned something about reading. Because I knew nothing about math, I made the decision to go to every workshop and spent one afternoon a week in the math coordinator's office at the division. I finally got some help in individualized reading. Because my memories are strong about my need for help as a first-year teacher, as a coordinator I am now making an attempt to help all new teachers, to answer their questions, provide support, and get stuff from the division for them. None of that was there for me.

Another coordinator helps colleagues with "problem children":

> In an emergency, teachers feel free to go to another teacher and say, "Get him [a disturbing child] out of my room." Many come to me. There's always somebody else in the school who can deal with the kid better than an upset teacher could at any one given moment. Children with problems can be shared among the faculty. Some teachers who are disturbed about kids have called me up in the evening. I make suggestions such as, "Have you talked with the parents? Would you like me to sit in on the conferences?" I do not do this with the idea of telling anyone what to do, but rather to find necessary information that would help the teacher and me do a better job with the child. If a teacher just wants to cry on someone's shoulder, there are plenty of people around. Everyone in the school has a buddy they can rely on.

Involvement of teachers as committee members and as coordinators, like ITEMS and the budget, has ripple effects. These formal responsibilities encourage teachers to relate directly, honestly, and frequently with one another over sensitive, conflict-laden issues. Teachers learn that assuming responsibility for school problems frequently means assuming responsibility for one another's problems. One visitor at a primary meeting observed:

> As they went around the table evaluating the placement procedure, one teacher stated she felt hurt about rumors regarding problems in her classroom. Significant to me was the teacher's willingness to share hurt feelings with colleagues. The teacher received sympathetic responses which, in turn, facilitated further examination of some of the complicated issues around placement.

The presence of many coordinators makes it not only acceptable and appropriate but expected that teachers will help one another. In fact, there are so many visible "helping" teachers that the question is more often to whom the problem should be taken than whether help should be sought.

Teacher committees and coordinators also set limits on other teachers, a far more difficult and controversial practice than the institutionalization of mutual help. Both committees and coordinators frequently determine acceptable behavior for teachers. Explicit expectations for teachers from teachers frequently appear in ITEMS:

> Item: We would like to clarify a new library rule. If more than six of your
> children visit the library at a specific time, in addition to notifying
> the volunteers you must accompany the group.
>
> Library Committee

Setting limits on one's peers is perilous. Yet when teachers have legitimate authority, sanctioned by principal and faculty, they find the courage to make demands on their colleagues in one instance and to comply with their colleagues' demands on them in another. I find in the ease and frequency with which teachers monitor and set limits on one another evidence of a sophisticated level of faculty relationships and staff development.

Over the years the committee and coordinator systems have passed through several developmental stages. At first there were multiple school-wide problems and, for each problem, conflicts within the staff about solutions. Committees were large and combative. As problems were resolved and teachers began to trust one another, membership on most committees diminished to two or three. Finally, in many instances, a single person became "the committee." Now many committees have lapsed altogether, and vestiges of many previous problems are handled a little bit by everyone, without an appointed monitor.

Nonteaching responsibilities, then, have become a large part of the life of the school and the lives of teachers. In discharging them, teachers have developed within the building an accessible, effective, mutual-support system through which they exchange help with their colleagues. Teachers are taking responsibility for themselves, for a portion of the school, and, perhaps most important, for the well-being of others.

Committees and coordinators have helped break down the isolation of teachers' lives. They have also relieved the principal's isolation. Administrators, like teachers, need accessible, effective support from others. Yet, like teachers, as long as principals make decisions in isolation, they will remain isolated. The only areas of decision making I continue to "control" are the evaluation of pupils and the evaluation of teachers. Even here I frequently seek out advice from committees and individual staff members. Inclusion of teachers in the important decisions of school life has blurred the distinction between administrator and teacher, management and union, superior and subordinate. It has counteracted the role distinctions that debilitate schools and schoolpeople. It is no clearer who runs the school than it is whether a classroom is open or traditional. This meshing of roles has allowed different members of the school community to contribute their strengths, sharing the power, the satisfaction — and the price.

Items, the budget, and the committee/coordinator structure have become important (if sometimes unintended) avenues for staff development. But there are many other activities, growing directly from the needs and experiences of teachers, that contribute to their personal and professional growth. Visits to other schools is one. Teachers tackling a new problem, such as running a mixed-age class, frequently benefit from observing others outside the school who have mastered similar situations. It is easier for teachers in the uncertain, vulnerable position of trying something for the first time to seek and utilize help from those with whom they are not in constant daily contact. We help teachers identify useful classrooms, arrange visits, and find coverage for their classrooms; this continual reexamination pays off in improved practice.

Promoting Self-Examination

Work with student teachers and schools of education also keeps us moving, learning, growing. We are cautious about research in the school, but not negative. If a request from a university researcher seems to be valuable to teachers and students and receives central-office approval, I pass it along to the staff. When teachers choose to participate in research, I find they look afresh at themselves, their students, and their classrooms and gain new insights into practices that may have become habitual.[4] Most projects are modest:

Students are invited to participate in a study of children's drawing techniques in their own classroom in a session taking an hour to an hour and a half. The children will be provided with drawing materials and asked to draw pictures of certain objects and scenes. Their pictures will be collected and analyzed to advance understanding of how children develop drawing skills. The analysis does not involve the child's personality, self-image, or emotional life; the results will, of course, not be evaluated as part of the child's regular schoolwork. Typical drawing assignments will be: draw a person brushing his teeth; draw a hill with several houses on it; draw a house on the side of a hill with a ball balanced on its roof; draw a happy face and a sad face; draw a group of children standing in a circle holding hands; draw a line of telephone poles along this road (the road is already drawn on the piece of paper the children are given). The results of the study will be shared with the Angier School.

Other proposals from university researchers have been more ambitious and ambiguous:

> We would want to be with you from about mid-February to mid-April. What we do has been evolving somewhat. We go into classrooms partly in the role of teacher aides and partly in that of observers. We do help the teachers in any way they ask us to, so long as it doesn't remove us from the scene of the action. We started out not taking any notes in the classroom and dictating from memory afterwards. But we soon found that in the midst of a busy classroom, no one noticed — or if they did notice, cared — if we took occasional notes — so we began to do that. It is a matter of judgment of course whether or not you are disturbing anyone. If you are, you stop. Up to now we have had wonderful relations with the teachers whose rooms we've been in. They soon discover that we are not part of the system of power which affects them; that we are absolutely close-mouthed about what anyone says to us; and that we are sympathetic listeners. We also have good relations with the kids — too good, on occasion. It's easy to become interested in particular children almost to the point of neglecting what you're really up to.

> Always subject to your decisions about what we may and may not do — the thing that makes your school especially interesting is that you have classroom options. I assume the group of parents you draw from is relatively homogeneous social class-wise. And a problem which fascinates me is: what differentiates children in more and less formal classrooms? (You probably have some damned good hypotheses about it by now.) I'd like to try to find out what differentiates them — and that might entail interviewing some parents.

> It is also interesting to think about the organizational problems of a school with options. What about the relations among teachers having different pedagogical views?

> The problem has some interesting implications. For instance, we are helping a new town to plan its educational system. And the question has been raised: what will happen if we put different educational options, each embodied in a small school, next to each other in an educational park? Would that be better, worse, or no different from separating them spatially?

> What we do mainly is spend time in classrooms; write up field notes; attend all school functions, since we like to know how the governance works, how the parents participate, how teachers work together, if they do, what the role of the aides is; how the district environment affects the school. We also interview as many different types of participants in the system as we can. Always with their consent, of course.

> Finally something we have gotten into and would like to pursue is a brief four-question, five-minute private interview with pupils in which we get sociometric data (Who are your best friends in the class?) and self-concept of ability data. We have two hypotheses. They are formulated "in favor" of the open classroom; but we are really neutral. (1) Peer groups are more flexible in the open classroom and less influenced by outside factors. Thus,

you'd expect to find more cross-sex, cross-social class, and cross-ethnic choices in 'open' than in 'traditional' classrooms. (2) Self-concept of ability is higher in the open than in the traditional classroom because there is less exposure of the self to public competition.

Ready access to the numerous colleges in the Boston area encourages teachers to enroll in graduate courses and pursue their own research projects, often making use of their opportunity to work with children and other teachers. Work in pre-service and in-service teacher training also has a powerful effect on teachers' professional development, which typically goes through several stages. Initially, of course, teachers take courses, practice teach, and learn the craft of teaching; then they assume positions as teachers and learn a great deal more from conducting their own classes. The next level in this developmental progression, seldom available to many teachers, is helping others become teachers—or become better teachers. Coordinators do this with our own staff, but teachers learn in new and particularly enriching ways when they work with colleagues outside the building.

Each year we at Angier contract with Brandeis University to cooperate in their undergraduate teacher-certification program. About a dozen students are placed with as many of our teachers. Student and teacher work together for several months; inevitably they come to know more about teaching, about each other, and about themselves. Bright student teachers examine, question, and challenge experienced teachers' educational ideas and practices, causing those teachers to examine, defend, and rethink what they do.

In addition to classroom training we run Brandeis Seminars, which help student teachers learn instructional methodology and theory. Each year I appoint a committee of teachers, paid by Brandeis, to lead these seminars. They, in turn, engage a considerable portion of the staff as faculty for the seminars. A variety of topics are covered: discipline, observing children, record keeping, curriculum, and—that riveting subject—getting a teaching job. Teachers have also assisted other teachers through the former Greater Boston Teacher Center, which used to offer faculty-led workshops and courses on a wide variety of topics for teachers in the Boston area. A committee of faculty assumed responsibility for planning and offering one of these courses each year.

In these situations teachers are paid to share what they know with prospective or practicing teachers. Remuneration conveys to teachers several important messages: "We are aware of the many good things you are doing; we value these things; we feel others would benefit from knowing what you are thinking and doing; we feel strongly enough about this and value your expertise enough so that we will pay you to share it." These messages, so seldom communicated to classroom teachers, affirm their importance, dignity, and accomplishment. When teachers receive this kind of recognition, they go to extraordinary lengths to justify it. They reflect on their practice, translating intuitive and unconscious behavior into more conscious, deliberate information that can be useful to others. And, of course, this process feeds back into improved classroom practice for the teachers themselves.

Teacher Evaluation

Most teachers welcome classroom observers who can diagnose instructional problems and offer helpful suggestions. Often a teacher will invite an outsider to observe for a specific purpose, perhaps to react to a new laboratory method of teaching science or a new grouping practice in reading, or to observe a misbehaving child. The teacher and observer experience the same events and can talk in a friendly way about what they have witnessed. The burden of judgment is off the teacher, and the burden of judging is off the visitor. Teachers who seek out this kind of assistance from other teachers, friends, coordinators, and sometimes even parents and principals, have already taken important steps toward professional growth. Consequently, the observation is likely to be profitable. Unfortunately, informal observation is rarely taken seriously in public elementary schools; formal, involuntary evaluation of teachers by principals and other supervisors is considered the primary means of promoting professional staff development. It is not clear to me why.

Studies of teacher evaluation and supervision have been reported for a half century. It is an interesting literature. At first, teachers were evaluated according to the success of their students at the next level of schooling or by proficiency examinations. Then attempts were made to measure teacher performance against some absolute model of "good teaching." The frequent futility of these efforts next led researchers to examine interactions between teacher, learner, and learning environment. Evaluators armed with lists would check off how frequently the teacher spoke, how frequently children moved from their seats, whether children were solving problems posed by books, by the teacher, or by children themselves. More recently, studies of teacher evaluation have focused on the relation between a specific teaching style and the specific learning styles of students. Now, as the inexorable cycle comes around again, attention has returned to evaluation of teachers through measures of student achievement.

Newton, like most school systems, has an official form used annually for evaluating nontenured teachers. Because over 80 percent of our teachers are now tenured, the system is also beginning systematic evaluation of tenured teachers. This formal evaluation has several familiar components. First, I observe in the classroom two or three times. Before each visit the teacher and I share ideas and afterward observations and more ideas. Then we each fill out the official form (shown in Appendix

G), commenting on work in the different subject areas and on relationships with parents, other teachers, and children. After that we bring the two sets of forms, reflecting our separate perceptions, to another conference. I am always particularly interested in discrepancies in our perceptions. I find few. When I point out difficulties or strengths I have observed, I usually find the teachers are also well aware of them. In fact, I have often found the teachers more exacting and more insightful than their evaluators. The last step is to incorporate both sets of observations into a final report, which goes to the personnel office with a recommendation for reappointment.

In theory, formal evaluation of teachers by principals and other supervisors is a powerful means of promoting professional growth. Many principals use it as an effective means of improving teacher performance. There have been many instances where I have been able to do so — especially where teachers were pushing toward their own goals for change and I was attempting to assist them. On balance, though, my feeling is that formal evaluation has only a limited influence upon staff development. Its possib'lities remain largely unfulfilled. Indeed, supervision often approaches a meaningless ritual. Or, even worse, it becomes the recurring occasion to heighten anxiety and distance between teacher and principal. Conflicts and inconsistencies inherent in the supervisory process, a confusion of goals, and the ambiguity and inconsistency of methods, all tend to limit the potential usefulness of formal supervision as a growth-producing process. Let me share some of the problems.[5]

First, there is a conflict of *role*. Formal supervision and evaluation take place under a cloud of retention or dismissal that frequently restricts possibilities for teacher growth. The question of reappointment has assumed a larger and larger place in formal supervision for two reasons. Only a few years ago a school was lucky to find anyone at all to fill a vacancy. Today an abundance of highly qualified teachers wait in the wings to fill the place of incompetent or undistinguished practitioners. Additionally, because of the precipitous decline in enrollment of elementary-school-age students, the number of teaching positions is also declining. Some schools have been able to cut staff as teachers retire and resign. But many systems must make an involuntary reduction in force. The most common criterion to emerge has been "last hired, first fired," which leads, sadly, to the dismissal of many young, energetic, and capable teachers and removes from schools some of their most important agents of staff renewal and invigoration.

The school principal, the person designated by most systems to help teachers grow, is the same person required to judge, to evaluate, and to "terminate" ineffective or surplus teachers. It is as though a priest who listens to transgressions is also made to serve as a policeman, charged with apprehending and punishing those who transgress. It is difficult for anyone to fill both roles simultaneously. Yet the principal, who holds the power of terminating professional life, is nonetheless expected to promote professional growth.

Second, there is a conflict of *purpose*—or rather of purposes. The supervisory process is supposed to change the behavior of teachers, to help each become more effective professionally. One might expect, therefore, that everything that occurs within the supervisory process supports the personal and professional growth of the teacher, complying with the criterion: "How is what we are doing now helping the teacher or going to help the teacher become better?" If these objectives are realized, why do so many teachers see supervision as something to endure, something done *to* them, rather than *for* them or *with* them? Don't teachers want to become better?

In fact, of course, supervision has multiple purposes, few of them related to teacher development and growth. Supervision is often used to induce teachers to adhere to a prescribed curriculum or comply with a supervisor's expectations, an intent diametrically opposed to individually defined professional growth. Supervision is frequently organized around the needs of the school system to assemble a competent staff; to determine who shall be hired, rehired, promoted, granted tenure, or dismissed; and to convince taxpayers and school committees that the system enforces rigorous expectations and is getting the most from its employees.

Evaluation and supervision also serve the particular needs of principals. For some, supervision is a means of maintaining authority and control over teachers. For some it is an opportunity to be accepted and liked—to break down the distance between teachers and administrators. For others, examination of teacher practice is a means of earning respect for expertise. And, for many principals, the overriding concern during the evaluation process is to avoid conflict—to perform an unpleasant, demanding task as quickly and inoffensively as possible. That is why many principals' evaluations of teachers—like teachers' evaluations of pupils—are milquetoast. They have no sharp edges, distress no one, and settle the stomach.

Just as children's needs in school seem to be attended only when adults' needs have been met, so teachers' needs in school systems are often attended only when those of their superiors have been met. The needs of the system and the supervisor compete with and frequently obscure the most important purpose of supervision: to help teachers become more effective. When students evaluate teachers, their interests are taken more seriously. Perhaps one way of establishing the primacy of teachers in the supervisory process might be to have them periodically evaluate their supervisors. Appendix H shows an instrument that makes this attempt.

Personal relationships also interfere with the supervisory process.

Despite what we may say, just as teachers like some of their pupils more than others, so principals enjoy some of their teachers more than others. How principal and teacher feel about each other has a powerful impact on the supervisory process. Is it possible to help someone you don't respect? I don't think so. Who helps the supervisor face and resolve feelings of frustration, anger, and hostility toward some members of the staff? Usually no one.

Effective supervision begins with an agreement that the only things that happened are what both teacher and principal agree happened. But this consensus of reality often fails to materialize. Neither principal nor teacher can detach themselves from the personal feelings and prejudices that color judgments. It is as difficult to see clearly the strengths of a person you dislike as to see clearly weaknesses in someone you like very much. Thus, many supervisory relationships deteriorate into warm hand-holding or cold acrimony — or into vacant motions of helping and being helped.

Values are at the root of a fourth area of inevitable supervisory conflict. I appreciate differences in teacher behavior if I feel they contribute to effective teaching. Still, like most supervisors, I appreciate some practices more than others. I find it neither possible nor honest to attempt to be unbiased and value free. If I allow and encourage teachers to practice their craft, employing educational means that they determine themselves, I find myself asking where do *I* stand? What is my own position on the important questions of instruction — on ability grouping, on individualized or group instruction, on teacher-directed or more student-centered classes, on desks in rows or interest areas? Or, to put it more personally, is there a second grade among the variety of second grades in which I would prefer my daughter to be placed? The principal who determines and enforces uniformity clearly takes a stand. There is a certain openness and honesty, if perhaps controversy, about making positions explicit. The principal who values diversity, on the other hand, has complex value problems to resolve. He is only a step away from valuing everything, and therefore nothing — of being an administrator/manager, a facilitator perhaps, but not an educator. How much of my own positions do I reveal to teachers and inject into the supervision process? What is the consequence for me and for teachers of making my positions explicit? Would such revelation enhance or inhibit the development of each teacher's philosophy? Would my position have a different effect upon teachers who agree with me than on those with whom I often disagree? These questions trouble me.

Implicit in the very act of observing is selecting, judging. To be effective we must know who we are and be clear about what we believe. How do supervisors become conscious and sure of their own values? How do we know what teachers' values are? How often do we assume teachers' values are compatible with our own when they are not; and how often do we assume that teachers' values are incompatible with ours when they are very much alike? When the values of teacher and principal are incompatible, should the supervisor try to change the teacher — whose actions may be thoughtful, consistent, and valued by others (children and parents, for instance)? Where is the line between supporting teachers in developing their own values and styles and projecting one's own values upon teachers? We as supervisors must begin to answer these extremely complex questions before formulating specific ideas about what we expect of teachers.

Finally, the supervisory process is marred by conflicts of *expectation*, the desire to maintain a relationship that combines social comfort with growth. Supervisors and supervisees spend much time together and want that time to be pleasant and free of conflict. It rarely works out that way. Learning can be joyous, but a process like supervision also involves hard insight and painful growth. Comfort is not a realistic expectation for a supervisory relationship. If principal and teacher role play their relationship, remaining objective and detached, they can perhaps insulate themselves from risk and pain — and from growth. Active engagement in supervision, as in any relationship, makes risk and pain inevitable. Nonetheless, the more one risks pain, failure, self-revelation, embarrassment, and judgment, the more competent one becomes in dealing with these difficult emotions. And the more one grows. Pain must not be wished away; it should be acknowledged and accepted by supervisor and supervisee alike.

Conflicts of this sort haunt formal efforts to supervise and evaluate teachers. They have diminished the success of supervisory relationships for me, and I suspect for others as well. Somehow, we will have to come to grips with these ambiguities if supervision and evaluation of teachers is ever to become a major force in promoting their professional growth.

Independence Training

I think of staff development in two ways, as the professional growth of individual teachers and the professional growth of a faculty. For both, my goal has been the same: independence training. The biggest problem besetting schools is the primitive quality of human relationships among children, parents, teachers, and administrators. Many schools perpetuate infantilism. School boards infantilize superintendents; superintendents, principals; principals, teachers; and teachers, children. The result is children and adults who frequently behave like infants, complying with authority out of fear or dependence, waiting until someone's back is turned to do something "naughty." Some systems have so thoroughly infantilized principals that many feel the need to clear every minor action with some higher authority; many teachers want principals to monitor every detail of their teaching, if only to relieve them of responsibility if things go wrong; and, of course, many children need teachers to direct their every move. Schoolpeople are badly in need of independence training.

The self-actualization of teachers is not a goal of schools because it appears to be unrelated to pupil achievement and literacy skills. I would argue that the self-actualization of teachers *ought* to be a goal of schools — not only because it enriches the lives of teachers, but because it also enriches the academic and personal lives of their students. To the extent that teachers can become responsible for their own teaching, they can help children become responsible for their own learning. One teacher put it this way:

> In the beginning, I did what I was told. I went by the book and planned every minute of every day for every child. Now I believe in the ability of children to do much for themselves. My job is to provide an enormous number of fruitful possibilities for them.

Just as independence training of individual teachers is enormously important to schools, so is independence training vital to a school faculty. A faculty becomes independent by becoming interdependent. A school should never become dependent on one adult to hold it together. A school may be a house of cards, a fragile interrelated social network, but principals who feel they cannot leave "their" building because they are certain something is going to go wrong are in trouble. They overestimate their own importance and demean their staff. There are always people around a school — usually several — who can make things work at least as well as the principal. The benefits to schools of interdependence are as important as they are to schoolpeople. Moeller and Mahan have shared research which demonstrates that

> members of groups who are strongly committed to common goals, who enjoy high peer-group loyalty, who express favorable attitudes between superiors and subordinates, and who demonstrate a high level of skill and interaction can clearly achieve far more than the same people acting as an aggregation of individuals.[6]

A school should be, above all else, a community of learners. Principals learn. Teachers learn. Parents learn. Student teachers learn. Visitors learn. And to the degree that they learn, students also learn. But the professional development of individual teachers is more than a means toward the end of delivering services to children and to society. It is also an end in itself. Schools are places to assist in the growth of *people*. Teachers are people, and their personal and professional growth is as legitimate a concern of schools as is the cognitive and affective growth of children. If we can help teachers figure out where they stand, and if they can stand there with dignity, security, satisfaction, and competence, then everyone benefits. Indeed, when a teacher becomes self-critical, self-monitoring, self-evaluative, and self-confident, there is little need for formal evaluation, or for supervision.

Lortie found that in the eyes of most teachers learning, success, and satisfaction came largely from students within their classrooms and that "*all* other persons [parents, the principal, colleagues] without exception, were connected with undesirable occurrences . . . Other adults have potential for hindrance but not for help."[7] This need not be so. Newsletters, budgets, committees, coordinators, and work with student teachers and fellow professionals all expand the realm of satisfying "others" and lead toward fruitful interdependence and adult independence. These kinds of activities relieve loneliness, emancipate teachers from dependence upon any single person within the hierarchy, and enable individual teachers to pose their own goals and enlist others to help attain them. For these reasons, I suspect, I have found that informal, indirect, modest activities — taken collectively — have a far greater capacity to stimulate personal and professional growth in teachers than more elaborate, direct attempts at formal staff development. In the final analysis, professional growth stems not from deliberate attempts to train teachers, but from a school culture that is adult, supportive, professional, cooperative, and humane.

CHAPTER NINE

The Principalship

Old principals never die; they just lose their faculties.

— Anonymous

A HUNDRED FIFTY YEARS AGO there were no school principals. Schools were run by masters, who taught, administered, ran the sports program, and lit the morning fires. With increasing population came larger schools, more complex administrative duties, and the practice of designating one of the masters *head* master, responsible for school-wide administration as well as teaching. Elsewhere, the terminology was "teacher" and "principal teacher." *Principal* and *head* were descriptive adjectives, not job-describing nouns.

Over the years, as administrative duties mounted and teaching responsibilities declined, the concept of "the principal" as full-time administrator evolved. Today, with the exception of teaching principals in small rural schools, principals are principals and teachers are teachers. Although we principals still like to think of ourselves as head or master teachers who frequently engage in the honorable craft of teaching, the principal has become a separate species, set apart from the instructional process by a desk covered with sedimentary deposits of memos, by a union-management rift, and by the size and complexity of modern schools.

Much of the history of the profession has been peaceful. Topics addressed by a 1950s textbook for prospective and practicing school principals suggest the simple, tranquil concerns of our predecessors:

The Place of Health Textbooks
The Matter of Party Treats, of Eats and Sweets
Slides, Swings, and Climbing Things: Erect Them or Eject Them?
The Creation of Wholesome Pupil Attitudes
The Principal as a Dispatcher and Director of Traffic[1]

173

A chapter on "School Spirit" offers principals this advice:

> How *can* school spirit be created and fostered?
> (1) Start off with a school song . . .
> (2) Establish official *school colors* . . . most likely *your* school colors will include at least one of these: red, blue, yellow.
> (3) Select a school mascot . . . Not a *live* one, of course! . . . (If your school is Roosevelt, your mascot could be Rosie; Jefferson, Jeff, etc.) . . . There should be only *one* in existence—that one at school. Better still, buy *two*, exactly alike. Put one away in moth balls against that day when the first one wears out! The children will never be the wiser! . . . These three, were there no other gestures made towards creating and maintaining a school spirit, have a discernible effect on the morale of a school staff and pupil body.[2]

And under "Some General Yardsticks in Measuring the Principal" the principal is asked:

> How does your appearance rate with that of other professional men and women in the community? Are you careful to wear attractive, tasteful clothing, to keep your shoes shined, to look "spick and span"? Do you give attention to habits of personal cleanliness?[3]

The chapter on "The Principal and Other Employees" concludes with the benediction: "The elementary principal works and co-operates with many other employees of the board of education. The larger the school system, the more numerous becomes the family of which he is a member."[4]

This text captures what some wistfully consider the golden age of the public-school principal—a period when schools were entrusted to veteran teachers who were accorded respect, responsibility, and authority with their title. Those principals could make the daily rounds, certain of a polite, deferential greeting from children and teachers in each classroom. No more. These passages supply the epitaph for an era in the history of the profession.

What kind of a ship is today's principalship? Since its emergence as a profession, the elementary school principalship has been defined, analyzed—and sometimes defamed.[5] Most observers describe a function somewhere between educational leader of the school and innocuous middle manager who translates the policies of superintendent and school board into schoolhouse practices. The literature is replete with attempts to list the duties and responsibilities of a school principal—see, for example, Appendix I. Yet no description can adequately capture the satisfactions, frustrations, possibilities, and impossibilities of this highly personalized job.

Although no two schools are alike, although each principal fulfills the job in an idiosyncratic way, most school administrators experience common conditions, problems, tasks, and worries. Each confronts the same constellation of parents, children, teachers, buildings, school board members, legal decisions, budget decisions, curriculum decisions, and the central office. The different roles that evolve for principals are heavily influenced, then, by similar realities.

The Realities of the Job

THE IMBALANCE OF RESPONSIBILITY AND AUTHORITY

The first reality of being a principal is the imbalance of responsibility and authority. Principals are ultimately responsible for almost everything that happens in school and out. We are responsible for personnel — making sure that employees are physically present and working to the best of their ability. We are in charge of program — making sure that teachers are teaching what they are supposed to and that children are learning it. We are accountable to parents — making sure that each is given an opportunity to express problems and that those problems are addressed and resolved. We are expected to protect the physical safety of children — making sure that the several hundred lively organisms who leave home each morning return, equally lively, in the afternoon.

Over the years principals have assumed one small additional responsibility after another — responsibility for the safe passage of children from home to school, responsibility for making sure the sidewalks are plowed of snow in winter, responsiblity for health education, sex education, moral education, responsibility for teaching children to evacuate school buses and to ride their bikes safely. We have taken on lunch programs, then breakfast programs; responsibility for the physical condition of the furnace, the wiring, the playground equipment. We are now accountable for children's achievement of minimum standards at each grade level, for the growth of children with special needs, of the gifted, and of those who are neither. The principal has become a provider of social services, food services, health care, recreation programs, and transportation — with a solid skills education worked in somehow.

There is an old story about a farm boy whose cow gave birth to a calf. Every day the boy would carry the calf up the mountain to the pasture and return with it in the evening. While at first the animal weighed only fifty pounds, each day the calf gained a pound or two — an inconsequential amount, of course, and an increment the boy could easily bear. He continued to carry the animal up the mountain, as it grew into a fifteen-hundred-pound cow. It was an extraordinary load, but the boy had been carrying the calf from its infancy; because each daily increment was small, it was possible for the boy to carry an animal ten times his own weight. There is a message here for principals. Each of our responsibilities is manageable, but the sum total forms an overwhelming load. This burden is not made lighter by the gradual erosion of the authority and resources necessary to fulfill the incremental responsibilities.

The school principal stands at the intersection of *needs* and *resources.* It is no longer possible to make a judicious match: resources are shrinking as needs expand. Today's principal somehow has to generate resources where there are none, and reduce needs as demands for services rise. And as principals try to mediate between growing needs and shrinking resources, we are faced with public demand that we account for our every act, a demand that is increasing as control over personnel, budget, and program diminishes.

It is not a cheerful picture. We take on a given faculty. Whatever we do, we cannot ask for more or different teachers. Principals are dealt a hand of cards to play as best we can; the rules are that the cards may be shuffled, but neither discarded nor added to. We take on a fixed budget. Whatever we do, we cannot ask for more — and we may get less. We take on a central curriculum guide. Schools, teachers, and principals are accountable for following these guides, and for publicly displaying results from them. Whatever we do, we may not disregard them.

A new principal gets a title, an office, responsibility, accountability, and obligations. Nothing more. The problems come with the territory, but the means necessary to solve them do not. Means — respect, authority, power, money, personnel, enthusiasm, commitment — must somehow be generated with the meager resources at hand. There are no magic tricks. It takes hundreds of thoughtful, considered, successful decisions before a principal is taken seriously by his constituents. Hundreds of "right" moves may set one ahead two weeks; a single "wrong" decision can throw one back two years. This imbalance of responsibility and authority makes many principals feel powerless and act helpless. As one principal put it, "I am responsible for everything and have control over nothing." Yet it is precisely the sense that one is in control, confident, and powerful that earns authority. The principal faces a dilemma: how to create a sense of authority within a role comprised of a giant bundle of responsibilities and accountabilities.

Isolation at the Top

To fulfill responsibilities successfully, a principal must establish and maintain close personal relationships with children, parents, teachers, and the central office. Ultimately these groups ascribe and accord authority and power to a principal; from them come resources as well as needs. Yet a second reality for principals is that relationships with others many times are characterized by isolation, loneliness, and fear. The job definition for principals requires us to impose some common expectations upon children and teachers. The enforcement of uniformity is all but incompatible with creating fruitful, satisfying human relationships with diverse individuals. It is no wonder that Becker found that "the largest number of problems identified by principals involves their difficulty in establishing and maintaining successful human relations."[6]

Many principals don't really feel close to anyone. Everyone is a potential adversary: parents, children, teachers, and central-office staff. Principals may feel close to one another, but there is sometimes the feeling that fellow principals also are potential adversaries, competitors for scarce resources and public recognition. Many principals agree with Philip W. Jackson's observation, reflecting his experience as director of the University of Chicago's laboratory schools:

> One of the chief residues of my own administrative experience is the memory of having felt alone, not in the simple physical sense of being by myself, without companions, but in the deeper psychological sense of being apart from others.[7]

Principals are inevitably set apart from the teachers we must constantly monitor, supervise, and evaluate. Furthermore, most principals are as much apart from those for whom we work as from those who work for us. Central offices give lip service to "participation" by principals in important decisions, but few principals feel like participants. In fact, many feel like glorified clerks in their relations with the larger system. Because the central office evaluates principals' performance, few feel comfortable sharing problems that might be interpreted as indications of weakness or incompetence. Thus, while a principal must establish and maintain close human relationships to gain the authority and respect necessary to fulfill many responsibilities, important institutional conditions required for the formation of those close relationships are absent.

THE TIME CRUNCH

The principal has little control over time. Much of it is devoted to "maintenance": making schedules, evaluating teachers, writing recommendations, interviewing and hiring teachers, placing children, ordering books and supplies. These routine duties are the foundation of efficient school operation. As we have seen, they are also exhausting and incredibly time-consuming. One account of a typical day suggests how little principals control either tasks or time:

> I got to school early this morning because I had a conference at 7:30 with two teachers, a child, a parent, and the guidance counselor. The conference lasted until about 8:15. Then I saw two more parents about placement of their children. At 9:00, the seventh- and eighth-grade teachers, the guidance counselor, and I saw two parents and a child about the child's progress. When that was over, I talked with a teacher and then I saw a man about changing the contract for school pictures. Between 11:00 in the morning and 1:30 in the afternoon, I dealt with five seventh-grade boys

and their teachers about various problems—mostly cutting classes and behavior problems. And then I taught a sixth-grade class. Next, I helped a teacher learn how to bonsai some plants. After that, I started my lunch, but before I could finish my sandwich, a little first grader got himself locked in the stairwell and couldn't get out. He pulled the fire alarm, which brought the entire Fire Department to the school. I tried to console that terrified, paralyzed child—to add to the confusion, he doesn't speak English—and tried to find out what had happened. I discovered that there is no exit from that particular stairwell because the door doesn't work, and so I immediately put in an order to get that fixed. It was a wild day, absolutely frenetic.[8]

The principal is commonly thought of as a rational manager—one who initiates. In actuality, what a principal is often bears greater similarity to the doctor on call in a hospital's emergency ward—he is one who responds.

One school system concerned by the spiraling responsibilities of its principals decided to make systematic observations to determine what they did all day. The study revealed:

(1) By far the greatest percentage of principals' time (58%) is devoted to the category of *Management* responsibilities.

(2) *Instructional leadership* responsibilities occupy the next largest portion of principals' time during the school day (17%). However, the time spent in this category is less than one-third of the amount spent on *Management* responsibilities.

(3) Nine percent of the principals' time is devoted to *Public Relations.*

(4) *Liaison* responsibilities occupy nearly as much time (8%) as *Public Relations.*

(5) *Outside Professional Activities, Personal Activities,* or activities which involve a combination of other areas of responsibility each occupies less than 5% of principals' observed school-day time.

(6) *Management* responsibilities outweigh all other categories of responsibility, even more in terms of actual numbers of activities than in terms of percentage distribution of time.

(7) On the average, a *Management* task is performed every eight minutes in the eight-hour school day, an *Instructional Leadership* task about once every 45 minutes, a *Liaison* task only once every four hours, and a *Personal* activity less than once every three hours.

(8) *Management* tasks are of the shortest duration, lasting only five minutes each, on the average. Thus, the greatest portion of a principal's time is divided among many brief management activities.

(9) *Liaison* activities last the longest (19 minutes on the average).

(10) *Staff evaluation* activities last relatively long on the average (17 minutes), particularly in senior highs (26 minutes).

(11) *Personal activities* last only seven minutes on the average. Principals were generally observed to spend only between five and ten minutes eating lunch or taking a rest break.[9]

This analysis of principals' duties and time-use patterns suggests the fragmentation of principals' time and the number of tasks that consume it. We spend each day moving from place to place, from problem to problem, making immediate, ad hoc decisions. The same study concluded:

> The principalship has become a very complex and demanding job. A principal is called upon to meet responsibilities in a dozen or more discernible areas during a typical school day. Further, there is little opportunity to devote uninterrupted attention to a single activity without interference from competing demands.[10]

Two forces compound the problem of time for principals. First, despite our frantic efforts to fulfill multiple responsibilities, others expect principals to do more, faster, and better. In the study discussed above, members of the school board appeared to want 300 percent of a person in the principal's office:

38% felt principals should spend *more* time in		executive management
46%	"	student and personnel management
16%	"	facilities and finances
47%	"	program evaluation
39%	"	staff evaluation
30%	"	liaison with central office
70%	"	outside professional activities[11]

Principals are asked to do more and to do it faster, while simultaneously keeping a weather eye out for the *legal* consequences of each decision we do or do not make. When the needs of constituents have not been met or when parents, teachers, and students don't think they have been met, more and more resort to the courts. In the past principals reached resolution by conference, consensus, agreement, or fiat. Now litigation is becoming a more common means of conflict settlement. Faced with multiple needs, with the necessity of making fast decisions in an atmosphere of fragmented time, administrators are liable for everything they do. We are cautioned by legal advisers not to allow students or faculty to move heavy equipment, not to administer prescription medications to students, not to take children on field trips or transport pupils in our own autos, not to allow potentially hazardous playground equipment, not to comply with central-office directives that have not been put in writing, and not to leave our buildings.

The major criterion used by the courts in cases of negligence is reasonableness: "Did the principal use good judgment, prudence, and reasonableness in carrying out his duties?" Unfortunately, the conditions under which most principals work hardly encourage care, reflection, premeditation, judgment, prudence, or reasonableness.

Instructional Leaders or Not?

There is a huge discrepancy between what principals would like to do and what we really do. Most want to be instructional leaders who work closely with teachers, children, and curriculum. Instead, as we have seen, principals spend the bulk of each fragmented day in an elaborate juggling act. We rarely control tasks, time, or location. Rather than initiating, principals respond to initiatives, demands, needs, and crises of others whenever and wherever they arise. As one principal put it, "You seldom know in advance what to be anxious about."

One school system advertising for a new principal sought someone with these qualities:

(1) Ability to see another's point of view
(2) Trust in teachers' judgments
(3) Supportive
(4) Relaxed and flexible
(5) Knowledgeable about curriculum areas
(6) Experienced in elementary administration
(7) Decisive
(8) Strength in one's own convictions
(9) Self-confident
(10) Ability to distinguish important issues from unimportant
(11) Sense of security
(12) Ability to set goals
(13) Ability to provide guidance for teacher growth
(14) Ability to promote staff communication by being open and communicative
(15) Personal warmth
(16) Understanding of human differences
(17) Ability to deal with pressure groups
(18) The staff practices a variety of approaches and teaching styles. They are strongly individualistic and independent, but seek strong leadership.

The goal was to achieve these objectives for students in the school:

Basic Skills. (1) to increase and master basic learning skills (oral, listening, computational, reading, and writing); (2) to increase fundamental skills in observation and inquiry; (3) to learn to accept and cope with change; and (4) to acquire self-direction in learning, with increased use of learning resources (for example, instructional media and libraries).

Social Community. (1) to develop an understanding of, and an ability to relate effectively with, a broad spectrum of other people; (2) to develop an understanding of the cultural heritage and social forces that shape their lives; and (3) to develop an understanding of citizenship and a commitment to participate in governance.

Personal Development. (1) to acquire sufficient understanding of self and others to cope adequately with life demands; (2) to develop an appreciation of the aesthetic values of life; (3) to understand one's unique worth and capabilities, and to establish both realistic and satisfying personal and occupational goals; and (4) to increase self-motivation and purposeful behavior throughout life.

Ethical. (1) to stimulate ethical and moral sensitivity that values the common good, the rights of others, and a free society; (2) to understand, conserve, and appropriately use their physical environment; and (3) to achieve satisfying human relationships through the development of sympathy and skill in assisting others.[12]

Given these exacting expectations and the range of intense pressures under which a principal must work, it is hardly surprising that many principals feel inadequate. Many live in fear that a puff of wind will demolish the precarious house of cards over which they preside. Some resort to slavish duplication of the system's job description, seeking to shift responsibility for their behavior to the central office. Some play it safe and take their legal responsibilities more seriously than their educational obligations. Many see themselves as glorified plant managers who maintain order, maximize production, and minimize dissonance. And, like teachers, many feel guilty because they know they are not doing — and cannot do — what is expected of them. Few are able to shape the job as much as it shapes them.

All principals have had the experience of attending a meeting in the superintendent's office when a secretary enters the room with a note and a worried look. She surveys the room looking for the right principal. You get the sinking sensation that the note is for you, that it says "Call your school immediately," that whatever you most feared might happen has happened. I remember a meeting with four principals in my office when the phone rang; all four leaped to their feet. The fears and fantasies principals carry around with them are staggering. One policy for professional liability insurance for principals offers these benefits: "attorney's fees, bail bonds, personal property damage during student disorders, disability income for assault upon the insured, and death benefits." The principalship requires a cross between a renaissance person, an optimist, and a masochist. Few exist. It is not surprising that many school principals, after living with these realities for a number of years, stop trying — realizing it is neither possible to cope with the job nor to afford to leave it.

It is a difficult time to be an authority figure. And no one doubts that being a principal is a tough job. Yet one state reported two hundred twenty-five principals' openings and over fifteen thousand certified educators applying for the jobs. Two or three hundred applicants commonly apply for a single position. If the difficulties, conflicts, and discouragements of being a principal are pronounced, so must be the satisfactions. No other position in the educational system involves close work each day with children, teachers, and parents. No other position offers as much hope for having such a vital influence on the life of a school. It is this hope, along with many other benefits, that ensures a long line of candidates for any principal's opening and sustains principals in the daily struggles. These possibilities and satisfactions can, much of the time, get us through the long haul.

The Potential of Leadership

I would feel uncomfortable explaining what I have tried to do over the last decade in abstract theoretical terms; too much would be obscured. A more concrete place to start is perhaps with a summary written by a Harvard graduate student who observed me for one full day:

SHADOWING ROLAND BARTH ON APRIL 29

7:40 A.M.	One of the Angier School teachers gave Roland a ride to school after Roland had left his car at a garage to be repaired. Car conversation concerned basically non-school matters.
8:00-8:10	Stopped in teachers' room to exchange social pleasantries and to discuss some specific matters with individual teachers. At this time (and several times later in the day), Roland tried to allay the concerns of many teachers over the possibility that three first-year teachers may be dismissed as a result of staff cuts. He wanted to convey his belief that the list of teachers-to-be-cut which was published in a local newssheet misrepresented the situation. He feels confident that the three teachers in question will be on the staff next year.
8:15-8:45	Went over the day's calendar in his office. Began to go through huge pile of correspondence. Many letters concerned parental desires for their child's placement for the coming school year. Several interruptions by staff: custodian needs info on upcoming program; teacher comes in to discuss student teacher's capability in taking over a class during her absence. Roland assures the regular teacher that he and the teacher aide will also be around to lend some help if the student teacher runs into any trouble. A prospective teacher calls to set up an interview.
8:45	Art teacher brings in student who has been misbehaving in class. This meeting and others like it take place only after Roland has previously discussed the situation with the teacher. The student is told that she will be sent to the office to spend the rest of the period there if she acts up again. (Later in the morning, the art teacher mentioned to Roland how well-behaved the girl had been today.)
8:50	A student teacher supervisor from a nearby university stops by to chat.

8:55	Goes down the hall to see teacher about a child whose mother has agreed to seek psychological counseling. Roland and the teacher agree that the school and the parents are finally beginning to act cooperatively.
9:00-10:00	Attacks correspondence pile for a few minutes. Begins a series of phone calls regarding a proposal to hire another custodian in order to keep the school open later for community affairs, and the complaint of a parent about a bra-less teacher. For this last situation, Roland called the superintendent's office to find out what existing policy is and to clue them in on the situation. Roland decides that he will ask the parent to explain how the teacher's dress is affecting her child's learning.
10:00-10:10	Peggy, the combination teacher's aide-secretary-typist, comes in with three copies of a review of a book on open education which Roland had written for a magazine. He dictates a letter to the magazine's editor and then begins to proofread the review.
10:10-11:00	A prospective parent comes in to discuss enrolling her two sons. She has brought along the children's present teacher. The parent is very concerned about finding the optimal learning environment for her sons. Roland discusses the school's placement policy and accepts the parent's concern with statements like, "Well, it sounds as though the question is . . . " He calls in the school's psychologist to discuss placement. He recognizes that he might not be able to satisfy every demand of the parent, but the parent seems to recognize that perhaps she is asking too much. The meeting ends with the appearance that the parent will enroll her children.
11:00-11:30	Two parents from another school system come to talk to Roland about one of the Angier School teachers who is a finalist in a principal search. The teacher in question, however, barely is mentioned. The parents explore Roland's philosophy and practices and complain about the poor situation in their own school. As the parents leave, Roland mentions the great faith he has in the teacher who has applied for the principal's position.
11:30-12:15 P.M.	Several meetings between Roland, the psychologist, and some teachers regarding the progress and future placement of several students.
12:15-1:00	Teacher aide-typist comes in to help prepare materials for the faculty meeting. Roland sounds her out on a few of the items which will come up at the meeting that afternoon.
1:00-1:35	Secretary brings in a school lunch. A steady stream of teachers enters with information, discipline problems, and requests.

1:40	Roland begins faculty meeting[13] in the library. Except for some announcements, Roland each week gives responsibility for conducting the meeting to some faculty committee or group. Today's workshop was on race awareness. Almost all faculty members contributed freely and Roland was treated as a member, not as the leader, at least during this situation.
3:10	Roland made several announcements, all of which stressed his desire to foster collaborative action among the faculty. The last few minutes were devoted to details of an upcoming fire drill which another teacher explained.
3:30-4:45	Roland meets with a number of parents and teachers. He tries to follow through on important correspondence. He spends the last half-hour counseling a former teacher. He is then given a ride back to the garage to pick up his car.

There is more to say about leadership than simply "Shadowing Roland Barth on April 29." There are many theories of leadership, complex models by which outsiders explain the inner workings of complex organizations. In concrete situations, however, I find that leadership arises from the interaction between a person and a context. It is different every time. At this point I should like to stand back for a moment and reflect upon my personal views of school leadership — reflections less dignified than a theory, yet more coherent than a series of appointments on a daily calendar. Ultimately, I believe, leadership is best defined not by the leader, but by those the leader attempts to lead. Leadership is in the eyes of the led. A principal's firm, decisive formulation of rules for playground behavior, for example, will seem a "courageous" act of leadership to some, but others may see the same judgment as autocratic or even tyrannical. There is often nothing inherent in a decision that qualifies it as an act of leadership or a lack of leadership.

The Elements of Leadership

WORKING FOR INDIVIDUALIZATION

Administrators attempting to provide equitable treatment or "opportunity" search for policies that will work for everyone. When we find something that looks like such a policy, we engrave it in stone. I find the quest for a way that works for all teachers or all parents in a school no more realistic than a quest for a way that works for all children in a class. The only difference is that children are more likely to submit when it is imposed on them than adults. Group solution of individual problems leads to grouptalk and groupthink, to passive compliance and active resentment. Attempts to lead by achieving consensus may result in a majority of tired hands raised above tired heads late in an afternoon faculty meeting; but when everyone reappears in the morning, little remains of that consensus beyond a vote recorded in the minutes. To proceed as if lasting agreement exists on such a tenuous basis I find both hazardous and foolish.

For me, leadership has been a process of individualization rather than collectivization. If agreement genuinely emerges from discussions and debates, I will acknowledge it — in fact, I will delight in it. I prefer to assume there is no consensus on *anything* in a school, that each individual sees the world through a unique "Swiss cheese," and the holes in one person's Swiss cheese are congruent with the holes in someone else's about as often as the planets are aligned. Occasionally I am surprised; I am seldom disappointed. It was four years before I called for a vote in a faculty meeting. The issue was coffee. The result: some teachers wanted a common pot, some a machine; others wanted to bring their own instant coffee, tea, or soup and needed only hot water. Still others argued that coffee and tea were malnutritious drugs and should not be allowed in schools. No consensus! Teachers' feelings about education are at least as disparate as their feelings about coffee.

Rather than trying to find or create consensus, I derive greater satisfaction and success from constantly talking with individual teachers to find out what each needs — and how close I can come to fulfilling those needs. One teacher may want a principal to produce authoritarian efficiency and mandated rules and procedures. Another needs support for his or her own innovations with no interference. When I must make a general decision, I do it in a careful, limited fashion. I check my perceptions against those of others, such as the school psychologist or the coordinators. If my perceptions are at variance with theirs, I go back and talk to teachers some more. Then, if resolution is clearly needed, I try to make a decision that will affect as few, not as many, as possible. For me, then, leadership is a constant search for the unique conditions under which each person best works, learns, and grows, and for the means — within my own limits and the limits of the school system — to provide those conditions.

LEARNING WHICH PROBLEMS ARE PROBLEMS

I used to lament, "If only someone would take care of all these intrusive demands of the job — memos, budgets, parents, discipline — then I could be a great principal." Gradually I realized that I was acting like the teacher who moans, "If only someone would remove all the troubled, troublesome children from my class, I'd be a great teacher." In both cases the supposed obstacles to performing the job *are* the job. They represent not a barrier, but the means, the occasion for exercising good teaching and good administration. The task is somehow to come to terms with these difficult elements of the job and sort them out, not to pretend one can eliminate them.

When my wife and I first bought our rambling, running-down farm in Maine, we felt overwhelmed by the number of problems and tasks demanding immediate attention. We worked frantically, finding neither much fun nor much success. And friends who visited during that period have not returned. Over the years I have discovered a taxonomy of difficulties. A few problems go away if left alone (the irregular line of stone posts supporting the shed evened up after the spring frost heave); some problems will be taken care of by others if we do nothing (for several years I wondered what to do with the junked auto abandoned by the edge of our road; then one day it was gone); some problems remain but don't get worse (the ugly asphalt shingles someone nailed on the end of the barn); and some problems scream for repair, then become all but invisible as you get used to them (the cracks in the plaster of most of the ceilings in the house; indeed, some of them now suggest patterns the children love to identify before they go to sleep at night).

Some problems, on the other hand, present gnawing uncertainties, like a portion of the stone foundation in our cellar that buckles inward at a cataclysmic angle. I remember fifteen years ago predicting that the wall would collapse at any minute and bring the house down with it. To date, however, there has been no shift in either the wall or the house. I have discovered that the house sits on a generous $12'' \times 12''$ sill, supported in turn by a large intact section of granite wall, testimony to the overkill with which nineteenth-century craftsmen constructed their buildings. I have come to accept the advice of the elderly native who, giving the threatening wall a kick, muttered, "If it falls in, then you can fix it." Indeed, why spend a month working on a wall that may not need attention during my lifetime? Why risk creating new problems, like rupturing the sewage lines that pass through the wall? This kind of analysis of problems leaves time to attend to the real crises, the ones that *will* get worse if you leave them alone (the major leak in the barn roof, for instance).

Leading a school, I find too, is knowing — or guessing — which problems are which, learning to ignore the "maybe" problems and the cosmetic problems in order to come to terms with those that will grow more severe if we wait. Leadership is attempting to hold the flood of daily administrivia — forms to fill out, meetings to attend, reports to submit — at arm's length so that other important issues like staff organization, placement, evaluation of students, and staff development can be closely addressed. In some ways a school is a fragile house of cards but healthy institutions usually are as resilient as healthy people, and as capable of dealing with difficulty. Most schools are protected with as much structural redundancy as an old farmhouse. They have a life of their own that does not depend upon administrative coddling.

Learning to Wait

If we have learned anything about educational change over the years, it is that substantive, lasting change comes only with the personal growth of educators. Personal and institutional growth takes time. It has taken several years — a generation of elementary-school children — for the practices outlined in this book to emerge and develop. But waiting can be worthwhile. Even instability, friction, and conflict are worthwhile, as long as growth continues. We who work in schools need to have ideals, to keep our eyes on a star; we also need the patience to ask not "How far are we from the star?" (which can be a depressing and painful question), but rather "How much closer are we to the star today than we were last week?" The incremental growth of individuals, less dramatic than sudden institutional reform, is more satisfying and lasts longer.

LEARNING TO REDUCE FEAR

Leadership for me is reducing fear so that those in the school may grow. No one learns well under conditions of fear. A teacher described one such oppressive atmosphere in this way:

> There was fear between teachers and administration. The principal used to keep cumulative reports on the teachers; any time a teacher did something less than right, it was written down in one of her reports. The principal would stand at the door and note those who walked in late. The teachers didn't feel comfortable in going to her with a problem as that was a sign of weakness which might later be held against them. Besides that, she had a tendency to say one thing and do another, so the teachers were very uncomfortable about asking for help. There was also fear between teachers. A grapevine existed. A casual comment from one teacher to another soon brought a call from the principal asking about the comment. An atmosphere of dishonesty existed. Parents, too, were afraid to question the administration and as a consequence, school-parental communication was weak. There was also fear of the custodians. They completely controlled what could occur in the classroom. There was no eating, drinking, or painting in the rooms. Supplies were strictly controlled and very difficult to get. And this atmosphere of fear was passed on to the children. Rules had to be strictly enforced, and there had to be lots of them.

Each of us has personal fears — fears that cannot be eliminated. But a principal can reduce rather than contribute to the fears of others so they do not become debilitating. I am learning that there are incentives for improving teacher performance more desirable than fear. I am learning when to be a *conductor* of information from the world outside and when to be an *insulator*, shielding teachers and students from pressures. By and large, I think it is essential for teachers to know what is going on. Yet do they need to know things that produce great anxiety and little benefit? (Does it do a teacher any good to know that test scores for her class are lower this year than last? Does it help children to learn, to be told they will repeat fourth grade if they don't learn?)

I know schools characterized by high productivity and high anxiety (some elite preparatory schools, for instance); I know schools characterized by low productivity and low anxiety (many so-called free schools, for instance). All too many schools, of course, are characterized by high anxiety and low productivity, a losing combination all around. Leadership for me is attempting to establish within a school conditions of low anxiety and high productivity for both children and teachers.

Selective Risk Taking

Leadership is learning to recognize risks in which the odds are favorable and the stakes are high. There are times when we must assume we have authority, whether it has been explicitly bestowed upon us or not. There are times we must act as if we are running things — until someone proves otherwise. If we use responsibility successfully, the chances are we will not be challenged. If we don't, we've risked and lost. Fred M. Hechinger has described the process well:

> One of the key tenets of the "new" principal is "never ask permission" of the system. If it appears useful to ask some parents to come in and teach some classes — go ahead, without asking a bureaucrat who is likely to say "no." The "new" principal sees himself as an autonomous executive while the "old" considers himself a member of middle management taking orders from above.[14]

Faced with accountability on all sides, principals frequently must choose between, on the one hand, taking risks that violate established policies in order to provide what we believe is the right education for children and humane working conditions for teachers; and, on the other hand, minimizing risks by becoming cautious, sometimes almost catatonic. The former course offers educational responsibility with the danger of legal irresponsibility; the latter offers legal responsibility at the expense of educational responsibility. Unfortunately, legal and educational responsibility are not always congruent.

Selective risk taking is somewhat like working on an old car. I once asked a neighbor who was helping me rebuild the engine of a Model A Ford how much I should tighten a head nut. "Stop a quarter of a turn before you strip it," he said. I think this is an apt way to think about school administration. I want to stop a quarter of a turn before I strip the organizational nut. But, of course, I've got to strip a few before I know my strength, the mechanical advantage of the wrench, and how much the nut can withstand. It takes a while before I know exactly how far to turn. In the meantime, risks will be taken and nuts will be either too loose — or stripped. Schools are places where principals, too, can learn.

Independence and Interdependence

Many administrators exercise an authoritarian, hierarchical kind of leadership: they arrange schedules that mandate who is supposed to be where doing what and when; they make rounds to check who is doing what, when, and where; they maintain tight personal control over money, supplies, and behavior; they dictate curriculum, goals, and means. An inevitable consequence of this model of leadership — aside from a certain amount of order, productivity, and consonance — is the creation of a dependent relationship between principal and teacher. Teachers learn not to move without orders from the principal; the principal learns that he cannot leave "his" building without constantly fearing that it will disintegrate in his absence. This dependency training immobilizes teacher and principal, when both need maximum flexibility and mobility.

My experiences suggest that a school based on the work of dependent adults can do little beyond minimizing dissonance and maximizing order. It is doubtful that genuine growth and change can be achieved through authoritarian means. The route to real personal growth begins with the rejection of complete control. As George A. Miller has observed:

> You do not need complete authority over a social organization in order to reform it. The important thing is not to control the system but to understand it. Someone who has a valid conception of the system as a whole can often introduce relatively minor changes that have extensive consequence throughout the entire organization.[15]

Leadership for me has meant independence training for children, parents, teachers — and for myself. We must try to extricate ourselves from the old, restricting, paternalistic framework. Teachers become independent and effective when they are expected to examine and challenge the educational system, when they are encouraged to develop their own curricula, when they are able to make important decisions about instructional practices, and when they have a part in making school-wide decisions.

Fred Shero, coach of the Stanley Cup-finalist New York Rangers, suggests that similar conditions produce good hockey teams, as well:

> A lot of coaches think they're God. They're afraid to delegate responsibility and think that they have to do every little thing themselves. I believe you hire good people, give them the responsibility and then trust them to carry it out.[16]

Most principals have in their bottom drawer a few marbles of power that come with their appointment and even more that they earn as time goes by. Some principals play these marbles alone — they determine what happens. Others don't play at all, making few decisions themselves and allowing others to make even fewer. I try to play all the marbles all the time. Sometimes I play by myself (when I evaluate teachers, for instance); some marbles I give to others to play (like the teachers who serve as curriculum coordinators); and some I share with teachers (like disciplining children). None are left sitting around. I have found that in schools, as almost anywhere, some decision (even a bad one) is usually better than no decision at all.

I am finding that the alternative to centralized, authoritarian control is not anarchy but cooperation. Sharing the marbles of power, giving everyone an opportunity to make decisions affecting everyone else, promotes faculty interdependence. Administrators and teachers alike often suffer from loneliness and isolation. Many tasks in schools these days—helping disturbed children, coordinating curriculum, evaluating pupils—are too big, too complex, and too frightening for any one person to deal with. If we are to fulfill these tasks, we must collaborate. Even though members of a staff do not agree about all problems or solutions, we can accept, respect, and care about one another, and help one another work out solutions. I have tried to foster interdependence by encouraging teachers to work in pairs, by appointing coordinators, by setting up committees, and by encouraging parent volunteers. All these interactions move the adults in the school away from detachment and indifference. A cartoon I once saw showed two fishermen in a sinking dory, one saying to the other, "I'm sure glad the leak's in *your* end of the boat!" Leadership for me has meant trying to move the adults in the school away from that kind of detachment and indifference and toward the realization that we're all in the same boat together.

THE COSTS OF SHARING POWER

Relinquishing the marbles of power to parents or teachers or students can be risky. Power may be used by others in a way harmful to the school—or to the administrator. Moeller and Mahan have said it well: "It is against human nature to give up power to someone else, especially when one is likely to be held responsible for others' actions."[17] Or power may be unwelcome. To give up power may lead to being viewed as powerless. Curiously, the principal who shares responsibility will meet resistance from teachers who prefer to be told what to do, even though they complain about such directives. The authoritarian principal conveniently relieves such teachers of accountability for their actions. For them, an opportunity to make decisions is an opportunity to fail and to be blamed for failing. Sidney Morison, a public-school principal in New York City, has observed:

> Principals' motives are always suspect in such an authoritarian system as ours, and it is most unusual for a principal to give up any controls that might threaten his (or her) authority. Even in our setting, where I had indeed relinquished some control and where teachers were free to make certain internal decisions, they had reason to mistrust me because they felt cut off from, and suspicious of, the decision-making process. One would expect, then, that they would be eager to accept the challenge and participate in this process. But that was not the case.[18]

The principal who shares power may also meet opposition from the central office. In systems dominated by adversarial relationships, competition, fear, and power struggles, principals are frequently pressured to choose sides. The principal who shares responsibility is sometimes assumed by other administrators to have sided with teachers—and therefore to be against administrators. Thus the administrator who supports teachers' efforts places himself in double jeopardy: he is an administrator and therefore assumed by teachers to be an adversary; he is supportive of teachers and therefore assumed by other administrators to have gone over to the enemy.

Even though a principal may share responsibility with teachers, he alone remains accountable to state laws, parents, minimum-competency measures, school committees, and a dozen other forces. It is the principal, not teachers, who has to defend teachers' programs with gerbils to a PTA meeting, and teachers' orders for tongue depressors to the school board.

Teachers who assume major school responsibilities also pay a price. I used to think that administrators were supposed to get as much as possible out of teachers. But I have found that when they are given support and responsibility, teachers may exhaust themselves. Many become too conscientious. They take on too much and try to do it all. I now think that there is an optimal level of investment of teachers' time and energy. Teachers who do more very often become disillusioned, tired, and sick. It's a serious problem, and one that I never expected to encounter.

A professor of education who brought her class of graduate students—all practicing teachers—to observe the school one day noted:

> The commitment in terms of time and energy that is required for teachers to be decision-makers about what goes on in their classrooms is the issue that offered to us the most puzzle. We're always talking about wanting to be able to decide what to teach, when and to whom to teach it, as well as what materials to purchase in order to do the job. However, when we actually saw your school in which teachers do in fact have that freedom *and responsibility*, we wondered if maybe it wouldn't be better to be able to blame someone else rather than have to be inventive ourselves. With freedom does come more work, and teachers will have to find ways to conserve their energy and enthusiasm so they won't burn out.

THE REWARDS OF SHARED POWER

By and large we have found that we prefer the risks and problems of independence and interdependence to those that come with isolation and patriarchal dependency. Participating in the instructional and management decisions of the school encourages teachers to take pedagogical stands and to come to terms with major educational issues. In the process they become more conscious of their own ideas about children and learning. These beliefs, translated into classroom practice, are continually developed and refined. With responsibility comes active adulthood—

something many never find in their work. As one of our teachers observed:

> The message was that he expected us to be grown up. But part of us would
> have liked it if he had come in and treated us like children, given us orders,
> told us what to do, and how to do it. We have had to learn that when he
> said he wanted us to be grown up, he meant it. And we have grown up.

Perhaps most important, I have seen considerable evidence that teachers who become agents of their own teaching can better help children become agents of their own learning. Responsibility, once shared and accepted, creates endless ripple effects within a school.

What ultimately relieves teachers (and principal) from pressures and constraints from both outside and inside the school is their performance. When parents, community, and central office are satisfied with what a faculty is doing, they tend to leave everyone alone. Because most teachers make thoughtful use of responsibility, they earn more freedom. Competent, responsible, adult behavior is self-rewarding and self-perpetuating.

Sharing power within a school brings as many rewards for the principal as for teachers. I have discovered that it is possible to be adviser as well as supervisor; colleague as well as superior; supporter as well as adversary; provider as well as requirer. Acting and reacting in this way breaks down the rigid role stereotypes that normally limit school relationships. Indeed, I find less risk in sharing responsibility than in not sharing it, since those who participate in joint decisions (for instance, in our placement sessions) care about and are willing to defend the outcomes as much as I. In many respects, principals do not possess power *until* they share it. Only by engaging teachers, counselors, and parents in the placement decisions, for instance, can I have a powerful influence in the placement of children. Were I to attempt to place children by myself, the decisions would be neither thoughtful nor lasting.

In a school where faculty is vitally concerned with the outcomes of decisions, where teachers work cooperatively more often than competitively, the life of a principal can be rich and satisfying. My greatest enjoyment derives from important things that happen without me; for example, when two sixth-grade teachers decide to take their classes on an extended field trip for several days and make all the arrangements themselves. I'm intrigued by how little of me is necessary these days—not in terms of hours per week, but in terms of monitoring teachers, children, and their parents. While I have my share of horrendous days, in general I find things are going better and better with less and less direction from me.

Still, I don't feel superfluous. I can be a bit more thoughtful, reflective, and in control of my own behavior when I don't feel I have to control everybody else's. I can work on orchestrating the school, enlisting disparate parties toward commonly valued ends. I can develop different ways of responding to different people. I can be accessible to teachers, to parents, to children, in a human, direct way. I can identify and react quickly to situations in the school that, like the leak in the barn roof, will turn into disasters if not attended to immediately. These kinds of responses are not necessary for the day-to-day survival of a principal, but they are the stuff of which a viable school is made. They come only when the time is there to develop them.

What is leadership for me? It is personal and idiosyncratic. It is not a planned way of behaving; it is different ways of responding to different people. It is risk taking, but checking the odds for success before taking the risks. It is supporting people. It is being accessible. It is individualizing contacts. It is learning how to be firm and clear in expressing expectations; learning how to respond rapidly to situations in the school of which I disapprove or problems that will get worse if nothing is done. Leadership is learning how to share responsibility for decisions, and determining who should be included in those decisions. It is validating my perceptions with others and developing trust in their perceptions. It is being consistent in actions and statements, so that people realize I mean what I say. Leadership is learning that teachers hold much of the power that ultimately makes a school succeed or fail. Leadership is carefully relinquishing control so creative powers may be released. Leadership is trying to look freshly at every problem as it comes up and searching persistently for solutions. And finally, leadership is keeping head in the clouds, feet on the ground, and hoping like hell that it all works.

CHAPTER TEN

Promoting Principal Effectiveness

A leader is best
When people barely know that he exists,
Not so good when people obey and acclaim him,
Worst when they despise him.
"Fail to honor people,
They fail to honor you";
But of a good leader, who talks little,
When his work is done, his aim fulfilled,
They will all say, "We did this ourselves."

— Lao Tzu

THE MATTER OF what conditions promote effective school leadership is critical, more so now than at any time in the history of the profession. Paul L. Houts, director of publications for the National Association of Elementary Principals, has observed that "expectations for skilled educational leadership by principals are rising just at a point when principals feel least qualified to fulfill them."[1]

What factors determine the success or failure of a school principal? Although we have come a long way from such specific virtues as polished shoes and well-maintained playground equipment, where we are now is not exactly clear. The fact that one principal can succeed in a school where others have failed suggests that personal characteristics are crucial. The fact that a principal can succeed in one school but fail in another suggests that conditions within individual school communities can also be determinants. And the fact that most principals in one system are able to supply effective leadership while most in another cannot suggests that circumstances within different school systems can affect the quality of leadership.

My experience indicates that several conditions can inhibit or enhance a principal's effectiveness: the size of a school or district, the distribution of power, the unit of management, the ways in which principals are trained, and the availability of support systems to foster professional development. Each of these is so important that it deserves discussion in some detail.

Conditions That Influence Effectiveness

SCHOOL SIZE

One of the most obvious determinants of a principal's effectiveness is the size of the school. Small schools and systems, like small businesses, have been thought of as inefficient by traditional measures of cost effectiveness. Large schools and systems have appeared to offer broader, richer educational programs at a smaller per-pupil cost.[2] The assumption that larger size leads to better education has stimulated legislation discouraging small schools and rewarding or mandating consolidation. This effort has been the most widespread educational reform since the founding of public education. Over the past eighty years schools and systems have grown in size as fast as they have diminished in number.

But as John Pittenger, former commissioner of education in Pennsylvania, points out, the view of schools as more or less economical units of production is not without its costs:

> This tendency obscured . . . whether schools are (or ought to be) like factories; whether educating children is in any useful way comparable to manufacturing barbed wire.

Pittenger goes on to catalogue some of the debilitating, frequently unanticipated disadvantages of large school systems:

(1) Consolidation means busing, and rising energy costs have made busing a huge expense. In Pennsylvania, for instance, transportation costs increased from $30 million in 1960 to $150 million in 1975;

(2) Large systems have led to decreased effectiveness of school boards, by limiting participation from different communities and by increasing the psychological distance between school-board members and the schools they control;

(3) Size has led to decreased parent involvement in schools. Parents do not find it easy to attend PTA meetings or parent conferences when the school is ten or fifteen miles away;

(4) Size has affected teacher morale. Bigger schools and bigger districts make teachers feel they have less and less control over the conditions under which they work;

(5) Size aggravates student alienation. While big schools may serve the needs of the few students who are academically and athletically talented, they may not be equally good for the large numbers without these obvious talents;

(6) Size has led to administrative impotence. In theory, administrators gain power and control through consolidation and centralization. But, in fact, most superintendents and principals in large districts and large schools find themselves with less control and reduced effectiveness in their jobs.[3]

Large schools accentuate all the debilitating realities of the principalship discussed earlier: imbalance of authority and responsibility, isolation at the top, the time crunch, and the inability of many principals to be instructional leaders. Large systems do less damage to principal effectiveness than do large schools. There are many first-rate principals in medium-sized schools, even in huge districts like Chicago and New York City. But the principal responsible for a fifteen-hundred-pupil school, or for three or four schools whose students number in the thousands, is forced into being a manager of supplies, budgets, and personnel. These principals become, as one put it, "shufflers of bodies"; they have little time to influence children's education.

Schools with less than five hundred elementary pupils or fewer than two thousand high-school pupils can provide far better conditions, not only for the principal's effectiveness, but for teachers and students as well. For instance, after carefully surveying four thousand schools throughout the country, a recent National Institute of Education study[4] found that student violence, property loss, burglary, theft, vandalism, and arson was significantly lower in small schools than in bigger ones. Larger schools may be more economical enterprises, but they are less effective places of learning. And there is increasing question about just how economical they are.

Distribution of Power

A second factor that influences the principal's effectiveness is the distribution of authority and responsibility within the school system. Principals are most crippled when they must deal with a bureaucracy in which each administrative layer is preoccupied with monitoring and controlling the layers below. Large size lends itself to this kind of layered bureaucracy, where control of principals' and teachers' behavior is the object. Administrative structure of this sort is not restricted to cities; many small districts labor under a centralized, authoritarian administration. Indeed, an authoritarian structure in a small system where constant surveillance is possible can be more stifling than the anomie of a large district.

Authoritarian bureaucracies appear to feel compelled to specify and enforce similar expectations for all schools, principals, teachers, and students. Instead of genuine communication, there are sets of procedures, policies, and expectations descending from on high and complaints, confusions, and noncompliances rising from below. A parent, unhappy about her child's math program, complains to the teacher, who says that she too questions that particular text, but it is the one the principal has told her to use. The principal tells the parent that he, too, questions the math series, but it is what the system's mathematics director has determined all schools will use. And the director of math explains that the assistant superintendent for curriculum chose that series because it is cheapest, newest, and written to accommodate the "behavioral objectives" that the superintendent requires. And so it goes.

The principal in an authoritarian district is something of a middle manager, responsible for implementing the decisions of the school board and central administration. Under these conditions a principal can be more or less effective as a transmitter and as an enforcer. In the matter of responding to the instructional needs and opportunities that present themselves each day, however, he is an educational eunuch.

If large units are associated with principal ineffectiveness, and if centralized, authority-wielding bureaucracies are associated with principal ineffectiveness, large *and* authoritarian bureaucracies produce virtual incapacity. The compounded effect upon principals of school size and authoritarianism is suggested by the list of issues that emerged from a recent elementary principals' conference in one large, centrally directed school system. The issues raised are typical ones:

> Principals are feeling an impossible time pressure as they attempt to fulfill their duties. How can building administrators provide quality education for children when low-priority tasks from the central office constantly impede these efforts?
>
> Principals are unanimous in feeling a lack of fast, frank communication from within the system. What can be done to improve (as well as reduce) memoranda, directives, questionnaires, and forms?
>
> Three-quarters of the principals believe the system is characterized by superior/subordinate relationships. How can we begin to see fellow educators in the central office as colleagues, rather than bosses?
>
> Many principals report that important decisions affecting their schools are made in the central office, without their involvement. How can the thinking and wishes of principals be represented in these major areas?
>
> The climate of the system is one of authority and obedience. Principals feel the need to relate to the central office on another basis, one characterized by more confidence and mutual respect.
>
> Principals feel that almost daily, new demands are made of them, new duties are expected to be performed. With all of these new duties is there anything *less* we will be expected to do, any relief that will enable us to fulfill the new responsibilities?
>
> The principals' group feels there has been a serious deterioration in morale over the past three years. What can be done to improve this situation?

The report of a consultant to another moderate-sized, centrally controlled system implies further institutional malaise:

> It is not clear who has what role in the preparation and management of the annual budget.
>
> Role description of central-office personnel and school people are needed so everyone will know who is responsible for doing what.
>
> From private conversations with several individuals, it is clear that many feel others are not "doing their share."
>
> It is unclear who is responsible for evaluating teachers, particularly the specialists. Everyone seems to have a part of it, but no one is clearly responsible for pulling all the parts together. Teachers are confused, and so am I.

I find problems in the "delivery system." Materials, books, diagnosis of children's needs, testing, and provision of special services are not getting to the teachers who need them. And by the time they arrive, the child may have moved on, or the teacher has moved to another unit of study. Who is responsible for monitoring all of this?

Principals are frustrated that they are being held accountable for delivering goods and services to teachers, children, and their parents, yet their relationship with the central office does not give them sufficient authority to command the goods and services needed in their buildings when they need them.

Large, centrally directed schools and systems are attempts to run an essentially human enterprise, teaching and learning, in an essentially dehumanized way. It is not surprising that they fail. The message is depressingly clear: attempts to centralize control begat bureaucracy; bureaucracy begat job descriptions; job descriptions begat conflicts about who was supposed to do what; conflicts begat low morale; low morale begat ineffectiveness and inefficiency. The obvious alternative to large controlling bureaucracies is democratization and decentralization. We need smaller districts, smaller schools, and school site management. This last shifts the locus of many educational decisions from the central office to the individual school, from the superintendent and his staff to the principal, faculty, and parent community.

School Site Management

There is growing support for the individual school as the appropriate unit for educational change, and therefore the most appropriate unit of control. Pittenger, for instance, is convinced that "delegating more authority to the school principal and his/her teaching staff . . . is the single most important step we could take to counteract the weaknesses inherent in administrative centralizing."[5]

John I. Goodlad and his associates at UCLA have spent over a decade developing a League of Good Schools, on the premise that the individual elementary school controls the quality of education and should therefore control many important educational decisions on which that quality rests.[6] California Superintendent of Public Instruction Wilson Riles has identified the building principal and the school staff as the most promising source of influence and change and has wagered considerable state funds on this conviction. And educators from across the nation at one recent conference saw greater autonomy for individual schools as one of the few promising solutions to the problems that beset schools, school systems, and principals.

School site management, like most ideas in education, is hardly new. American schools were decentralized for far longer than they have been centralized. Except for the last fifty years, practitioners have run their own schools. Principals and teachers have been responsible for decisions about program, budget, and personnel. Only recently, with dramatic increases in population, expanding schools and districts, and increased local, state, and federal regulations, have schoolpeople been shut out of the important decision-making processes.

Now the idea of school site management, as it is currently called, is coming around again.[7] Of course, that is not sufficient to assure its implementation. The educational establishment is conservative and self-protecting, beset with inertia and caution. The occasion to shift educational responsibility back to individual schools is the occasion to take unknown risks with unknown stakes at unknown odds. Present conditions, if intolerable, are at least known. Resistance therefore comes from all quarters. Superintendents and school boards, accountable under state laws for providing specified educational services, already may feel impotent; they hardly welcome a reduction in power and control. Many are reluctant to give power to schoolpeople, feeling, as Joseph Featherstone puts it, that "autonomy granted to incompetents and petty tyrants can be a mixed blessing."[8] A number of central-office administrators are unable to accept the argument that a shift of responsibility is necessary, not because they are incompetent, but because the bureaucratic nature of their job determines that they cannot be effective.

Many principals fear a shift from a centralized bureaucratic system to a more decentralized one in which they must be leaders. They feel safer accounting to a remote, toothless bureaucracy than to local, toothy parents. Many worry about who will take power within the school community. Will parents control teacher hiring? organizing the staff? placing children into teachers' classes? Will teachers have the power to dismiss an incompetent principal?

Much apprehension is legitimately focused on the notion of "autonomy." It is a poor choice of word. In schools there is no such thing as autonomy. There cannot be. There should not be. No educator has unconditional control over what happens in a school, to other people's children, in a society full of other people upon whose support the educational enterprise rests. "Autonomy" is the wrong word, the wrong concept, for a discussion of school site management. Administrative decentralization is not a matter of determining who gets autonomy and who loses it, but rather how authority shall be distributed. The move toward school site management is a move to redistribute responsibility, to determine anew which responsibilities need to stay in the central office and which ought to be kept in the local school.

In my judgment individual schools should have *all* responsibilities unless there are strong reasons for the central office to handle them. I see valid reasons why the central office should continue to be responsible for research, for testing, for determining the amount of money allocated to each school, for seeking out highly qualified teaching applicants, for informing schools of local, state, and federal statues, for providing food and health services, and for coordinating material and personnel resources for the schools. I believe individual schools should select teachers, evaluate pupils, adopt curricula, and determine how appropriated funds are used. To my mind, this is a simple, logical division of power.

Principals seem ready to assume greater responsibility. One survey[9] asked elementary-school principals to indicate which of three descriptions best fitted their place in the school system:

(a) The principal is recognized publicly as the head of his school, with considerable authority to plan, organize, and administer the educational program in it.

(b) The principal is viewed as the administrative head of the school, assigned primarily to carry out the policies of the central office. He is given some encouragement to plan for his school community.

(c) The principal is neither encouraged nor authorized to proceed independently to alter his own school's program in any significant manner.

Of the twenty-four hundred principals who participated in the survey, 54 percent reported they were leaders, 41 percent reported they were supporters, and 5 percent reported they were followers. Clearly, half the American principals have considerable responsibility for school leadership — or at least think they do. Other countries have had substantial, successful experience with school site management. For example, the British educational system, discussed in Chapter 1, accords individual schools important responsibilities and supports them in exercising those responsibilities.

My primary experiences with local school decision making have been in Massachusetts, in the Newton public schools. This is not to suggest that Newton has achieved school site management or is even consciously working toward that end. Indeed, if anything, in recent years the pendulum seems to be swinging toward greater centralization. My point of reference is Newton because I am familiar with this system and because principals and teachers there traditionally have been vested with considerable authority and responsibility. Principals in other school districts undoubtedly could relate similar experiences; I can speak only from mine. The descriptions of Newton given in this book are selective, intended to document some of the educational consequences of local decision making. At times the accounts may appear idealistic or incomplete. They are. The reader may be assured that administrators and teachers within the Newton schools engage in their share of grumbling, griping, and groaning.

Newton, with about fifteen thousand pupils, is the fourth largest school system in Massachusetts. While large, it has somehow eluded many of the problems of bigness. There are two high schools and five junior highs. The twenty-two elementary schools, scattered among thirteen villages, average about three hundred students apiece. The small size of each school has overcome the large number of schools in maintaining a human scale. Each elementary school is a neighborhood school, to which almost all children can walk and to which a coherent community can relate.

Newton superintendents over the years have conveyed an implicit message to principals: "You have a building, a staff, three hundred pupils, a unique community, a budget, a set of curriculum guides for the system. Now you put them all together and make it work. Speak up if you need help." With this charge, the elementary schools have gone in twenty-two distinctive directions, each one reflecting the views, values, and personality of the principal; the strengths and weaknesses of the staff; the ethnic, racial, and economic characteristics of the neighborhood; and the needs and interests of the pupils. The instructional programs are remarkably diverse. Most currently fashionable modes of instruction—team teaching, nongrading, individualized instruction, programmed instruction, self-contained classrooms—are found in the district. Frequently, many of them can be found within a single school. Ideology has given way to practicality; uniformity to diversity. While the character of each school is idiosyncratic, by and large the quality is uniformly high. While means differ, the goals of good education are commonly held.

Like diversity within a school, the presence of disparate ideas and practices within a school system brings reflection and examination of practice, the challenge of goals and ideologies, and the cross-pollination of people, ideas, and methods. This often results in stimulating, ongoing, unplanned staff development.

Those most familiar with children and their needs—teachers, principals, and counselors—have major responsibility not only for identifying those needs, but for determining how they can best be met and for tracking down the necessary resources. Teachers are expected to use the system's curriculum guidelines unless they have developed their own and can show that theirs offer greater promise for them and their students—which, as we have seen, many do.

Relations between principal and teachers in general are mutually supportive. Relations between principals and central-office personnel, by and large, are collegial and cooperative, with those "above" supporting those "below," as well as making demands upon them. School faculties have a significant role in selecting principals. Not surprisingly, about half the new principals emerge from the system's teaching ranks and most are sympathetic to teachers, assisting and encouraging teacher growth as well as directing their performance.

The Newton system operates remarkably effectively, despite the marked differences among schools. Few mandates, policies, and procedures are handed down from above, and, curiously — despite the generally upper-middle-class community — relatively few problems concerning children and parents move from the individual school to the superintendent. Fires are usually put out where they occur, at the classroom level. For instance, a parent dissatisfied with her child's math program speaks to the teacher, whose likely response is, "What seems to be the problem? Is there a better way we can provide for Helen in mathematics? A different book? A different approach? Different peers to work with?" And the teacher makes some changes. Perhaps the most important consequence, then, of shared authority between the central office and the school is that schools become directly and immediately accountable to parents and students for the success of their efforts and methods. Local responsibility leads to local responsiveness. The teacher whose student is not learning math cannot pass the buck. When teachers have authority, they continually adapt and refine their instructional practices in response to what is happening to children in their classroom.

Clearly, the alternative to centralized, authoritarian control for a superintendent is not anarchy. The alternative is selective sharing. The central office that delegates responsibility to individual schools — like the principal who delegates responsibility to individual teachers — enlists the support of many professionals in determining and defending practices. The superintendent who does not make unilateral decisions is not faced with unilateral accountability. Superintendents who worry less about control often gain more real influence than those who attempt to influence by controlling.

Just as most teachers within a school respond to the combination of responsibility and clear limits with enthusiasm, maturity, commitment, and energy, so most principals within a district can be more effective under similar conditions. School practices represent a logical extension of district practices. I would not — nor could I — have carved out my role as principal in a context that provided neither the conditions nor the legitimacy for its development. Probably the most powerful determinant of a principal's effectiveness is the larger institutional context within which he works. School leadership is heavily influenced by the "culture" of the school system. The mores, the taboos, the overt and covert reward systems, and the quality of the personal relations are far more significant than the organizational chart on the wall of the school committee room. Just as the culture of the school has a far more powerful effect upon the growth of the faculty than contrived attempts at in-service training, so the culture of the system has a far greater influence upon the effective leadership of principals than administrative workshops. Most educators in most school systems have strong tendencies toward responsible, imaginative behavior. The question is how these tendencies may be acknowledged, legitimized, nurtured, and realized.

TRAINING OF PRINCIPALS

The culture of a school system cannot of itself ensure principals' effectiveness. Much depends upon the professional growth of capable principals. The pre-service preparation of principals by universities and school systems is usually ineffective. Despite university efforts to certify thousands of aspiring principals, their programs alone will never be sufficient—because no one knows what the principal will face until the situation presents itself. No one can anticipate which forces, which issues, which problems a particular principal in a particular school will find debilitating and which will be manageable. Most beginning principals probably agree with one of their colleagues completing her first year, who said, "My preparation for the job was woefully inadequate. There is no other way to describe it."[10]

The most effective pre-service preparation of principals takes place in schools, not in universities. Most of what principals must know is better learned under the roof of a school than by taking courses or reading books. If schools are to be well used as training grounds for future administrators, present principals must learn to recognize staff members with administrative potential and deliberately encourage and support them. Principals must see teachers with strong leadership characteristics as future colleagues rather than as present threats and share with them as much responsibility as both can manage in the day-to-day aspects of running the school.

We principals often find it hard to delegate or trust. But we can't do it all, and we certainly can't do it all well. Moreover, if we try to do it all, then no one else gets a chance to do any of it. That leaves fine people uninvolved in important aspects of the life of the school, and professionally unprepared when a principalship opens in the next school or the next town.

For several years an Angier teacher served as my assistant principal, although she was called primary coordinator. I couldn't have done my job nearly so well without her. For example, she was much better at making teachers' schedules than I. Had I insisted on doing the scheduling myself, because I was the principal and scheduling is supposed to be the principal's responsibility, the result would have been a time-consuming chore for me, poor schedules, and a missed opportunity for her.

When teachers with these kinds of administrative experiences are interviewed for principals' openings and asked what they would do in certain situations, they don't give hypothetical answers. They've been there. A lot of confidence develops when one has already dealt with the hassles that confront a principal. Prior experiences not only help able people land jobs but reduce their transitional anguish to a much shorter and less painful period. My former "assistant" is now an elementary principal.

When a new principal is appointed, everyone breathes a deep sigh. The central-office administrators are relieved because they can now say, "You were hired for the school because among hundreds of qualified applicants we felt you could do the job. Now do it." But this relief is (or should be) short-lived. Once the principal is on the job, he or she needs support and assistance. To school systems, in fact, pre-service training is far less vital than the professional development and renewal of practicing principals. Every principal—novice and veteran—is in and out of hot water all the time. These situations provide all the ingredients for personal and professional growth: difficulties, a context for resolving them, and a person who really wants them resolved. These moments of conflict and pain hold great potential for learning. What the principal needs is helpful, nonjudgmental, nonpunitive assistance in sorting out, reflecting upon, and sharpening professional practice. Unfortunately, what most principals find is at best benign neglect, at worst in-service training.

In-service training usually occurs when someone in the central office decides that principals in the district need to improve their teacher evaluations, curriculum development, budgeting techniques or whatever. All principals are then required to attend a course euphemistically called "professional development" an hour each week for six weeks. They may even receive some kind of credit. When it's over everyone feels virtuous and relieved. The only problem is that little has really changed.

Those who push in-service training on principals generally do so because they feel some principals are not doing their jobs well. They don't want to hear what *my* problems are; they want relief from *their* problems. They want to know why the test scores aren't higher. They want to know why parents don't seem to like the social-studies course. They are preoccupied with the discrepancy between what I am doing and what they want me to do, while I care mainly about the gap between what I am doing and what I want to be able to do. There is little connection between my needs and theirs; consequently, little personal or professional growth occurs.

In-service training should begin with the identification by principals, not superintendents, of areas in which principals need help. What do I do if two teachers across the hall from each other are constantly hassling each other? Do I talk to other teachers, the secretary, or the custodian about it? A course in faculty relations and a hundred books on administration aren't going to solve the problem for me either. I can talk to the two teachers, but what do I say to them? A principal needs helpful counsel in handling this and scores of other problems. Few principals have a support system, a group of other experienced and caring adults who can give them this kind of advice.

Principals, like teachers, need to learn to share problems without worrying about appearing inadequate. They need to feel that adult learning is legitimate. They need help in becoming more secure about their values, goals, ideas, and practices so they can act forcefully, consistently, and confidently. In short, they need to learn to act with authority, for only by doing so will they come to have authority. And all this learning requires a series of support systems: within the school, from other principals, from the central office, and from outside the system. Let us consider each in turn.

Support within the School

Every principal needs staff members in whom he can confide, people with whom he can bounce around ideas, problems, and solutions. Otherwise, only one person assesses situations, anticipates consequences, and formulates decisions — a perilous situation. A school-based support system is crucial, because it means that teachers are part of solutions as well as part of problems. Support from staff carries with it support from parents, students, and the central office.

One would think that in a staff of twenty or thirty, several close and nurturing relationships would emerge. But because personnel problems are often the toughest issues principals must confront, because there is always potentially an adversary relationship between union and management, helping relationships are difficult to establish and maintain. Sharing responsibility with staff members is a potent way to build collegial, interdependent, and supportive relationships between principal and teacher. I have already discussed how coordinators and committees foster relationships that legitimize discussion of many kinds of problems. Shared responsibilities can help move a school from "him versus us" to "we're all in this together."

Support from Other Principals

Principals also need support from one another. Many principals live in a climate of suspicion, mistrust, and competition among their colleagues in the system. Like teachers and students, principals compete for resources and recognition. They are judged not only by how well they do, but by how well they do in relation to other principals. Therefore, "smart" principals sometimes learn to hide successful ideas and practices. A taboo exists among principals against sharing either problem or solution. Public-school principals thus become parochial. How many principals have been observers in the schools of their colleagues within the past year? Incredibly, many have seen more schools in England than in their own districts. One woman who left the ranks of principals to become a consultant reported:

[I] discovered more about my peers than I had in seven years as a fellow principal. I realized how isolated we were from one another and how simple it was to break through this isolation. All it had taken was a genuine interest in finding out something real about the other person. For seven years, I had listened to these principals talk at our meetings and I didn't know them. In one and a half hours, I listened to them talk about their years as principals and I felt we were friends.

Unfortunately, few achieve this breakthrough — a monumental waste. Yet the potential is there. Like teachers, principals have a great capacity to stimulate professional growth and effective practice in their colleagues. Principals can help one another because they occupy the same rung on the bureaucratic ladder, deal with similar problems, face similar pressures, and evolve different solutions. Principals neither evaluate nor are evaluated by one another. And a fellow principal is always there; at almost any time of day, a principal may be quite sure that his colleague down the road is "in the building."

I have glimpsed the ability of principals to increase one another's effectiveness. For many years the Newton Elementary Principals Group has influenced to a remarkable degree both individual members and the system. The group annually elects a chairperson under whose leadership it meets two mornings a month. In addition, each of the twenty-two principals is assigned to one of three committees — Program, Personnel, or Business Services — that meet periodically to consider appropriate issues. The officers of the group and the chairpersons of the subcommittees constitute the executive committee, which meets twice a month to plan the agenda for the principals' meetings. Frequently the superintendent, curriculum coordinators, and budget directors are invited to address a specific topic at a meeting, or may request to do so. In addition, educators from outside the district — researchers, professors, state educational officials — have been invited to meet with the group. But the meetings belong to the principals; no one else may attend without executive committee approval.

The group often issues statements or makes proposals to the superintendent or to the school committee. For instance, after polling members to determine whether space was available, the group requested (and received) a marked increase in the number of black children bused into Newton from Boston through a voluntary program. Requests for budget increases in specific areas have been frequently initiated by the principals (and occasionally approved by the central office). The principals' group has made joint requests for assistance and materials from district curriculum coordinators. They have been heavily involved in screening candidates for principals' openings, developing teacher evaluation procedures, and planning a series of workshops to develop skills in supervising teachers.

In short, the principals' group paves a two-way street in which policy recommendations and innovative activities are initiated by principals for central-office response, as well as the other way around. The principals' group provides a means by which principals can collectively influence district policy and practice. In a sense, the principal of each school throughout the district is a "senator," representing teachers, pupils, and their parents. If and when this senate has the support of its constituents, and if the senators can agree among themselves, the group can exercise enormous influence, more so than any other single force in a school system. Like individual administrators, groups of principals have as much authority as they are willing to assume. In Newton the principals' group has been a creative vehicle for the development and exercise of authority.

An equally important outcome of the principals' group has been the support system it has provided its members. Exercising collective authority has brought principals closer together. There are times when each looks out for his own needs. On the other hand, principals have also found that each can often receive more of the needed resources if they act together than if they act competitively. Thus the group has fostered interdependence. When individual principals take responsibility for achieving certain things for the group, the members come to depend upon one another. Caring in one form leads to caring in another. A buddy system for principals new to the system has evolved, and a support group of new and experienced principals meets regularly. Many principals' meetings devote time to sharing common problems and promising solutions. Talking with colleagues about how they evaluate teachers, what limits they set, how they prepare budgets, or how they respond to parents at placement time, all help challenge and refine one's personal and professional behavior. Although principals desperately need support, they cannot depend upon others to hand it to them. Ultimately, the responsibility for developing a support system rests upon their own shoulders.

Support from the Central Administration

The relationship between central administration and school principal customarily is one of superior to subordinate. The typical central message from superintendent to principal is "Here's what I expect of you." The central question asked is "How well are you doing it?" This approach tends to close off communication, curtail trust, and inhibit rather than promote the professional growth of principals. However, the central administration of a school system can also become a valuable support system for principals. The Newton experience again is instructive. A central message from superintendent to principals has been:

> Though we provide services and supportive school programs, try to provide continuity in program through curriculum development and teacher

training, and monitor progress to the best of our ability through frequent visits to the schools, we still must depend primarily on the principal to maintain a valid program for each student in his school . . . [and] to set the tone in that school.[11]

The central questions asked of principals by the superintendent have been:

In what general direction do you as principal believe your school is going?

What specific goals have you and your staff set for this year?

What long-range goals have you established?

How can you and your staff determine the extent to which they are being met?

What are your major concerns this year?

What factors (personnel, program, plant, community) may serve to inhibit the attainment of goals you and your faculty have set for yourselves?

How can the Central Staff of the School Department help you with these problems?[12]

This statement and these questions stem from two core premises: that the principalship is a pivotal position in the school system, and that each school community is unique. When principal and staff are asked to determine the direction in which the school is moving and identify means for measuring progress, diversity is made legitimate. Problems may be addressed in diverse ways.

Furthermore, systematic feedback between the central office and principals has intrinsic merits. Central-office personnel sharpen their performance when they are evaluated by those most directly affected by it, just as principals improve when they are evaluated by their staffs. As the Newton superintendent has observed, "Such an assessment process works in both directions. The essential purpose is to create a climate in which people in schools are encouraged to look at themselves and where they are going . . . and to convey to us where we may be of some assistance to them."[13]

Few central-office administrators who have fought their way up the pecking order feel comfortable with the ambiguity and unpredictability of running a service agency for school principals. Yet central-office administrators in Newton have found that when they bring their power and resources to bear in support of principals, they are rewarded with increased principal effectiveness and educational quality. They find when the central office runs a service agency for principals, then principals are able to set up service agencies for teachers, and teachers for children. The "chain of command" can become a "chain of support." While support from the top is not required for principal effectiveness, principals can do a better job because of (rather than in spite of) efforts of the central office. This can be a source of considerable satisfaction for both principal and central administrator.

A central office can have an especially significant influence upon principals' behavior and effectiveness through the procedure it employs to evaluate principals. Principals as a rule try to comply with what is expected of them. If they are rated according to how well they carry out standard district policies, they are likely to try to carry them out. The district that rewards principals for sticking to a uniform curriculum will get a uniform curriculum. It is equally possible for a system to use its reward system to get divergent leadership, tailored to specific needs of individual schools. The Newton Guidelines for Evaluation of Principals reveal the system's leadership bias:

1. Program Leadership

Leadership in the administration of the school is most important. Teachers and other personnel wish to believe that progress is being made within the school, and in the school system as a whole. Most teachers look for challenges that will interest them, for activities connected with significant school problems, and for tangible results. In any organization people need to feel that they are part of a worthwhile endeavor.

Examples:

Seeks to define aims for the school and to have faculty members share in the search.

Secures the best people possible for the organization.

Works with the staff as a team, helping subordinates and others to improve their performance.

Makes known own position on relevant issues.

Works with individual staff members to improve instruction.

2. Relationships with Staff and Students

The principal has the task of establishing a school atmosphere and tone wherein all members of the school community can work effectively. People do their best work when they know what is expected of them and when they feel encouraged to assume responsibilities appropriate to their abilities.

Examples:

Evaluates and discusses each staff member's work in terms of school purposes.

Keeps faculty informed of policy and regulations of the school organization.

Encourages an atmosphere favorable to the voicing of ideas and opinions.

Provides opportunities for people and groups to discuss conflicts and to arrive at compromises.

3. Relationships with Parents and Community

The principal must see that the parents are well informed about the school's program and goals. Parents need to feel that their own ideas and concerns are heard and are taken into account.

The school can usually serve the wider community in many ways — educational, social, recreational — and the principal should be alert to such needs.

Examples:

Encourages an effective parent organization through which the educational aims, program and policies of the school may be interpreted to the public.

Recognizes possibilities for parent education and urges appropriate parent participation.

Seeks to have parents and others assist in the school's daily program.

. . . .

4. Operation of the School

One of the principal's tasks is to facilitate learning and teaching by operating the school in an efficient manner.

Examples:

Procedures

Is efficient in the scheduling of staff duties and use of school plant and equipment.

Maintains free and open channels for communication:
bulletins, meetings, and conferences.

Works cooperatively with other administrators in the school system.

. . . .

Budget

Uses the budget effectively to further the aims of the school.

Seeks to have faculty members participate in budget decisions and procedures.

Materials and Services

Makes readily accessible materials, equipment, and supplies.

Works with teachers to develop effective techniques for selection and use of good instructional materials.

Provides and encourages the use of a variety of resources — professional publications, consultants in special fields, committee resources.[14]

These criteria form a description of an effective principal, whose skills are at once idealistic and realistic, uniform and individualized. Nowhere is there a reference to "complies with district curriculum guides or policies, etc." It is not that the central-office people feel their policies are unimportant; rather, they recognize that other functions of a school principal are more important to effective leadership.

Support from Outside the System

External attempts to influence principal effectiveness have been largely limited to university courses and intervention by consultants, who tend to do crisis and patch-up work with only short-term, limited influence upon performance and little effect on fundamental growth. One promising exception has been the work of the Leadership Learning Cooperative in Lincoln, Massachusetts. This group focuses on questions like What kind of help do school principals need in developing effective leadership capabilities? How can this assistance be supplied? Unlike so many attempts to improve the performance of principals, LLC has been successful because its staff helps principals identify their own goals and find their own means of working toward them. The partners at LLC work on a "developmental" rather than a "deficiency" model of change. They start where their clients are, then move toward where principals want to go and are capable of going. LLC's developmental, imaginative approach fosters honest, highly motivated interactions. There is much to be said for an independent group providing this kind of assistance. An organization outside the school system does not threaten, since it has no responsibility to evaluate or judge. Even though many of its member school systems underwrite expenses for principals to work with LLC, it is with the understanding that everything said in the course of that work is confidential. As trust is established, principals reveal problems, fears, frustrations, fantasies—and begin to examine their own leadership. Appendix J gives some examples of LLC activities throughout New England.

In assessing my own participation in LLC, I have observed:

> Most people I talk with at school are potential (and actual) critics of me, what I do, and what I don't do—teachers, parents, children, higher administration. This reality (or at least my perception of it) is seldom conducive to a thoughtful, honest, ongoing examination by me of my place in this extremely complicated social institution. In fact, a defensive posture—the official posture of a public school principal—is not conducive to much of anything.
>
> So with whom does a school principal talk and ventilate in confidence, without threat, and with satisfaction? I find this kind of activity no incidental luxury but rather a professional and personal necessity. The opportunity has seldom been available for a series of periodic, systematic conferences with a thoughtful, noncritical, reflective, sympathetic "other" who is familiar with the constraints under which a school principal operates.
>
> Out of these many open, sharing, and risk-taking sessions many things have emerged for me—and continue to emerge. What is my leadership style? How have I handled recalcitrant teachers? How will I bring my school into a busing program? Discussions around these topics have helped

me to deal successfully with each. Perhaps more important, I feel I have become more self-conscious of my operating style as I have made these and scores of other ad hoc day-to-day decisions. This has helped me to anticipate with more precision the consequences of my decisions (and the process I use in arriving at these decisions) and thereby reduced the frequency of unwanted and unanticipated fall-out.

In addition, a mutual, thoughtful reflection on these issues has exposed for me a good deal about how certain personality characteristics of mine influence (interfere with/help) in decision making and providing leadership. I have found much to ponder over concerning such distinctions as: being firm and being rigid; being a leader and being directive; being angry and being hostile; facilitating and copping out; and being personal and being professional.

While LLC is firmly dedicated to developmental theories of leadership and organizational change, the group is unencumbered by traditional assumptions, goals, or methods. Although public-school systems cannot replicate the conditions under which LLC has worked so successfully, they can certainly borrow some of these refreshing ideas and methods — and maybe even some of the philosophy and values underlying this model — in providing support and assistance for their school principals.

How Important is the Principal?

I once worked with a group whose task it was to determine the importance of the school principal. To examine this question we decided to set it in a dramatic context, asking "What would happen if the principal were to disappear from your school tomorrow?" Our group generated a list of two dozen tasks normally fulfilled by the school principal — building management, community relations, curriculum development, staff evaluation, placement of children, and so on. We tried to sort these tasks into three categories:

(1) *The task is not essential.* The task exists because the principal exists. If there were no principal to deal with naughty kids sent to the office by teachers, naughty kids would be handled in the classroom or at home. Or maybe there would be no naughty kids. There were a few entries in this category.

(2) *The task is essential and someone else could do it.* Central-office administrators, individual teachers, or committees of teachers could hire teachers, prepare budgets, manage the building, do the scheduling. Most entries fell in this category.

(3) *Tasks the principal and only the principal could perform.* There were *no* entries in this category. We could not find a single function presently performed by the school principal that could not be either eliminated or performed by another employee of the system.

Eliminating principals is not just an imaginative exercise. Recently the Rye Neck district in New York operated for a year without principals. Their experience was sufficiently successful that they decided to eliminate the position from the educational organization. The superintendent said he had come to believe that "a principalship is a series of functions, and not necessarily a person." According to his plan, teachers, called "leaders," work in teams to fulfill that series of functions. Although the leader/teachers are paid extra, the plan saves the district thousands of dollars, at the same time giving the faculty a larger role in decision making. Perhaps it was this realization that principals might be dispensable that motivated New York City principals, who could have had year-long sabbaticals written into their contracts, to bargain instead for six-month sabbaticals. Many principals feared that if they left for a year they would be replaced or their positions eliminated.

The principal's position is tenuous indeed. Principals don't really have a clientele or a constituency that will function as their advocate. How many parents are going to be really upset if the principal leaves? How many teachers are going to protest? Will the school board resign in outrage? Parents and children care primarily about who the child's teacher is. "If you pull that teacher away," the parents say, "I'll scream and yell." But the community seldom sees the direct effect of an effective principal on the school. Leadership is often invisible. If the school seems to be running well, parents assume that school is as it should be. The principal often becomes visible only when things go wrong.

What would happen if the principal vanished? I would predict both positive and negative consequences. One advantage, in addition to saving money, might be development of greater faculty participation in the life of the school. The imperial model might give way to interdependence and a greater responsibility of each member for the welfare of the group and the institution. But there would be disadvantages as well. Many more decisions would be made by the central office, increasing the centralization of schools. And, as responsibilities were increasingly assumed by teachers and committees of teachers, less energy would be available for teaching. Evaluation of teachers would be difficult. The central office is too far removed to deal with teaching in individual classrooms, and teachers would be reluctant to evaluate their peers.

The most pronounced difficulty would probably be the absence of a single person at the top. Many decisions must be made in the course of each school day and children, parents, and teachers all want to know "who's in charge." They want it to be an identifiable person. A school could undoubtedly function under a league of teachers or parents, although organizations run by committees don't have good track records. Committees can analyze, make recommendations, and present majority and minority reports, but they can't make immediate, tough, controversial decisions. On the rare occasions when they do, their decisions are torn apart by their own members and by those whom they represent.

I have little patience with romantic critics who tell us that if only children, teachers, and parents could do what they want, everyone would live happily ever after. It is as simplistic to suppose that the problems of schools will be solved by liberating teachers from the "oppression" of administrators as it is to believe that children's learning problems can be solved by liberating them from the "oppression" of teachers. Both sound reasonable; neither happens to be true.

The question is not whether to abolish the principal's role. That has been done effectively in many school districts. Where the body remains, many central offices have succeeded all too well in creating "principal-proof" schools, leaving only subordinate middle managers. And with declining enrollment and increasing budget shortages, there is a renewed attempt to assign one principal to several schools, leaving even less possibility for principals to develop educational leadership. The question for many of the nation's schools is not an agonizing, "Should we get rid of an effective, responsible principalship?" The question is whether to abolish the title as well as the creative function.

In other places an alternative question is under consideration: "Should we have a principal whose work is worth the title?" In the way that many are beginning to view the individual school as the proper unit for educational change, many are looking to the principal to become the influential agent of change within that unit. Attention has shifted to the school principal because effective principals make better schools.[15] The able principal has the capacity to create conditions that elicit the best from most schoolpeople most of the time. Principals, more than anyone else, can insulate teachers from distracting, debilitating outside pressures so they may devote their precious energies to students. Principals can orchestrate the school's constellation of unique needs and resources so that most generally get what they need. And principals have the capacity to stimulate the growth of the school community, to lead by responding thoughtfully and purposefully to children, teachers, and parents.

The most important educational issue of the future is certain to be the most important educational issue of the past: how to improve the performance of the children who attend the public schools. Within the school there are two important influences upon children's performance: teachers, who work closely with children; and principals, who shape the environment in which children and teachers work. Three primary relationships within a school determine the quality of education: teacher to child; teacher to teacher; and teacher to principal. More and more educational theorists are learning that what teachers teach and what children learn, for better or for worse, is heavily influenced by the school principal. As one university observer discovered:

> What I personally came to see was something I have been fighting against for a long time: the leadership of the principal is important to the quality of the teacher-pupil relationship. I have wanted to believe that a teacher could make changes *alone*, with or without an effective principal. Perhaps so, but quantum leaps can be made if teachers see themselves as part of a whole, with a supportive leader.

This reluctant but inevitable realization has come to many educators. I have visited a large number of schools and worked in several, and I have found an unmistakable correlation between the way a principal works with faculty and the way teachers work with students. I'm not sure exactly what the dynamic is, or precisely how these effects are transmitted, but the relation between principal and teacher seems crucial to the educational process.

The salient question then is not whether to expel principals from the rolls of American education, but rather how to improve their effectiveness as educational leaders. The question is not whether to liberate schools from principals, but rather how to liberate principals from institutional constraints and provide conditions that will allow them to fulfill their potential for school leadership.

Even with the best of conditions—responsibility and support from teachers, central office, parents, and students—a principal may still botch it up. And, with the worst of conditions, some principals can still make it work for everyone. The personal and professional quality of the individual principal is, of course, at the root of effectiveness. Superintendents, teachers, parents, students, and school committees now realize that when they decide *who* is to be the next principal, they have effectively decided *how* the principal will do the job. Everyone knows that subsequent attempts to change a principal have limited effect. So incredibly elaborate selection processes are routinely launched, in which candidates must brave complex application procedures and a maze of exhausting interviews. The growing cry for teacher control of schools, for community control, for student rights, and for accountability suggests that many would like the principal's job. I don't believe it. I think few want the principal's job, but everyone wants to control how the principal does that job. Therefore everyone has a vital concern in the appointment of the right person.

People who want to influence what happens in schools are beginning to discover that one has to live under the roof of a school to have an influence on it. Those who are concerned about the quality of public education want to be closer to it and to teachers. And it is becoming evident that the principal is extraordinarily close to the educational epicenter. They see what effective principals have known all along — that it is not the critics or the central-office people or the university people who really make schools what they are. It is whoever occupies the principal's office. I'm encouraged that many of the most talented people I know in schools and universities are working hard to become principals. Serving as a school principal is becoming recognized as a legitimate occupation for capable people.

Afterthoughts

We are faced with insurmountable opportunities.

—Pogo

OVER THE PAST SIX YEARS—nearly a generation of elementary-school students—I have taken part in a school's passage through several developmental stages. We began those years with a belief that there was a One Best Pedagogy that all right-thinking people would follow. This rigid view was gradually transformed by the recognition of alternative points of view—open and traditional. Then came acceptance of variations of open and traditional. Now we see that there are as many different kinds of good classrooms in a school as there are good teachers. If anything distinguishes the school I have described, it is the diversity of teachers, teaching styles, and philosophies coexisting under the same roof, and the fact that somehow it works. In the midst of great differences, children and parents and schoolpeople grow and get along together most of the time. This has become for me and for other members of the school community a source of immense satisfaction.

I began to write this book hoping that a somewhat ordered account of events, excitements, perturbations, and satisfactions by one school practitioner might be useful to others. But the writing has been more of an education for me than I could have imagined. Many of us who are educators appear to operate from incident to incident, day to day, year to year, without a coherent philosophy. Many of us even believe we have no philosophy. And indeed many may have no philosophy. Still, an examination of what we do and say suggests that some sort of underlying rationale lies behind most of our day-to-day activities and decisions.

Philosophies arise in various ways. Some are formed out of reading

217

and reflection and the attempt to live and practice what has been created in the mind. For me — and I suspect for many schoolpeople — philosophy more often emerges pragmatically from being placed in a problematic situation with whatever values, goals, and know-how one has and trying as best one can to get the job done. From time to time, if we have the opportunity, we sit down and think about what we did, and how, and why — and what we wish we had done. I am now beginning to think that I have more of a philosophy of school leadership in me — yet to be developed — than I had supposed. It has been the occasion to write that has made elements of my personal philosophy, long buried, more explicit for me.

As a principal I learned early that diversity is a fact of school life. Variability of people can be masked over, driven under, acknowledged, or cultivated, but it cannot be legislated or administrated away. I have learned that some minimum, uniform standards are essential for an institution to function — and survive. And I have learned of the productive problems and fruitful consequences that come from honoring diversity in educational method. I have tilted toward pluralism, diversity, and individuality rather than orthodoxy, uniformity, and collectivism; I am beginning to understand why. I now see clearly that there is much more to school administration and school effectiveness than "requiring" in some places and "allowing" in others. That is only the beginning. Enlisting and assisting the diverse parties involved in the life of a school — teachers, parents, students — in a coalition each member of which respects that same diversity in others, is a larger part of making the process work. The life of pluralistic institutions rests upon the recognition that respect for any person's uniqueness and integrity depends upon that person's honoring all others in the same way. The democratization of a school, then, like the success of a classroom, emerges from a careful, deliberate balance between structure and lack of structure.

As much as those of us at Angier have learned, as far as we have come, I don't feel we are "there." In education if you think you're there, you don't know where you are. All of us, especially in this day of upsets and assaults on tradition, and confusion about personal and institutional direction, are engaged in a perpetual process of becoming. I feel the next developmental stage in the evolution of a pluralistic school — the one most difficult to attain — is the recognition that effective teaching is a function not only of honoring teacher idiosyncracy, philosophy, conviction, and preference but of its appropriateness and suitability to the learning characteristics of each child. This is a stage dominated by the teacher's question, "Am I doing it this way for me or for the student?" It is a stage in which children are matched with teachers *and* teachers adapt their instruction to children. Evolution from adult-centeredness to child-centeredness probably comes only with considerable personal security and the skills of keen introspection and careful observation of children. I am beginning to see signs that this more altruistic stage may logically follow the steps we have already taken.

Institutions, like individuals, pass through critical life stages: birth, growth, decay, and death. Schools contain seeds of both self-regeneration and self-destruction. The source of most of the problems that afflict schools lies within the schools themselves—in the quality of their human relationships. And the source of most solutions resides within the schools as well. We have passed through a decade or more during which policy debates on schools reflected the macro themes of large-scale, quantitative social science. The macro realm of public policy is important; we've learned a good deal about the systemic constraints on schools—the effects of race, social class, and inequality. Yet much macro talk is counsel of despair. If the system is to change, where do we begin? The macro realm only sets the stage. What goes on the stage occurs at the school level.

I believe the important educational advances of the future will not come from new technologies, alternatives to standardized tests, the institution or abolishment of behavioral objectives, or refinement of minimum competencies. Significant change in schools will come from a reweaving of the lives of pupil, teacher, principal, and parent into a richer social fabric. Significant change will come with a measure of self-determination for schools and the independence and interdependence of individuals within schools. Change will come when we learn to establish conditions within schools that will help schoolpeople welcome responsibility and use it wisely.

A fundamental purpose of public education is to prepare children to live in a pluralistic society. A good way to prepare for social diversity is to learn to live with it early, in an approximation of a pluralistic society where differences are acknowledged, respected, and used to advantage. If teachers, principals, and parents can acknowledge and value personal authenticity and accept the accompanying differences, I think we will all find more success and satisfaction than if uniform standards and compliant behavior remain the dominant characteristics of education. Uniformity in schools is usually associated with stability; diversity with instability. My experience suggests that schools can be both diverse and stable, and that a dynamically stable diversity is the best condition of all.

Appendixes
Notes
Selected Bibliography
Index

A Comparison of Young Pupils in Single-Grade and Multigrade Classes

Vincent Silluzio's paper, "A Study of Kindergarten and First Grade Children in Multi and Single Grade Classes" (Newton School Department, 1977, pp. 1-2), reveals these findings:

(1) Newton primary-grade students developed skills in reading, mathematics, word analysis, and listening equally well whether assigned to K-1 or to single-grade classes.

(2) The number of years spent in multigrade classes had no effect on the development of basic skills. Students in multigrade classes for one, two, or three years between kindergarten and grade three developed skills at a rate no different from students who had been in only single-grade classes during the same period.

(3) Basic skill development in multigrade classes did not depend on the amount of experience the teacher had had with this type of class. Classes taught by teachers with no multigrade experience did as well as classes taught by experienced multigrade teachers.

(4) Neither multigrade nor single-grade classes favored one sex over the other in reading achievement. Boys and girls developed skills equally well regardless of the type of classroom to which they were assigned.

(5) In reading, first-grade students in K-1 classes from lower socioeconomic backgrounds achieved significantly higher than students from similar backgrounds in grade-one-only classes. This significant difference persisted through grade two, but disappeared by the end of grade three. In all other skills measured, children from similar socioeconomic backgrounds in K-1 and single-grade classes did not differ in achievement.

(6) Students in both multigrade and single-grade classes had strong, positive feelings about school. However, after completing one year in kindergarten-first-grade combination classes, first-grade children had significantly less positive school attitudes than first-grade children in single-grade classes. Most of these attitude differences were only temporary. When tested two years later with the same instruments and by the same investigator, most of these attitude differences were no longer significant.

(7) The results of sixty-one teacher interviews showed that teachers with multigrade experience tended to favor multigrade classes, teachers with no multigrade experience tended to favor single-grade classes.

Examples of Teachers' Curriculum Outlines

CURRICULUM OUTLINE K-1-2 CLASS Mr. Roche
Mrs. Porter-Englehart

The educational program for the K-1-2 is designed to provide maximum opportunity for each child to respond creatively to the learning environment. The foundation of the curriculum is the conviction that the development of certain skills is essential to the learning process, and that this development will proceed according to the individual needs of every child. The environment, which provides free access to a wide variety of materials, allows for and encourages continuous and integrated learning involving diverse subject matter and disciplines. The materials presented for discovery and exploration are a combination of predetermined, teacher-developed subject matter and skill programs, and child-initiated interests and questions.

Even though the curriculum will be flexible and constantly expanding, there will be a developing theme throughout the year. The focus will be to help each child develop a positive awareness of the total environment through observation, experimentation, and discussion. Basic development of skills and tools will also be related to creative experiences within the individual's expanding awareness, making further understanding possible. By pursuing this curriculum the desired results for each individual could be identified as follows:

(1) An appreciation of some of the realities in our environment including the usefulness of the natural environment to humans. (We shall begin by studying "color"—its properties, its presence in the natural environ-

225

ment such as seasons, animals, its impact upon the emotions and imaginations of the individual. Following this will be an investigation of shapes—observation of their presence in nature, awareness of the natural origins of man-made shapes, the usefulness of shapes in developing tools for continued learning such as geometry and measurement. The third phase of this part of the curriculum will be an exploration of movement in nature—possibly a study of the universe or solar system, the sea, the life cycle of animals and their environment, and some understanding of man's application of these ideas to his own creations—the construction of some simple machines, electricity.)

(2) The development of a positive self-image by establishing an understanding of the importance of the individual and his relation to everything in the environment. (Here we shall need to explore the five senses of the human being, and other physical characteristics as well as emotional responses. This will necessitate an attempt to become aware of and try to understand "you" as well as "me.")

(3) A positive acceptance of differences in the environment with particular emphasis on one individual's relationship with others. During this evaluation of differences each child will hopefully be able to begin to establish for himself the relevance of everything in the world from a vantage point of expanded positive awareness.

(4) We are aware of and appreciate the importance for creating a special sense of unity and security within the context of our environment for our ten kindergarten-aged children, and look forward to participating jointly with a variety of group experiences, designed for this purpose.

(5) For children who are continuing their educational experiences in the described environment, we look forward to assisting them with continued growth and more in-depth experiences.

The following lists by subject areas are indicative of some of the directions we expect to follow during the year, understanding that each child's individual pursuits will probably not include all of this material.

Reading and Language Arts: The goal is to help each child to develop the skills he can master which will open to him the world of the printed word and effective verbal and written communication.

Letter recognition: upper and lower case
Development of sequential thinking
Letter sequence and alphabetizing
Color names and recognition
Visual discrimination and rhyming words
Development of skill in oral communication
Development of an interest in creative writing
Comprehension of stories
Individualized reading programs utilizing both basal reading texts and independent reading books, including practice in phonics skills and the development of sight vocabulary

Making of books, creative writing and illustrating; sharing with peers

Dictating stories and poems as a group and individually

Group experience charts

Alphabet, vocabulary, and phonics games

Group experiences such as listening to stories read aloud, discussions of pictures, theater games, writing and performing of plays and puppet shows, dramatic interpretations of stories and poetry, sharing of ideas and experiences

Reading of: signs which ask questions, provide information, give directions, and announce special projects; cooking recipes

Instruction in the writing of letters and continual practice through the recording of experiments and observations, the writing of stories, poems, and songs, the development of phonics skills, completion of crossword puzzles, keeping a daily diary

Use of the typewriter, printing sets, and tape recorders

Instruction in the use of resource material to assist children to use the printed word to find answers to their questions.

Mathematics: Through an emphasis upon manipulative materials (chips, Dienes blocks, Cuisenaire rods, pattern blocks, Attribute blocks, cards, tangrams, geo-boards, balances, scales, dice, Mirror cards) each child is helped to develop his analytical and quantitative abilities and concurrent computational skills.

Recognition of shapes, patterns, numerals, number sequence, number-numeral relationship, parts of the whole (fractions)

Categorization

One-to-one correspondence

Concept of set (classifying and sorting)

Combinations of sets

Concepts of addition and subtraction

Equality and inequality of sets

Calendar skills

Weighing and measuring

Money

Place value

Concepts of greater than-less than, bigger-smaller, before-after, and between

Relationship of structure, balance, symmetry

Addends to 10 or 20

Computational skills using equations and symbols (x, $+$, $-$, $=$, box, etc.)

Graphs

Through games each child develops his abstract thinking abilities in both independent and group situations. A catalogue of games would be cumbersome here, but a sampling might be useful: checkers, chess, Kalah, Wari, Attribute blocks, lottos of all kinds, cards, dice, construction, balance, and a wide variety of strategy games.

Science: Our aim is to increase each child's awareness of his environment through specific observation and exploration of the world around him.

The seasons: weather, climate, and temperature; their effect upon the life cycles of trees, plants, and animals; pollution; ecology

Planting of seeds, bulbs, slips

Animals: the habits of and care for animals in the classroom (guinea pigs, fish, and ????); collections and observations of wild animals and insects (spiders, caterpillars, ants, frogs, toads, and ????); studying animals' environments, habits, and life cycles

The sea and sea life

Machines: study and construction of simple machines (pulleys, levers, gears)

Electrical circuits

Magnets

Magnification

Weighing and balancing

Application of scientific principles in the exploration of colors and solutions, shapes, construction, recipes

The five senses

Solar system

Social Studies: Special emphasis is placed upon increasing one's awareness of self and one's own feelings, and relating them to the needs and feelings of others—individually and in groups.

Ability to work out one's own social encounters in the family, school, neighborhood, and greater community

An awareness of other cultures and ethnic groups

Exploration of geographic distances, maps, map-making

Music and Movement: Music is an integral part of the classroom environment. A record player, rhythm instruments, piano, and tape recorder are available for children's use. Almost daily participation is encouraged to help develop musical feeling and internalization of rhythms.

Development of gross motor skills

Exploring the expression of feelings, thoughts, moods, dramatics, story and poetry telling and interpretation through body movement, singing, and simple instruments

Singing and learning of new songs

Introduction to composition

Introduction to musical notations

Listening to and making use of a wide variety of sounds including environmental, electronic, and self-made ones

Art: A wide variety of art activities is always available in the classroom, supplemented by frequent special projects. Considerable use is made of "junk" in creative endeavors.

Paper products: construction, tissue, preglued and crepe paper; corrugation and cardboard; boxes and tubes; papier mache

Paint: tempera, finger, watercolors

Crayons, craypas, chalk, colored pencils, sugar-water chalk, ink, printing

Plaster-of-paris, plasticene, clay, playdough

Material, yarn, ribbon, plastic film, styrofoam, string

Instruction is provided in weaving (individual looms, floor looms), braiding, and sewing

Construction projects are encouraged in building, making of puppets, and creating from boxes

Experimentation and expression of feelings is encouraged in all projects

CURRICULUM OUTLINE   5-6 CLASS   Mr. Weisenfreund

Language Arts: The general goal of the language arts curriculum is that each child be able to send and receive, both orally and in writing, the eight types of discourses that make up all our speech and writing:

(1) True stories (biography, autobiography, chronicle, reportage, etc.)
(2) Made-up stories (fiction, fables, tales, poetry)
(3) Conversation (oral improvisation, discussion, play acting)
(4) Information (generalized facts)
(5) Directions
(6) Labels and captions (words used in conjunction with pictures, graphs, maps, etc.)
(7) Word play (rhyme, rhythm, puns, riddles, tongue twisters, poetic manipulation of sound and sense, crossword puzzles, etc.)
(8) Ideas (generalized opinion and statement, theory)

These goals will be manifest in the full-length book selections which will be required each week, weekly and daily writing assignments, oral reading and group discussion of material presented, newspaper and periodical reading, discussion of current events, monthly research reports, weekly book projects, and daily entries in personal diaries.

There will be emphasis on proofreading, on vocabulary building, spelling, and accurate punctuation.

You can encourage your child to choose and read books at his/her level at home, to read aloud to the family.

Math: The math curriculum will include:

Emphasis on place value

Reading numbers through 1,000,000

Writing numbers through 1,000,000

Mastery of multiplication facts up to 12 x 12, and related division facts

Multiplication with one-, two-, and three-digit multipliers

Division using one- and two-place divisors

Addition: mastery of facts from 1-10; column addition of five-digit numbers

Subtraction: mastery of borrowing; subtraction of five figures

Decimal fractions—meaning, operations, naming

Bar and line graphs

Scale measure—accurate plotting with a ruler
Perimeter
Area
Word problem solving
Use of compass and protractor
Vocabulary—geometric terms, quantitative terms
Number bases

Children will work as individuals, in small groups, and as a whole class. They will be encouraged to think logically and creatively in a math medium, to see more vividly elementary math concepts and spatial relationships, and to appreciate the use of math in their daily lives.

All students will be required to focus on the mastery of the four operations on whole numbers. There will be periodic quizzes and tests to identify strengths and weaknesses in these areas.

In addition to regularly planned, teacher-directed lessons in academic subject areas, each Wednesday each child will begin a weekly "contract." Each contract (whether prepared by the student or the teacher) *must* include: reading a book, completing a book project, a writing experience, a creative project, a math reinforcement or enrichment activity, and some ongoing work in an interest area. The interest areas will include science projects (planting, cooking, physical science experiments, human body systems, astronomy, etc.), social studies projects (map skills, current affairs, economics, geography, American history, etc.), and, for some students, penmanship practice, spelling activities, and the like.

Students will take an active part in the decision-making process, especially as regards the use of time. The contract system builds in a clear record of progress, as each child increases his ability to deal with a variety of choices.

In evaluating individual student progress, answers to the following questions will become important:

Do the students talk with each other about their work?

Do they initiate activities which are new to the classroom?

Do they persist over a period of days, weeks, or months on things that capture their interest?

Do they demonstrate real interests of their own?

Are they able to say, "I don't know," with the expectation that they are going to do something about finding out?

Do they exhibit any initiative, have they developed any skill, in finding out what they want to know?

Do they continue to wonder?

Can they deal with differences of opinion or differences in results on a reasonably objective basis, without being completely swayed by considerations of social status?

Are they capable of intense involvement? Do they demonstrate a passion-
ate commitment to anything?

Do they display a sense of humor which can find expression in relation to
things which are important to them?

Do they continue to explore things which are not assigned—outside of
school as well as within?

Can they afford to make mistakes freely and profit from them? Do they
challenge ideas and interpretations with the purpose of reaching deeper
understandings?

Your questions, comments, and concerns are welcome at any time. Please
feel free to visit the classroom at ANY TIME, or call me at home.

A Typical Angier Greensheet

[The Greensheet, so named because it is reproduced on green paper, is a weekly newsletter for students, faculty, and parents that is compiled and issued by parents.]

November 22, 1976

ANGIER ENGLISH COMMITTEE

For several years I have felt a piece missing in discussions between school and home. This piece has to do with curriculum. Classroom teachers discuss with parents each fall their curriculum outlines for the year. Twice a year we hold parent conferences during which curriculum is frequently discussed in terms of a child's progress. From time to time the PTA arranges a program around a particular area—for instance, the math meeting which took place last week. These meetings tend to focus a good deal of attention and concern on an area for a brief time, and they are over.

The missing piece, I believe, is an occasion for parents and school personnel to engage in periodic, sustained discussion about what is taught here and how it is taught—at the same time enlisting the assistance of the many parents in the community to help us better provide for our children.

I have suggested to the Angier faculty and to the PTA Board that we establish an Angier English Committee as the first of many possible subject-area committees. The purpose of this committee will be to provide a regular forum for discussion between staff and parents about the teaching of English and to help identify and provide resources from the community to further enrich and strengthen Angier's

English program. I am delighted that Ellie Hackett (whose credentials in English are well known to readers of this periodical) has agreed to chair this committee. Ruth Elkins, Barbara Feldstein, Debby Horwitz, and I will also serve on the committee. We invite parents interested in English at Angier (and willing to make a sustained commitment) to join us. We hope that you will return the tear-off at the bottom of this letter.

We have no "erector set" plans for this committee. Thus far Ellie and I have agreed:
•That the world has enough—more than enough—committees already. If the response to this idea initially (or later on) is not strong, the committee will be abolished.
•That the continued life of this committee will be reassessed at the end of the year. If tangible results do not emerge, the committee will not continue.
•That the committee will meet for one or two hours once a month at times and places to be announced in the Greensheet beginning with the first meeting, Monday, December 13th, at 3:15. Most of the meetings will be held after school on Monday or Wednesday afternoon.
•That all meetings of the committee will be open.
•That while this committee may be influential, it will not make decisions about what to teach and how to teach it at Angier. These responsibilities are delegated by the School Committee to the Newton professional staff. We cannot, even if we wanted to, abdicate them by conveying them to parents, children, or anyone else.

Thus the Angier English Committee is a trial balloon which may or may not fly and may or may not serve a useful purpose for parents and the school. Let's try it and see what happens.

Roland

A FEW MORE WORDS ABOUT THE NASCENT ANGIER ENGLISH COMMITTEE

My credentials are limited to being reasonably articulate, conversant enough with the rudiments of grammar to diagram a sentence, and able to use a dictionary to check my spelling. I am, nonetheless, a concerned and active parent. I pray that the written word will not become obsolete in the foreseeable future. If it continues to live, I would like to see it used effectively by my children and my children's children.

Maybe if each of us thinks about what we consider important in a language-arts curriculum and about what we are willing to do to implement the best possible English program at Angier, we may have some influence. If you have anything to say on subjects from spelling to sentence structure, from oratory to original Haiku, from semicolon to sonnet, from acting to adverb, from reading to reciting, or from calligraphy to careful creativity—you name it—please return the sheet below to the Greensheet box. I guarantee that our first job as a committee will be to look through your responses and comments. I would like to be able to speak for you, so please return the form below to ensure that I will have some things to say. If for any reason you would rather not sign, please return the form anyway. We can only be influential if we (1) speak up and (2) listen.

Ellie Hackett

____I would like to serve on the Angier English Committee.

____I am unable to serve as a regular member, but I am interested and would like to attend meetings from time to time.

____I am unable to attend meetings, but am interested in English at Angier and would like to make a contribution in some other way.

Some things about which I am concerned and which I would like to have discussed are:

NAME_____PHONE_____

OUR NEXT BOOK DISCUSSION MEETING WILL BE HELD ON THURSDAY, DECEMBER 16, at 10:15 in the library. The book to be discussed is *Tuck Everlasting* by Natalie Babbitt. It is available in a paperback edition published by Bantam. There are also copies available in the library. It's a provocative book. We look forward to discussing it with you.

Barbara, Gail, Gini, and Irene

IF YOU GUESSED THAT JACK MCLEOD'S FATHER IS JACK MCLEOD, formerly principal of Warren Junior High and now principal of the Bowen School in Newton, you were correct. Now try this one: Which teacher has a son twelve years old, a daughter two years old, a spouse who is also a teacher, and a master's degree in community organization? Additional hint: This teacher has taught children in grades K, 1, 2, 3, 4, 5, 6, 7, and 8.

Roland

PLEASE CHECK THE PARENT BULLETIN BOARD WHEN YOU PASS THROUGH SCHOOL. There are all sorts of notices of activities from skating to fine arts and crafts demonstrations—offerings of the Newton Recreational Department and the Newton Free Library.

MISSING—ONE PAIR OF NEW TAN HIGH-TOP BOY'S SHOES—SIZE 2½ They have the initials ALB inside. Please call 123-4567 (Blankenship) if found.

METCO COORDINATOR NAMED

Ulysses G. Shelton, Jr., was appointed coordinator of the Metco Program in Newton by the School Committee on November 8th, on the recommendation of Superintendent of Newton Public Schools Aaron Fink. Mr. Shelton will coordinate the program for the 350 Metco children attending 26 Newton schools. He began his new job last Monday.

LOST—CURLY-HAIRED FEMALE WELSH TERRIER WITH TAN HEAD AND FEET AND

black body, about 14" high, short tail, floppy ears, whitish (because of cataracts) eyes. Answers to Gwyneth. Has Fanwood, New Jersey, dog license number 143. Last seen south of Beacon Street in Waban. Reward.

Gwyneth's Owner
234-5678

FOR SALE: GIRL'S BANANA SEAT BICYCLE

Excellent condition, very reasonable price. Light green in color. If interested, please call

Mrs. Zucker
345-6789

FOR SALE: CB RADIO!!

Mark Leibovich, Room B, has won a PACE CB 144 radio as a raffle prize. Although valued at over $120 retail, he will sell it for $100. If interested, please call

Mark Leibovich
456-7890

THERE IS A NEWTON SCHOOL POLICY ON THE ADMINISTRATION OF MEDICINES

in the schools. If you have any questions about the policy, please consult your Angier handbook or pick up a copy of the rules and regulations from Ann Finnelli in the office.

NEW FAMILIES NIGHT

Mark your calendar now for this meeting on Tuesday, December 14, at 7:30 P.M. This meeting is planned for parents to talk with teachers and Roland Barth about how we feel about Angier. This is an opportunity to have various questions answered. We look forward to meeting you.

George and Pat Piper

THE NEXT MEETING OF THE NUTRITION COMMITTEE WILL TAKE PLACE

at 1:30, Tuesday, November 23. All interested parents and teachers are invited to join us. There will be a series of nutrition workshops at Horace Mann School, especially for parents. They will deal with basic nutrition, nutrient labeling, and nutrition for children. The workshops will take place on three successive Tuesday mornings—November 30, December 7, and December 14—from 10 until 12. If you would like to participate, please call me at 567-8901 by Tuesday, November 23.

Bev Blicher

THANKSGIVING RECESS BEGINS ON WEDNESDAY, NOVEMBER 24TH, AT NOON.
SCHOOL RESUMES MONDAY MORNING, NOVEMBER 29TH. HAPPY THANKSGIVING!!

NO SNOWBALLS

At a recent faculty meeting, the staff adopted a new snowball policy for the Angier School. Throwing snow anywhere on school grounds during the school day is not permitted unless this activity occurs under the direct supervision of the classroom teacher.

IF MS. STEELE'S FIFTH-GRADE CLASS IS STRINGING YOU UP

with their string figures, it is all because Wilma Klass (under the aegis of the Creative Arts Committee) showed them this popular activity of Alaskan children on November 12th. If you need information on Alaska, contact the fifth graders in Room 17.

Gloria Smith

THE PTA PROGRAM COMMITTEE WANTS TO HEAR FROM YOU.

Please share your reactions to last Monday's math meeting. What did you think of the format? Do you have any suggestions for future programs? Send your comments to the PTA box in the office or call me.

Judy Freedman
678-9012

TEST YOUR KNOWLEDGE ABOUT THE PAST PRESIDENTS OF

the United States. Try the quiz in the library.

GREENSHEET PRESSES WILL BE SILENT FOR A WEEK. NEXT GREENSHEET 12/6.

APPENDIX D

PTA Questionnaire
to Evaluate Angier School

[This letter and questionnaire were sent to Angier parents. A similar set of materials was distributed to Angier graduates attending junior high school.]

Dear Parents:

As discussed with you on the telephone recently, the Angier School PTA would like to assess the transition from elementary to junior high school, and the areas of elementary curriculum strength and weakness by asking some recent graduates and their parents about their experiences at Angier School. Toward this end we are asking both you and your child to complete the enclosed anonymous questionnaires. You will notice that the questionnaires inquire about specific curriculum areas and general impressions. We are truly interested in both, and should you wish to comment at greater length, please feel free to do so. The results of this survey will be published in the Greensheet before the end of this school year.

It is our feeling that a school "community" exists not only for those currently in attendance, but for yesterday's and tomorrow's students and their families as well. Consistent with this feeling, it is our expectation that the results of the survey will provide an interesting and informative perspective to present Angier parents, and will also be of some help in the school's evaluation of curriculum and the effectiveness of parent/teacher communications.

We are most appreciative of the effort you and your child are putting into this

endeavor. Should you have any questions about the questionnaire, please call.*
Thank you once again.

Very truly yours,

Pat and George Piper
Presidents, Angier School PTA

*Direct all questions to _____

PARENT QUESTIONNAIRE

Please answer the following questions by checking the appropriate spaces. Feel
free to comment on any of the items, and/or to attach any written comments you
care to make.

[For questions 1-7, parents were given the option of checking Satisfied, Somewhat Satisfied, Somewhat Dissatisfied, Dissatisfied, or Does Not Apply.]

Applies to Angier School

1. Communication with principal

   a. Responsive to parental concerns
   b. Resolution of parental concerns

2. Communication with teachers

   a. Responsive to parental concerns
   b. Resolution of parental concerns
   c. My child's evaluation conference
   d. My child's evaluation report

3. Communication with support staff
   (i.e., special teachers, psychologists, coordinators)

   a. Responsive to parental concerns
   b. Resolution of parental concerns
   c. My child's evaluation conference
   d. My child's evaluation report

4. My child's achievement in the
   following skills

   a. Writing
   b. Reading
   c. Mathematics

5. My child's knowledge or appreciation of the following subjects

   a. Science
   b. History
   c. Geography
   d. Music
   e. Art

6. My child's

   a. Ability to think through
      a problem
   b. General study habits
   c. Acceptance of responsibility
      for his school work
   d. Sense of personal initiative

7. The amount of homework my child
   receives

   a. If dissatisfied, is the amount
      too much ( )
      too little ( )

[For question 8 the choices of answer were More Emphasis, Same, Less Emphasis, or Don't Know.]

8. How much emphasis should be placed on the following educational goals at the elementary school level?

   a. Achievement in:
      (1) Writing
      (2) Reading
      (3) Mathematics

   b. Knowledge/appreciation of:
      (1) Science
      (2) History
      (3) Geography
      (4) Music
      (5) Art

   c. Learning about current events
   d. Learning to get along with other children
   e. Broadening of interests
   f. Gaining a sense of independence
   g. Developing a sense of self-discipline
   h. Other_____
      _____

9. What did you consider the major strength of Angier School?_____
   _____

10. What did you consider the major weakness of Angier School?_____
    _____

11. Do you feel that periodic questionnaires like this are useful? Yes____No____

Suggested Ways
to Help Your Child at Home

Concord (Massachusetts) Public Schools, 1970

Learning is a cooperative venture involving parent, child, and teacher. At school the child does required work under teacher supervision. In order for learning to be a continuous process, children do need home study. This means helping a child set reasonable goals and giving him a time and a place to study. Parent interest will be the cohesive factor in promoting voluntary home study. The following is a list of activities that may be undertaken to help your child at home.

(1) Help your child learn to follow directions.

(2) Help your child develop listening skills.

(3) Discuss varied topics with your child to help him develop critical thinking skills.

(4) Encourage your child to be aware of current events, newspapers, magazines, and TV news programs.

(5) Suggest projects which enrich science and social studies.

(6) Hear your child practice oral reports.

(7) Help your child develop proofreading skills.

(8) Have your child practice number facts and other arithmetic skills.

(9) Help your child use the library.

(10) Play games to develop reading, vocabulary, map skills, arithmetic skills, etc.

(11) Develop vocabulary by giving your child a new word to use each day.

(12) Encourage your child to seek a pen pal.

(13) Help your child learn to summarize the main idea of a book, a story, or a TV program.

Guidelines for Discussion at Parent-Teacher Conferences

Concord (Massachusetts) Public Schools, 1970

PARENTS' GUIDELINES

Knowing the relationships a child has with his environment at home or in the neighborhood can give the teacher a great deal of insight into the child's social and academic adjustment at school. With this in mind, would you consider the following points in preparation for your conferences with your child's teachers. Please remember that this is not necessarily an outline for the conference. Topics will be discussed only as parents or teachers feel they apply to the particular child. It is hoped that the conference will be an exchange of information on the part of both parent and teacher.

I. Social adjustment of the child
    A. How the child sees himself
    B. The child's relationships with other children
    C. The child's relationships with adults
    D. Acceptance of individual responsibilities
    E. Characteristics that might affect school performance

II. Adjustment to academic tasks
    A. Attitudes and work habits
    B. Motivation
    C. Skills in independent situations
    D. Skills in group situations

III. Academic performance in relation to self or total group
   A. Progress in skills areas
   B. Performance in other academic areas
   C. Specific suggestions for improvement

IV. Physical problems
   A. Temporary
   B. Permanent

V. Possibilities for home enrichment

GENERAL INFORMATION ON CONFERENCES [FOR TEACHERS]

(1) It is an emotional and factual exchange to fill in knowledge and to offer special knowledge.

(2) Listen completely to what the child or parents have to say. Make no judgment or interpretation. Do not jump to conclusions.

(3) Never label a child, even in a joking way.

(4) Never mention another child by name or give information about other children.

(5) Avoid giving personal opinions.

(6) Use professional experiences as samples. Avoid using personal experiences.

(7) Keep an open mind about the validity of your own judgment.

(8) *Do not give false reassurance.*

(9) Do not give suggestions without a good understanding of the child and his situation.

(10) No one has all the answers. Make referrals to the social worker, the school nurse, the family physician, or other appropriate resources.

(11) The parent-teacher-child conference can be a valuable tool when used correctly. It requires a thorough knowledge of the parent and the child, however. In considering such a conference the teacher should consider carefully the feelings of the child and the predictable outcomes. If such a conference seems likely to put the child in the middle, it should not be held.

(12) The manner in which the teacher marks the daily work also reflects the philosophy to which the system is committed. Papers are diagnostic devices and judgments made regarding their quality indicate their positive rather than negative value.

(13) *Be observant*—What he says. What he doesn't say. What significant gaps there are in the conversation. Body tension. Excitement. Dejection.

(14) *Be a good listener*—Begin with child's or parent's concerns and interests. Let them express themselves first. Indicate your understanding by brief comments and significant questions. Parents may reveal their anger or dissatisfaction with the child's school experience. Listen carefully. Give explanations and facts. Do not take sides.

(15) *To Question*—the central method of conferences is the fine art of questioning:

The wording of the question is often less important than the manner and tone of voice in which it is put.

Do not ask too many or too few questions.

Ask questions in order to understand and be of assistance, to obtain specific information, and to keep the conference going.

Keep pace with the child or parents. Don't push for information. Do not try to get all the information from one conference.

(16) *To Talk*—Talk to reassure, to encourage, to explain, to offer information, to give answers.

Answer personal questions in a frank, brief, truthful way. This should be followed by an immediate redirection of the child's or parent's attention back to the conference.

Support positive feelings, reduce misunderstanding, and discourage unrealistic expectations.

(17) *To Conclude*—"Maybe my answer wasn't clear to you." "Is there something else you wish to ask/talk about?"

Parents often ask, "What do you think we can do?" Sometimes it is well to answer, "What do you think you can do?" thereby involving the parents in planning and decision making.

Teachers and parents should see eye to eye on their goals and should be completely comfortable with one another, and noncompetitive.

Plans must be realistic to the child's and parents' ability and capacity to carry them out.

Do not give suggestions when the child or parents is/are unable to act upon them.

(18) *To Summarize—Keep the Academic, Social, and Physical in mind.*

Where did the child/parents agree with what the teacher said?
Where disagree?
What did the child/parents say with the most feeling?
To what did the child/parents show no response?
What did the child/parents want to talk about most?

How did the child/parent explain the child's school performance?
What do the parents expect of the child in school?
What did the child/parents suggest should be done by the parents, the teachers, and the child?
How is the teacher's view the same or different from the parents?
What intellectual and social stimulations are provided for the child at home?

Evaluation of the Nontenured Teacher

Newton (Massachusetts) Public Schools

Date_____197___

Teacher_____School_____

Subject, grade, or position_____

Started teaching in Newton_____197___

I. Instructional Competence   SATISFACTORY   UNSATISFACTORY

   A. *Planning and preparation*   ☐   ☐
      General observations_____

      Suggestions for improvement_____

   B. *Learning environment*   ☐   ☐
      General observations_____

      Suggestions for improvement_____

   C. *Methodology*   ☐   ☐
      General observations_____

      Suggestions for improvement_____

	SATISFACTORY	UNSATISFACTORY

D. *Subject matter*   ☐   ☐
General observations_____

_____

Suggestions for improvement_____

_____

II. Professional Characteristics

A. *Quality of relationships*   ☐   ☐
General observations_____

_____

Suggestions for improvement_____

_____

B. *Professional growth*   ☐   ☐
General observations_____

_____

Suggestions for improvement_____

_____

C. *Managerial responsibilities*   ☐   ☐
General observations_____

_____

Suggestions for improvement_____

_____

RECOMMENDATION (Check either 1 or 2)

(1) A position for the teacher is available
next year in this school or division, and
my recommendation follows:

Should the teacher be given:

	yes	no
(a) a first annual appointment (for teachers here only part of the year)?		
(b) a first annual reappointment?		
(c) a second annual reappointment?		
(d) appointment to tenure?		

(2) A position is not available in this school
or division, therefore no recommendation
on reappointment can be made.   ☐

Comments:_____

_____

Signed_____Position_____
School_____Date_____

Signature of teacher_____

(The signature does not indicate agreement or disagreement with the content of the report.)

Communication Inventory
for Supervisor

[Of the forty-eight items included in the original communication inventory, a representative sampling is given here. The inventory was distributed by the Brookline (Massachusetts) Public Schools in 1970.]

Name_____ School_____

Directions: Please read each question carefully. Indicate your honest answer by placing a check mark under the *yes* or *no*. Please answer every question.

YES   NO

( )   ( )   Do you generally find talking with your supervisor an enjoyable experience?

( )   ( )   Does your supervisor talk too much?

( )   ( )   Is your supervisor the type of person who does *not* welcome your suggestions?

( )   ( )   Is your supervisor as willing to compliment you for good work as he is to find fault with your mistakes?

( )   ( )   Does your supervisor realize the problems and difficulties that confront you in carrying out your responsibilities?

( )   ( )   When you make a mistake, does your supervisor—in a pleasant and constructive way—tell you how you can avoid such mistakes in the future?

( ) ( )   Does your supervisor make you feel that you are an important person?

( ) ( )   When you talk with your supervisor, do you generally have the feeling that you end up discussing only those things that he is interested in?

( ) ( )   When you are dealing with your supervisor on a problem, does he have the ability to ask questions that get at the heart of the matter?

( ) ( )   Does your supervisor usually keep you informed about how you are doing?

( ) ( )   Is your supervisor always finding fault with you?

( ) ( )   Can you depend on your supervisor doing what he says he will do?

( ) ( )   When you have something rather difficult to discuss, does your supervisor make it easy for you to say what's on your mind?

( ) ( )   When you want to talk with your supervisor, does he usually give you the opportunity to do so?

( ) ( )   Does your supervisor practice what he preaches?

( ) ( )   Does your supervisor usually admit it when he is wrong?

APPENDIX I
Principals and Their Duties

[Portions of a resolution adopted by the Newton (Massachusetts) School Committee on September 22, 1975.]

Sec. 9   Principals shall be responsible to and serve under the direction of the Superintendent.

Sec. 10   Principals shall be the chief supervisory and administrative officers in their respective buildings.

Sec. 11   Subject to the rules and action of the Committee and the supervision of the Superintendent, principals shall in their respective buildings and school districts:

  (a)   supervise instruction and special services;

  (b)   organize and supervise curriculum and its improvement within the limits prescribed by state regulations and School Committee policy;

  (c)   assign, supervise, and evaluate teachers;

  (d)   provide supervision of students;

  (e)   supervise the keeping of enrollment, attendance, and other records, and preparation of reports;

  (f)   supervise clerical and building service personnel;

  (g)   supervise grounds, buildings, and appurtenances of their schools;

  (h)   cause the proper officials to investigate and report on cases of truancy;

  (i)   make requisition in writing at such times as designated for necessary books, supplies, and equipment;

(j)   keep an inventory of books, supplies, and equipment;

(k)   exercise a watchful care over all school property;

(l)   prepare budget pursuant to the instructions of the Superintendent or his delegate;

(m)   promulgate regulations affecting traffic at and near the school and transportation of pupils, consistent with applicable ordinances and advice of the Police Department and contracts for bus transportation;

(n)   supervise observance of and compliance with the rules of the Newton Board of Health applicable to the schools.

Learning Activities Offered by the LLC

[This material is based on private correspondence with Barry C. Jentz and Joan W. Wofford, partners in the Leadership and Learning Cooperative, Lincoln, Massachusetts. The LLC is further described in their book, *Leadership and Learning: Personal Change in a Professional Setting* (New York: McGraw-Hill, 1979).]

We think about the learning activities we offer in two broad categories: long-term activities (a year or more in length) and short-term activities (less than a year).

Long-Term Activities

These activities are of three kinds: interdistrict groups, professional growth consultation with individual leaders, individual and group consultation work in school systems.

INTERDISTRICT GROUPS: Two examples of interdistrict groups, made up of individual administrators from different systems, are:

Examining Organizational Tasks and Processes. Seven principals from 4 districts met to examine how they use their time during the school year. Members mapped their calendars a year in advance; examined the discrepancy between the anticipated use of time and the unexpected events that conflicted; practiced setting priorities; and created new ways of responding to the unexpected events.

Learning about Your Performance as a Leader. Seven principals from 6 districts designed a survey instrument to collect information from their faculties about how teachers see them offering leadership in their buildings.

In all, 240 staff responded to a questionnaire in the 6 elementary schools and one junior high school, and 40 teachers were interviewed. The data collected in each school were organized and reported back to the principals and their staffs, and mechanisms were created to allow for a continuing flow of information to the principals about the staffs' perception of their leadership.

PROFESSIONAL GROWTH CONSULTATION: The professional growth consultation is a regular bimonthly meeting between a leader and an LLC consultant in the leader's school or office. These consultations provide the leader with an opportunity: (1) to examine his or her practice and the assumptions that inform it; and (2) to formulate and try out alternative ways of responding to day-to-day events. A "case" example follows:

The Case of Ms. C

Ms. C is in her early forties and has been principal for five years. The school is large (500 pupils) and old (1927). Ms. C sees her leadership as "affiliatory," not "autocratic," and values child-centered teachers, flexibility, consensus decisions, openness, and a rational search for and explanation of behavior.

Mrs. M teaches grade one, and has been in the school for twenty-two years. She has worked under two previous male principals. She runs a "structured" class, values goodness, cleanliness, order, work over play, the two-parent home, and male authority figures.

Ms. C wants Mrs. M to change. Her strategies have included encouraging Mrs. M to talk in faculty meetings, visiting her classroom, making positive comments about what she sees there, suggesting new materials and procedures, and placing a teacher aide in the room part time. Mrs. M has countered. She does not talk in faculty meetings and never voluntarily initiates a conversation with her principal. When Ms. C enters her classroom, Mrs. M immediately leaves whatever she is doing and stands by her desk. Mrs. M talks with other teachers about the good old days when you "knew the rules."

Ms. C and the LLC consultant talk in a series of bimonthly meetings over a period of a year and a half. Ms. C is frustrated by her attempts to "move" Mrs. M. She is ashamed of her "failure." If she were a good administrator, she would know how to deal with the Mrs. M's of her school. She has used up all her alternatives, all those learned from books, previous courses, and workshops. No one in her district helps. Ms. C makes some "learnings":

•Talking out loud about her problem seems to help her think of some other alternatives for Mrs. M. She talks privately with Mrs. M and shares some of the frustration.

•She discovers that many teachers do not understand her particular leadership style and are waiting to hear about her expectations. She begins to accept that some teachers need to "be told."

•She finds herself thinking about the good things that have happened in the school under her tenure. She becomes less defensive about being young, a woman, and childless.

•She discovers that she has been expecting Mrs. M to make all the changes; she begins to see that some changes will begin within herself.

•She learns that some teachers find her autocratic because she has insisted upon a consensus decision-making process. She begins to question some of her underlying assumptions about leadership.

•She begins a process of separation—of seeing the world from a number of different perspectives. She separates those values she shares with Mrs. M— such as children learning to read, a sense of order, and a genuine caring for children—from those that divide them. She can now support Mrs. M from her sense of shared values and still insist upon some changes.

•She separates decisions; some she makes herself quickly and efficiently, and others that affect teachers are taken to faculty meetings for joint deliberations.

•She begins to value thinking about her job, and to understand that changes for Mrs. M and for herself will come slowly and quietly.

INDIVIDUAL AND GROUP CONSULTATION WORK IN SCHOOL SYSTEMS: The focus here is on working simultaneously with members of different parts of the administrative hierarchy, individually and in groups. An example is:

System X

A. *Administrative Staff.* LLC attended regular bimonthly meetings of the senior administrators and helped them analyze their organizational problem-solving, decision-making, and communication processes, and engaged them in inventing and practicing new forms of dialogue.

B. *Professional Growth Consultations.* LLC met monthly with each administrator to help him/her examine and respond in new ways to administrative problems located in a particular setting.

C. *Third-Party Intervention.* LLC enabled two administrators who were locked in a debilitating conflict to meet together in a series of four sessions over two months and work through the conflict.

D. *Workshops and Courses.* LLC developed and ran for 17 principals meeting bimonthly a skill training course in the evaluation of tenured teachers. LLC developed a system for evaluating a new budget system, collected information, and fed it back in a two-day workshop.

E. *Mediation and Negotiation:* LLC mediated a dispute between a principal and faculty and met with Teachers Association representatives, School Committee, faculty factions, and central administration.

Short-Term Activities

Short-term activities vary enormously in form and content. A few illustrations follow:

Principal Effectiveness Survey. Using LLC's Principal Effectiveness Survey model, the principal/superintendent and the chairman of the School Committee of this high school distributed a case questionnaire to the faculty, designed to provide the principal/superintendent with information about how the staff sees him offering leadership. LLC collated the data and wrote a report to the principal and staff.

Leadership in a Time of Decline. LLC led a one-day workshop for 100 elementary principals at an annual conference, focused on what leadership strategies are called for in a time of retrenchment.

Sexism in Schools. LLC led a one-day meeting at a week-long Title IX-financed conference where 60 teachers and administrators examined the evidence and consequences of sexism in their school system.

Conflict Management. LLC met in a concentrated series of meetings with three self-identified central office administrators whose interpersonal conflicts were undermining the superintendent's expectation that they would work together.

Notes

Chapter 1 Uniformity and Diversity

1. David B. Tyack, *The One Best System: A History of American Urban Education* (Cambridge, Massachusetts: Harvard University Press, 1974).

2. See Roland S. Barth, "Teaching—The Way It Is/The Way It Could Be," *Grade Teacher* 87 (1970):98-101.

3. "Report to the School Committee" by Aaron Fink, superintendent of the Newton (Massachusetts) public schools, June 26, 1973.

4. Ferndale (Michigan) Board of Education; statement adopted August 18, 1958.

5. Carman Clark, "The Best Asparagus Bed in Knox County," *Country Journal* 4 (May 1977):60.

6. *White Teacher* (Cambridge, Massachusetts: Harvard University Press, 1979), p. 56.

7. Gerald Becker and others, under the direction of Keith Goldhammer, *Elementary Principals and Their Schools: Beacons of Brilliance and Potholes of Pestilence* (Eugene, Oregon: Center for the Advanced Study of Educational Administration, 1971).

Chapter 2 Alternatives to Uniformity

1. For a particularly good analysis of such a school, see Clement S. Seldin, *Schools within Schools: An Answer to the Public School Dilemma* (Croton-on-Hudson, New York: Blythe-Pennington, 1978).

2. South Row School, Chelmsford (Massachusetts) public schools, *Final Report of the Ad Hoc Advisory Committee for Alternative Education*, March 1977.

3. However, I have seen evidence that aligning children by teaching style may also align them by the voting tendency of their parents. For instance, I once observed that the majority of parents of children in a more informal third grade

voted for George McGovern, while the majority of those in a more teacher-directed class voted for Richard Nixon.

4. Quoted by education editor James Cass in *Saturday Review/World* (November 6, 1973):53.

Chapter 3 Organization

1. *Rules and Regulations of the Newton School Committee;* adopted September 22, 1975, p. 16.

2. "Some Thoughts on What Schools Should Be," May 1970, p. 4, mimeographed.

3. Although few agree on what constitutes "good teaching" and although educational research is vast and confusing, we do know *something* about effective instruction. See, for example, Goodwin Watson, *What Psychology Can We Trust?* (New York: Teachers College, Columbia University, 1961) and Nathaniel L. Gage, *The Scientific Basis of the Art of Teaching* (New York: Teachers College Press, 1978).

Chapter 4 Placement

1. I have even seen a situation where a principal deliberately stacked a class with difficult children, in an attempt to drive the teacher into early retirement.

2. In Newton a primary and an intermediate teacher may be selected by the principal to serve as primary coordinator and intermediate coordinator, in addition to their teaching responsibilities. These positions—kind of assistant principalships—are supported by a small stipend and official appointment by the school committee. A fuller discussion appears in Chapter 8.

3. Our experience is that this rule is necessary, otherwise receiving teachers may attempt to influence the makeup of their class. Although lobbying is not permitted, anyone present at these meetings may contribute to the deliberations.

4. In this case the possibilities were a combined 3-4 class taught by a male teacher; a more teacher-directed, straight fourth grade taught by a team of two women teachers; and a more informal, self-contained 4-5 taught by a woman teacher.

5. Usually there are only two or three of these children in a class of twenty-five. We are confident that about a third of the children from each class would do well in any of the learning environments available.

6. "A Study of Kindergarten and First Grade Children in Multi and Single Grade Classes" (Newton public schools, Newton, Massachusetts, 1977), p. 1.

7. *Teaching Styles and Pupil Progress* (Cambridge, Massachusetts: Harvard University Press, 1976), pp. 152-155.

8. Ibid., p. 162.

Chapter 5 The Instructional Program

1. From "Curriculum Reform Revisited," a lecture delivered by Henry Rosovsky, Harvard's Dean of the Faculty of Arts and Sciences, at the Askwith Symposium, Harvard Graduate School of Education, May 16, 1977.

2. A recent federal government memorandum reports: "The Office for Civil Rights has recently reviewed and analyzed certain data on student discipline actions . . . This data shows that, in many hundreds of school systems throughout

the Nation, minority children are receiving a disproportionate number of discipline actions in the form of expulsions and suspensions and are being suspended for longer periods than nonminority children" (United States Department of Health, Education and Welfare, Office for Civil Rights, Acting Director, "Memorandum for Chief State School Officers from Martin Gerry; Subject: Record Keeping on Student-Discipline Procedures and Actions in School Districts," 1975).

3. *Rules and Regulations of the Newton School Committee.*

Chapter 6 Parents

1. See Don Davies, ed., *Schools Where Parents Make a Difference* (New York: Citation Press, 1976).

2. "Making Citizen Participation Work," *National Elementary Principal* 55 (March/April 1976):22.

3. John V. Gilmore, "Parental Influences in Academic Achievement," *Normline* 2(2) (New York: Harcourt, Brace and World Test Department, n.d.), not paginated.

4. *Elementary Principals,* p. 37.

5. One apprehensive principal at a convention observed, in an unguarded moment, "Parent involvement in schools is like making love to a gorilla—once you start, you don't stop until the gorilla is ready to."

Chapter 7 Pupil Evaluation

1. The National Consortium on Testing (of Arlington, Virginia), representing over forty national educational organizations, is examining the nature of standardized testing and its effect upon American education and is exploring and encouraging the development of alternative evaluation procedures. This material was excerpted from a proposal written by Paul L. Houts to the Carnegie Corporation of New York, April 6, 1977.

2. See, for example, James S. Coleman, *Equality of Educational Opportunity* (Washington, D.C.: United States Office of Education, 1966).

3. *What Schools Can Do* (New York: Liveright, 1976), p. 14.

4. Quoted at a National Academy of School Executives seminar by *Education USA* (June 6, 1977):307.

5. Provided in private correspondence by Leonard Solo, principal of the Cambridge (Massachusetts) Alternative Public School.

6. A class list is valuable in observing a classroom and can be used in a variety of ways: (1) as a checklist to record who has participated in or completed a specific task; (2) as a place to jot down specific behaviors observed during the day; (3) as a reminder for the teacher to help a child overcome a problem or pursue an interest.

7. Workshops 2, 3, 4, and 6 were planned and conducted by Dr. Nancy Lankford, psychologist with the Newton public schools. I am indebted to her now, as I was then, for the value of these seminars to teachers.

8. The Concord (Massachusetts) public school system has developed useful guidelines for parent-teacher conferences, which are given in Appendix F. I recommend also Gerda Lawrence and Madeline Hunter, *Parent-Teacher Conferencing* (El Segundo, California: TIP Publications, 1978).

Chapter 8   Staff Development

1. Dan C. Lortie, *School Teacher* (Chicago: University of Chicago Press, 1975), p. 106.

2. *What Schools Can Do*, p. 19.

3. I see no reason why this system could not work even more effectively on a district-wide basis. Each teacher could have an account, perhaps backed by a charge card in the amount of $400, which could be used at a central supermarket of commonly needed educational supplies and materials, from masking tape to dictionaries to posters. These items, purchased in bulk, would bring more into each classroom for less.

4. William J. Tikunoff and Beatrice A. Ward give a striking example of the influence on teachers' professional development when they are "worked with" rather than "worked on" in the educational research process. The following quotation is from their "Research and Development: A Resource in the Resolution of Conflict," *IR&DT Bulletin* 1 (October 1977), San Francisco: Far West Laboratory for Educational Research and Development.

Interactive Research and Development on Teaching (IR&DT) is an R&D strategy that places teachers, researchers, and trainer/developers together to inquire as a team into . . . questions, problems, and concerns of the classroom teacher. Decisions are made collaboratively regarding research issues and strategies and the concurrent development of training that grows from the research. Each member of an IR&DT team has parity and shares equal responsibility for decisions made by the team, from identification of the question/problem to the completion of all resultant R&D activities.

5. For these insights, and for his confidence and vision that "supervision can be systematic, rational, goal-directed, pleasant, predictable while at the same time being growth-producing," I am grateful for my work with David F. Weeks of University Center, Inc., Boston.

6. Gerald H. Moeller and David J. Mahan, *The Faculty Team* (Chicago: Science Research Associates, 1971), p. 51.

7. *School Teacher*, p. 169.

Chapter 9   The Principalship

1. W. V. Hicks and M. C. Jameson, *The Elementary School Principal at Work* (Englewood Cliffs, New Jersey: Prentice-Hall, 1957), pp. xi-xv.

2. Ibid., pp. 129-132.

3. Ibid., p. 209.

4. Ibid., p. 106.

5. The Chautauqua Series ("Remaking the Principalship") of the *National Elementary Principal* comes as close as any attempt to capturing the essence of the public elementary-school principal today. See vols. 53 (3, 4, 5) and 54 (1), 1974.

6. *Elementary Principals*, p. 8.

7. "Lonely At the Top," *National Elementary Principal* 56 (July/August 1977):29.

8. Roland S. Barth, "On Becoming a Principal: Conversations with Helen Herzog," *National Elementary Principal* 56 (March/April 1977):35.

9. *Report of Findings of a Study of the Principalship in Action in the Montgomery County Public Schools* (Rockville, Maryland: Montgomery County public schools, 1975), p. 6.

10. Ibid., p. 45.

11. Ibid., p. 34.

12. From the job description for principal of the Runkel School, Brookline (Massachusetts) public schools, March 1975.

13. Elementary pupils in Newton are dismissed at 1:00 P.M. on Tuesdays and Thursdays (3:00 P.M. on the other days) in order to provide the staff with weekly opportunities for meetings, workshops, and contact time with individual children. Careful adjustment of the schedule ensures that pupils receive hours of instruction each week comparable to those of students in other districts.

14. "Principals: Call for New Breed of School Leaders," *New York Times*, educational supplement, March 21, 1971, p. 7.

15. "On Turning Psychology Over to the Unwashed," *Psychology Today* 3 (December 1969):70.

16. As quoted in "The Miracle on 33rd Street," *Time*, May 21, 1979, p. 77.

17. *The Faculty Team*, p. 99.

18. "Decentralization 5 Years On: A Principal's View," *Urban Review* (July 1974):204.

Chapter 10 Promoting Principal Effectiveness

1. "The Changing Role of the Elementary School Principal: Report of a Conference," *National Elementary Principal* 55 (November/December 1975):67.

2. Both assumptions have been challenged by recent research. For example, see the study of rural school consolidation by Jonathan Sher, ed., *Education in Rural America: A Reassessment of Conventional Wisdom* (Boulder, Colorado: Westview Press, 1977).

3. John Pittenger, "Big Schools, Big Problems," *Harvard Graduate School of Education Association Bulletin* 21 (spring/summer 1977):14-15.

4. *Violent Schools—Safe Schools: The Safe School Study Report to Congress* (Washington, D.C.: Government Printing Office, January 1978).

5. "Big Schools, Big Problems," p. 16.

6. See Goodlad, "Schools *Can* Make a Difference," *Educational Leadership* (November 1975).

7. See Lawrence C. Pierce, "School Site Management" (Aspen, Colorado: Aspen Institute for Humanistic Studies, 1977).

8. *What Schools Can Do*, p. 16.

9. National Education Association Research Division, "The Principal and Administration," *The Elementary School Principalship—A Research Study*, Thirty-Seventh Yearbook, *National Elementary Principal* 38 (September 1958):38-39.

10. Barth, "On Becoming a Principal," p. 38.

11. "Report to the School Committee" by Aaron Fink, superintendent of the Newton public schools, September 9, 1974.

12. "School Assessment," Newton public schools, 1971-72 (mimeographed).

13. Fink, "Report to the School Committee," June 26, 1973.

14. From *Criteria for Evaluation of School Principals*, Newton public schools, 1970.

15. For instance, from *Violent Schools—Safe Schools* (p. iv):

The single most important difference between safe schools and violent schools was found to be a strong, dedicated principal who served as a role model for both students and teachers, and who instituted a firm, fair, and consistent system of discipline.

For an earlier study of the school principal's considerable influence upon staff and pupil performance, see Neil Gross and Robert Herriott, *Staff Leadership in Public Schools: A Sociological Inquiry* (New York: John Wiley and Sons, 1965).

Selected Bibliography

BARTH, ROLAND S. 1972. *Open Education and the American School*. New York: Schocken Books.

BECKER, GERALD, AND OTHERS, UNDER THE DIRECTION OF KEITH GOLDHAMMER. 1971. *Elementary Principals and Their Schools: Beacons of Brilliance and Potholes of Pestilence*. Eugene, Oregon: Center for the Advanced Study of Educational Administration.

BENNETT, NEVILLE. 1976. *Teaching Styles and Pupil Progress*. Cambridge, Massachusetts: Harvard University Press.

DAVIES, DON, ED. 1976. *Schools Where Parents Make a Difference*. New York: Citation Press.

FANTINI, MARIO. 1973. *Public Schools of Choice*. New York: Simon and Schuster.

FEATHERSTONE, JOSEPH. 1976. *What Schools Can Do*. New York: Liveright Publishing Corporation.

GOODLAD, JOHN I. 1974. *Towards a Mankind School: An Adventure in Humanistic Education*. New York: McGraw-Hill.

—— AND ROBERT H. ANDERSON. 1963. *The Nongraded Elementary School*. New York: Harcourt, Brace, Jovanovich.

GROSS, NEIL, AND ROBERT HERRIOTT. 1965. *Staff Leadership in Public Schools: A Sociological Inquiry*. New York: John Wiley and Sons.

HOUTS, PAUL, ED. 1977. *The Myth of Measurability*. New York: Hart Publishing Company.

HUNTER, MADELINE. 1972. *Continuous Progress, Nongrading, Team Teaching*. El Segundo, California: TIP Publications.

JACKSON, PHILIP W. 1968. *Life in Classrooms*. New York: Holt, Rinehart and Winston.

JENTZ, BARRY C., AND JOAN W. WOFFORD. 1979. *Leadership and Learning: Personal Change in a Professional Setting*. New York: McGraw-Hill.

KOHL, HERBERT. 1978. *Growing with Your Children.* Boston: Little, Brown and Company.

LAWRENCE, GERDA, AND MADELINE HUNTER. 1978. *Parent-Teacher Conferencing.* El Segundo, California: TIP Publications.

LIGHTFOOT, SARA LAWRENCE. 1978. *Worlds Apart: Relationships between Families and Schools.* New York: Basic Books.

LORTIE, DAN C. 1975. *School Teacher: A Sociological Study.* Chicago: University of Chicago Press.

MARSHALL, KIMBOROUGH. 1972. *Law and Order in Grade 6-E: Chaos and Innovation in a Ghetto School.* Boston: Little, Brown and Company.

MOELLER, GERALD H., AND DAVID J. MAHAN. 1971. *The Faculty Team.* Chicago: Science Research Associates.

PIERCE, LAWRENCE C. 1977. "School Site Management." Aspen, Colorado: Aspen Institute for Humanistic Studies. Occasional paper.

PURPEL, DAVID E., AND MAURICE BELANGER, EDS. 1972. *Curriculum and the Cultural Revolution.* Berkeley, California: McCutchan Publishing Corporation.

ROGERS, VINCENT, AND BUD CHURCH, EDS. 1975. *Open Education: Critique and Assessment.* Washington, D.C.: Association for Supervision and Curriculum Development.

SARASON, SEYMOUR B. 1971. *The Culture of the School and the Problem of Change.* Boston: Allyn and Bacon.

———. 1972. *The Creation of Settings and the Future Societies.* San Francisco: Jossey-Boss.

SCHEFFLER, ISRAEL. 1974. *Four Pragmatists: A Critical Introduction to Peirce, James, Mead, and Dewey.* New York: Humanities Press.

SELDIN, CLEMENT A. 1978. *Schools within Schools: An Answer to the Public School Dilemma.* Croton-on-Hudson, New York: Blythe-Pennington.

SHER, JONATHAN, ED. 1977. *Education in Rural America: A Reassessment of Conventional Wisdom.* Boulder, Colorado: Westview Press.

SILBERMAN, CHARLES E. 1970. *Crisis in the Classroom.* New York: Random House.

SILLUZIO, VINCENT. 1977. "A Study of Kindergarten and First Grade Children in Multi and Single Grade Classes." Newton (Massachusetts) School Department. Unpublished.

TYACK, DAVID B. 1974. *The One Best System: A History of American Urban Education.* Cambridge, Massachusetts: Harvard University Press.

WOLCOTT, HARRY F. 1973. *The Man in the Principal's Office: An Ethnography.* New York: Holt, Rinehart and Winston.

Index